Creating the Empress:
Politics and Poetry in the Age of Catherine II

Ars Rossika

Series Editor: **David BETHEA**
(University of Wisconsin — Madison and Oxford University)

CREATING THE EMPRESS:
Politics and Poetry in the Age of Catherine II

VERA PROSKURINA

BOSTON / 2011

Library of Congress Cataloging-in-Publication Data:
A catalog record for this book as available from the Library of Congress.

The book is supported by Mikhail Prokhorov Foundation
(translation program TRANSCRIPT).

Copyright © 2011 Academic Studies Press
All rights reserved

ISBN - 978-1-61811-805-9

Book design by Ivan Grave

Published by Academic Studies Press in 2011
28 Montfern Avenue
Brighton, MA 02135, USA
press@academicstudiespress.com
www.academicstudiespress.com

Acknowledgments

*I*t is a great pleasure to show gratitude to my colleagues, friends, and institutions for the help I have received in writing this book. First of all, I want to thank my husband **Dr. Oleg Proskurin** for his never-ending dedication to scholarship and his generosity in sharing ideas, inspirations, and perceptions. I want to thank my colleagues **Mark Altshuller** (University of Pittsburgh), **Marcus Levitt** (University of Southern California), **Andrei Zorin** (University of Oxford, UK), **Joachim Klein** (Leiden University), **Aleksandr Levitsky** (Brown University), **Michael Wachtel** (Princeton University), and **Karen Evans-Romaine** (University of Wisconsin, Madison) for their endless intellectual support and everlasting encouragement. I have to express my sincere gratitude to my friends and colleagues at Emory University, especially to **Michael Epstein** and **Elena Glazova-Corrigan**, for their spiritual encouragement and enthusiastic support.

The book was drafted while I was a Regional Fellow at Davis Center for Russian and Eurasian Studies, Harvard University in 2002-2003. I owe countless thanks to **Prof. William Mills Todd III** and all members of the Davis Center, as well as to the entire faculty of the Slavic Department at Harvard, who supported me at the first steps of my research.

I owe infinite thanks to the chief editor of *Novoe Literaturnoe obozrenie*, **Dr. Irina Prokhorova**, for giving me an opportunity to publish the Russian version of my book (2006.) I have to express my genuine appreciation to **Melissa Miller** (University of Wisconsin, Madison) whose careful editing made the publication of this book possible.

Contents

Acknowledgments	5
Introduction	9
Chapter One *Coup d'état as Cross-dressing*	13
Chapter Two *Astraea's coming to the Russian Throne*	49
Chapter Three *Catherine the Healer*	86
Chapter Four *Toppling the* Bronze Horseman	109
Chapter Five *The War in Greek Garb*	150
Chapter Six *The Birth of* Felitsa	182
Chapter Seven *Politics as Carnival in Derzhavin's Ode to Fortune*	218
Chapter Eight *Ridiculing the Monarch*	256
Bibliography	286
Index	303

Introduction

The main topic discussed in this book is the relationship between political and literary symbolism during the reign of Catherine II. Much has been written about Catherine's political and social ideas; this work, however, takes a drastically different approach. I intend to examine not the relationship between literary texts and political ideas, but the ways in which literary texts interacted with a kind of political symbolism which manifested itself in various forms of verbal and non-verbal discourse. This political symbolism created its own mechanisms of representation through an entire system of images, metaphors, and mythic allegories. Although they centered on relevant political symbols borrowed from the European tradition, they manifested themselves differently in the Russian context. I discuss these manifestations and their development in Russian culture in this work as well.

I interpret diverse forms of political imagery not as a mystification of reality, but as an important part of that reality itself, no less real than economic forces of social practices. I admire the statement of Ernst Cassirer who referred to the history of man as the actions of *animal simbolicum*. Cassirer rejected anthropological and psychoanalytical models for history, an approach which stemmed from the neo-Kantian opposition of the rational and irrational. He considered the myth not only a constant of all primitive civilizations, whether they are ancient or not, but an inherent essence of any modern culture as well. The rise of totalitarianism in Europe as well as the imperialistic wars definitively showed that "myths of state"

(Cassirer's *Myth of State* was published in 1945) have a tendency to undergo a permanent *renovatio*.

Cassirer's *The Philosophy of Symbolic Forms* (1928–1940) allowed for a structuring of culture based on a system of mythological projections. This approach proved fruitful for both analyzing political myths as well as for decoding a hidden symbolic mode in literary texts. In the forties and fifties, historians of the Warburg School (Edgar Wind, Frances Yates, and Aby Warburg) successfully applied this concept to their brilliant study of Renaissance arts, philosophy, literature, and politics. They also became interested in the theme of Empire that is in the theme of an eternal return of Roman Imperial allegories and metaphors, the reincarnation of classical paradigms, and the reinterpretation of previously established epic models. These scholars' discourse (I should also mention an excellent work by Frank Kermode *The Classic. Literary Images of Permanence and Change*) proved extremely useful in helping me define my task as a careful explication and close consideration of the political imagination developed in Catherine's time in both the political and artistic spheres.

The flourishing of neo-classicism in this period encouraged more elaborate imperial representations, which corresponded well with an ideological *translatio imperii* onto Russia. The revival of neo-classical images during Catherine's rule saw the first translations of Homer's *The Iliad* and Virgil's *The Aeneid* into Russian. These texts "deeded to posterity the poetic matrix out of which Western imperial iconography was to be continuously recreated."[1]

The Imperial idea, like Janus the two-faced god, always looked in opposite directions. One side corresponded with a rational component made up of real politics, geo-political interests, and economic benefits. The other side, the irrational one, turned toward the past: to dynastic myths and the rewriting of history, to the moving of capital cities, to the renaming of towns, to the adoption of outlandish titles and emblems, and to the reenactment of distant victories and defeats of yore. Empire perceives and understands

---

[1] Marie Tanner, *The Last Descendant of Aeneas. The Hapsburgs and the Mythic Image of the Emperor* (New Haven & London, 1993), 11.

itself only in the mirror of the past — against the background of events and artifacts transpired. A novice Empire plans its domination over other nations using the old maps. It inevitably looks over its shoulder at the past, carrying along universal phantoms and chimeras into the future, whose heritage is eventually passed onto it. Frances A. Yates writes: "Every revival of the Empire, in the person of some great emperor, carried with it, as a phantom, the revival of a universal imperialist hope".[2]

In 1787, Prince de Ligne, a witty Austrian diplomat traveling with Catherine II to a recently incorporated Crimea, witnessed her conversation with the Austrian king Joseph II, who held the honorary title of Emperor of the Holy Roman Empire. Joseph II, as a guest of honor on this first royal trip to the ancient land of Taurida, was obliged to listen to Catherine's constant, ambitious remarks on the future Russian conquest of Constantinople. Prince de Ligne remembered the situation: "Their Royal Majesties shared their views for awhile concerning those cursed Ottomans. As a great admirer of the glories of antiquity and hardly a fan of modernity, I spoke about the restoration of Greece. Catherine speculated about the necessity to revive Lycurguses and Solons. I leaned towards Alchiviad. Finally, Joseph II, who preferred the future to the past, as something material to a chimera, remarked, 'What the hell are we busying ourselves with Constantinople for?'[3]

Russia, as a young Empire, was still infused with the "political energy" of mythmaking and converted its political pragmatism (access to warm-water ports, acquisition of new lands, the security of its southern borders, etc.) into an inspiring tale about the restoration of ancient Hellas and its philosophy, Olympic Games, and wise rulers. I use the term "convert" fully realizing that the process of forming and asserting an imperial imagination will always oscillate between two poles—the rational and the irrational. The formation of any type of political "phantom" into a "symbolic form" is a creative process.

---

[2] Frances A. Yates, *Astraea. The Imperial Theme in the Sixteenth Century* (London, 1993), 1.
[3] Prince de Ligne, *Letters à la Marquise de Coigny* (Paris, 1914), 38—39.

Empire will always co-opt representatives from the literary world into its service. Paradoxically, artists and humanists of the Renaissance eagerly participated in the creation and development of imperial symbols and allegories by attaching the whole rediscovered repertory of classical antiquity to the emperor. "Ephemeral spectacles," ballets, and the art of decorating were all normal means for expressing the political reality of Renaissance culture.[4] As artifacts were more convincing than actual facts, the people were attracted to the emperors more for their "peaceful eloquence" than for any tyrannical exercise of power.[5] Intellectuals of the seventeenth century inherited the urge to serve the king, seeing such service as a way to become respectable members of the "king's body," in other words, by the end of the reign of Louis XIV, members of the "state's body."[6]

In eighteenth-century Russia, the world of politics completely controlled the world of literature. The latter, however, created the mode of reception of the former. It was the literary works which generated the symbols, metaphors, and allegories which the political world appropriated for its own use. Eventually, the "symbolic capital" of the Empire and its political imagination became not only socially and economically converted; it often stood as its sole achievement. Summing up the reign of Catherine II, Vasilii Kliuchevskii shrewdly noted that her success lay not so much in her inconsistent internal reforms and aggressive foreign policy as in the "force of public excitement."[7] This "political energy," which corresponded in various complex ways with literary imagination, will be the subject of my book.

---

[4] Roy Strong, *Art and Power. Renaissance Festivals 1450-1650* (Berkely & Los Angeles, 1984), 5.

[5] Frances A. Yates, *Astraea. The Imperial Theme in the Sixteenth Century*, 210.

[6] Jean-Marie Apostolidès, *Le roi-machine. Spectacle et politique au temps de Louis XIV* (Paris, 1981), 25.

[7] V. O. Kliuchevskii, *Sochineniia v deviati tomakh*, V (Moscow, 1989), 312.

Chapter One

COUP D'ÉTAT AS CROSS-DRESSING

The eighteenth century was, for the most part, a time of female rule in Russia. In order to attain the throne and maintain power, however, the female monarchs had to exhibit masculine behavior. The French diplomat Charles Masson devoted a whole chapter of his *Secret Memoirs of the Court of St. Petersburg* to women in positions of power at the Russian court. Repudiating the "gynecocracy," as he called the reign of six successive Russian tsarinas in the seventeenth and eighteenth centuries (Sophia, Catherine I, Anna Ivanovna, Anna Leopol'dovna, Elizabeth, and Catherine II), he compared Russia to the kingdom of the Amazons: "The existence of the Amazons no longer seemed a fable after I beheld the Russian women. Had the succession of empresses continued, we might perhaps have seen this nation of female warriors replicated on Russian soil, in the same climate where they had previously flourished."[1]

The medieval formula of "the King's two bodies," which implied the notion of the Emperor as God-Man,[2] developed in interesting fashion in the Russian context. The church, which equated the tsar with Christ and considered him an incarnation of celestial rule, denied women the right to be anointed sovereign.[3]

---

[1] Charles François P. Masson, *Secret Memoirs of the Court of Petersburg, particularly towards the end of the reign of Catherine II and the commencement of that of Paul I* (London, 1801), 307.

[2] Ernst H. Kantorowicz, *The King's Two Bodies. A Study in Medieval Political Theology* (Princeton, 1957), 20–21.

[3] V. M. Zhivov, V. A. Uspenskii, "Tsar' i Bog: Semioticheskie aspekty sakralizatsii

Chapter One

Traditional Russian ideology, influenced by the Russian Orthodox Church, interpreted the "man-woman" opposition to be one of "sacred-profane." Women were often assigned pagan attributes and considered to be dependent and subordinate creatures.[4] Church and society both cultivated the concept of a "blessed womb" and assigned to royal women the task of producing a male heir.[5] An influential theologian, statesman, and admirer of Peter the Great, the archbishop Feofan Prokopovich, had to find eloquent excuses to justify the coronation of Catherine I, Peter's widow and heir. In his *Speech on the Funeral of Peter the Great* (1725), addressing Catherine I, he declared: "The whole world sees that your female flesh does not prevent you from being like Peter the Great."[6] His skillful rhetoric was meant as a defense of "female flesh" as suitable enough (but not ideal for the embodiment of God on Earth) in order to legitimize Catherine I's right to be the new Russian ruler. To Russians, the sacred, divine nature of kingship was always masculine. Russian female rulers of the eighteenth century inherited this medieval role distribution and had to reckon with it. Notably, the usual scenario for any palace revolution in the eighteenth century involved a ritual act of cross-dressing.[7]

Anna Ivanovna, the Duchess of Courland and the daughter of Peter's step-brother Ivan V, came to the Russian throne in 1730 with the help of the Supreme Privy Council. She began her coup d'état with a symbolic change in gender. She repudiated the "conditions" set for her rule by certain boyar elites ("verhovniki") by deciding

---

monarkha v Rossii," in Uspenskii B. A. *Izbrannye trudy*, 1 (Moscow, 1994), 141.

[4] Eve Levin, *Sex and Society in the World of the Orthodox Slavs. 900-1700* (Ithaca & London, 1989), 19.

[5] Isolde Thyret, *Between God and Tsar. Religious Symbolism and the Royal Women of Muscovite Russia* (DeKalb, 2001), 16–46.

[6] Feofan Prokopovich, *Sochineniia* (Moscow – Leningrad, 1961), 128. Unless noted, all translations are mine.

[7] See the brief, but very important notes by Iu. M. Lotman: Iu. M. Lotman, *Kul'tura i vzryv* (Moscow, 1992), 140–141. The Amazon image of Catherine II has been examined in the article: John T. Alexander, "Amazon Autocratrixes: Images of Female Rule in the Eighteenth Century," in *Gender and Sexuality in Russian Civilization* (London, 2001), 33–54.

to rely on the capital guards. Assuming the most suitable image for a new legitimate sovereign of Russia, she performed several ritual acts of cross-dressing. She called for the guards of the Preobrazhenskii regiment and introduced herself to them as their colonel. Later, she was awarded the order of Saint Apostle Andrew the First Called (with a blue ribbon), which was conferred only upon the highest-ranking male officials of the state. The choice of this particular order was rather peculiar. Another order existed — the order of Saint Catherine the Martyr of God (the female equivalent of the order of Saint Andrew), with a red ribbon — which Peter I had established in 1714 as a way to commemorate the brave deeds of his wife Catherine during the military campaign against the Turks in 1711. Both the masculine (Saint Andrew) and feminine (Saint Catherine) high orders existed from Peter I's time until the end of the eighteenth century. The matter of male-female orders and those who held them became so important for the succession that in 1797, Paul I issued strict instruction that the orders forbid the intermingling of the genders. According to the decree, all male royal children were to receive the Saint Andrew orders while all female ones were to receive the Saint Catherine orders. Paul I was trying to prevent female pretenders to the throne from using the male orders as a symbolic tool for establishing their sovereignty.

Anna Ivanovna's performance served as a model for the next round of female usurpers. The Empress Elizabeth (Elizaveta Petrovna, 1741—1762), the daughter of Peter I, executed her coup d'état using a similar scenario. Although the rulers whom she had to dethrone were a rather powerless and inept pairing of mother and son and not a strong, independent ruler, she nevertheless made use of all the symbolic aspects of a man's accession. During the night of November 25th, 1741, the infant tsar Ivan Antonovich VI and his mother-regent Anna Leopol'dovna, Princess Brounshweig-Bevern (who had ruled from 1740—1741) were deposed quietly and without bloodshed. Elizabeth also relied on the support of the military. Before setting out for the barracks of her loyal regiments, Elizabeth put a cuirass over her usual clothing.[8] It was not that she feared

---

[8] S. M. Soloviev, *Istoria Rossii s drevneishikh vremen*, XI : 21—22 (Moscow, 1963), 124.

physical injury; the change in dress was purely a symbolic one. The coup consisted of the army's peaceful arrival at the Winter Palace with Elizabeth carried aloft by grenadiers. The royal family (the Brounshweigs) were pulled asleep from their beds and physically removed. The cuirass, a piece of armor covering the body from neck to waist, was part of military dress. There was a cuirassier regiment among those loyal to Elizabeth's army. When the revolution was over, Elizabeth placed an Andrew ribbon on her clothes. Then, early the next morning, she announced that she was the colonel of the three infantry regiments, the cuirassier regiment, and the cavalry guard. At the same time, she took the title of captain of her favorite grenadier company in the Preobrazhenskii regiment.[9] Later, she would follow the same ritual in celebrating the anniversaries of her accession by dressing in their uniform and visiting their barracks.[10]

Elizabeth loved luxury and entertainment, something to which many of her contemporaries attested. The play with cross-dressing became one of her favorite amusements, especially the masquerade balls. The Empress liked to change into men's military dress, which stressed her beautiful proportions. Elizabeth did not strive to create an overtly erotic atmosphere through her acts of cross-dressing, as many did in Europe.[11] Hence, the choices for costumes for others were always strictly controlled. The Empress punished anyone who violated her rules, her particular mood, or her tastes.

Catherine II, then Grand Duchess, was a keen observer and student of her predecessor's acts of cross-dressing. She wrote about one particularly intimidating masquerade ball in her *Memoirs*:

> "In 1744 in Moscow, as I have already related, the Empress had a fancy to have all men appear at the Court balls dressed as women and the women as men, without masks; it was like a Court day metamorphosed. The men wore whalebone petticoats, the women the Court costume of men. The men disliked these reversals of their sex and were in the worst

---

[9] Ibid.

[10] *Teatral'naia zhizn' Rossii v epokhu Elizavety Petrovny*, 2 (Moscow, 2005), 541.

[11] Terry Castle, *Masquerade and Civilization. The Carnivalesque in Eighteenth-Century English Culture and Fiction* (Stanford, 1986), 40.

possible humor, because they felt hideous in their disguises. The women looked like scrubby little boys, while the more aged had thick short legs, which were anything but attractive. The only woman who looked really well and completely a man was the Empress herself. As she was tall and powerful, male attire suited her. She had the handsomest leg I have ever seen on any man and her feet were admirably proportioned. She dressed to perfection and everything she did had the same special grace whether she dressed as a man or as a woman."[12]

Cross-dressing in the time of Elizabeth became one of the most representative features of courtly culture. She loved not only cross-dressing masquerades (a routine, weekly event, according to court journals), but hunting as well. The Empress chased down her prey in Izmailovo near Moscow on horseback and in masculine dress."[13]

Catherine began to develop her own strategies even in those early, difficult years at Elizabeth's court. Given the situation, her main function (as far as establishing a legitimate position in the Russian royal family) was to produce a male heir. Her ambitions, however, could not be limited to the traditional roles of mother and wife. Catherine the Great began establishing and projecting an image of her as Emperor (as opposed to Empress) as she strove to justify contemporary pronouncements that she was indeed Catherine *le Grand*, as the Prince de Ligne, an Austrian diplomat, referred to her. [14]

In *Memoirs*, written later, in the 1770s, Catherine draws her retrospective portrait carefully, emphasizing the masculine traits

---

[12] *The Memoirs of Catherine the Great*. Transl. from French by Moura Budberg (New York, 1955), 185—186. See a very interesting work on the history of Catherine's *Memoirs*: Monika Greenleaf, "Performing Autobiography: The Multiple Memoirs of Catherine the Great (1756-96)," in *The Russian Review*, 63 (2004), 407—426.

[13] *Teatral'naia zhizn' Rossii v epokhu Elizavety Petrovny*, 2, 531.

[14] In 1787, Prince de Ligne, in his letters to Marquise de Coigny, written during his trip to Crimea with Catherine II, called the empress "Catherine **le Grand**": "La simplicité confiante et séduisante de Catherine Le Grand m'enchanté, et c'est son génie enchanteur qui m'a conduit dans ce séjour enchanté" (Prince de Ligne, *Lettres à la Marquise de Coigny* (Paris, 1914), 53).

of her image. She changed her pale features as a young Grand Duchess to correspond to the necessary stereotypes of her later masculine strategy. From the beginning of her *Memoirs* on, she develops a myth about a "perfect child." According to this myth, her parents had wanted a son and were not pleased by the birth of a baby girl. Catherine goes on to stress that books were the main source of pleasure in her life. She read not only French novels, but political, "masculine" literature as well, specifically Plutarch's *Lives of the Noble Greeks and Romans*, *On the Spirit of the Laws* and *Considerations on the Causes of the Greatness of the Romans and of Their Decadence* by Montesquieu. Count Louis-Philippe Ségur, appointed French ambassador to the Russian court in 1785, believed that nature, reluctant to bestow any gifts on her husband Peter III, had showered them on Catherine, who had the "talent, courage, and firmness of a man born to command."[15]

Catherine II's favorite pastime was horseback riding. Elizabeth had also loved riding and dressing as a man. However, whereas Elizabeth dressed as a man and rode horses to demonstrate her beauty and grace, Catherine did the same for different reasons. She had to project her unique personality and her ambition to be more than a wife of the Emperor and the mother of an heir to the throne. The masculine style of the young Duchess was most likely fashioned after the persona of the well-known libertine (and mistress of Voltaire), Countess Sophie Bentinck (1715–1800). Catherine devoted a number of pages in her *Memoirs* to a description of this acquaintance from her early years.[16] Separated from her husband and with an illegitimate child, the Countess exerted a huge influence on the thirteen year-old Catherine. Against the will of her parents, Catherine spent many days with the Countess, who gave the future Russian empress her first lessons on emancipation. Catherine recounts that she looked "like a man" and rode like

---

[15] *Memoirs and Recollections of Count Ségur, ambassador from France to the court of Russia and Prussia, written by himself,* II (London, 1826), 159.

[16] Catherine wrote: "Countess Bentinck came riding to meet us. — I had never seen a woman on a horse; she fascinated me, for she rode astride. When we arrived at Varel, I never left her side. This attachment displeased my mother and my father even more" (*The Memoirs of Catherine the Great*, 43).

a "riding-master."[17] It was Countess Bentinck who gave Catherine a taste for riding.

Catherine became a splendid rider; according to her *Memoirs*, she could spend days on horseback. At the same time, the young Duchess began to take on an additional role. She underlined her loneliness and her undeserved humiliation at the hands of a capricious and suspicious Elizabeth who clearly feared the growing popularity of the extravagant Grand Duchess. Catherine played the role of "insulted Prince" (stepping in for her husband Peter III): she rode alone and read books:

> "To tell the truth, hunting did not interest me at all, but I passionately loved riding; the more violent that exercise the more I enjoyed it, so that if a horse ever broke away I galloped after it and brought it back. Also I always carried a book in my pocket in those days; any moment I had to myself I spent in reading."[18]

One incident at court was particularly significant. Elizabeth prohibited Catherine from using a man's saddle. Catherine remembers:

> "It was during that year that I invented for myself saddles upon which I could sit as I wanted. They had the English crook and one could swing one's leg to sit astride; the pommel, furthermore, could be screwed off and one of the stirrups raised or lowered as one required. If the grooms were asked how I rode, they could truthfully say: "In a lady's saddle, according to the Empress's wish. I switched my leg only when I was sure that I was no going to be observed <...>"[19]

At the same time, as Grand Duchess, Catherine was inverting gender roles; she created an image of herself as a strong and intelligent political figure. She appeared far more masculine than her weak, politically incompetent (and sexually impotent) husband. Thus, even before he was overthrown, she had begun to claim Peter III's place in terms of both power and gender. The Amazon motif

---

[17] Ibid, 23.
[18] Ibid, 183.
[19] Ibid.

had gained political significance by the time of her coup d'état in 1762. Catherine the Great had transformed Elizabeth's acts of cross-dressing at court into a serious political strategy.

Coup d'état as cross-dressing

Catherine's accession to the throne was accompanied by a series of acts of cross-dressing. The initiative and range of this power play belonged, for the most part, to the young Countess Catherine Dashkova (1744—1810). Her role in the events of 1762, many scholars believe, was somewhat exaggerated by Dashkova herself as well as by memoirists who relied on her story. In this case, however, who played the prominent role in the organizing of the complot is less important than the ideological gestures that the participants in the revolution of 1762 demonstrated, and later described in their memoirs.

The evening before the main event, after one of the participants in the conspiracy, Captain Peter Passek, had been arrested, Dashkova urged her ally Nikita Ivanovich Panin (1718—1783), an influential politician, to take immediate action aimed to incite the people and the army to revolt. Meanwhile, Panin, the observant courtier appointed as mentor to Catherine's son Pavel Petrovich in 1760, decided to bide his time. Then, an eighteen year-old woman "lost no time in donning a man's greatcoat and setting out on foot"[20] to the place where the plotters usually gathered. She insisted that Catherine come back to St. Petersburg from Peterhof (a carriage had secretly been readied for just such a trip). When the courageous Dashkova returned home, her tailor informed her to her disappointment that the officer uniform which she had ordered ahead of time was not yet ready.[21] According to her designs, this masculine attire would play an important role in all events of the revolution.

Dashkova appeared at the Winter Palace early in the morning. There she met up with Catherine, who had just returned from the Kazan Cathedral where she had taken the oath of Empress earlier

---

[20] *The Memoirs of Princess Dashkov.* Transl. by Kyril Fitzlyon (London, 1958), 70.
[21] Ibid, 71

in the day before members of the clergy. Dashkova, however, was much more occupied with a ceremony of a different kind. She carefully observed the tradition of all previous palace coups which contained a ritual act of cross-dressing; a female pretender dresses as a man (or dons significant elements of male attire), removes her "female" ribbons and decorations and substitutes "male" ones. Dashkova took off Catherine's ribbon, the symbol of the order of Saint Catherine, and pinned the blue ribbon of the "male" order of Saint Andrew, which she had borrowed from Nikita Panin, on Catherine's clothing:

> "Suddenly I noticed that she (Catherine. — V. P.) was still wearing the Order of St. Catherine and had not yet put on the blue ribbon of the Cross of St. Andrew. (The wife of the Emperor did not wear the blue ribbon; she was entitled only to the Order of St. Catherine, who had been founded by Peter I for his wife, and the Emperor Alexander followed his example in this respect.) I ran to Mr. Panin to borrow his blue ribbon, which I put on the Empress's shoulder. Thereupon she took off her own insignia of the Order of St. Catherine and asked me to put them in my pocket."[22]

Then, both women changed out of their dresses and put on uniforms from one of the Guards regiments; Dashkova borrowed Captain Talyzin's uniform for the purpose and Catherine took one of Lieutenant Pushkin's, as these two officers were roughly similar to them in height.[23] Apart from the cross-dressing, there were other ideological connotations connected with the uniforms. Dashkova made a special note:

> "These uniforms, by the way, were those the Preobrazhenski Regiment formerly worn from the time of Peter the Great down to the reign of Peter III, who abolished them in favor of Prussian type uniform. And it is a peculiar thing that no sooner did the Empress arrive in Petersburg than soldiers threw off new Prussian uniforms and donned their old ones which they somehow managed to find."[24]

---

[22] Ibid, 73.
[23] Ibid.
[24] Ibid, 73–74.

This donning of the green uniform of the Preobrazhenskii regiment, with its three-cornered hat decorated with oak leaves, had a double meaning. It demonstrated not only a change in status — the Grand Duchess had become the Empress — but manifested her political strategy as well. Peter III, who idolized Frederick II, had instated a new type of uniform for the Guards, one patterned after the Prussian model. The uniform was embroidered with gold, very uncomfortable, and very expensive. The Guards had hated it, associating the uniform with a new political orientation towards Prussia, a recent enemy. By dressing up in the uniform of the Preobrazhenskii regiment (the founding of which Peter I regarded as his proudest achievement in the military sphere), Catherine II exhibited a return to Peter's "behests." It was most likely Dashkova who masterminded this symbolic action. Such a kind of uniform was apparently ordered to a sluggish tailor. Early in the morning both ladies, dressed as men, set off on horseback ahead of the army bound for Peterhof to meet a deposed Peter III and his allies. It was significant that on the night of June 30th, 1762, after the coup was over, drunken soldiers from the Izmailovskii regiment, incited by malicious gossip, came to the Summer Palace (where the new Empress was resting) and demanded to see her. Despite her fatigue at not having slept in several days, Catherine rose, put on the Preobrazhenskii regiment uniform and set out on horseback from the palace to accompany the soldiers to their quarters. The political show had been performed to the very end.

The image of an Amazon-like Russian Empress, riding a horse in front of her loyal regiments, became an immutable political emblem in eighteenth-century Russia. The image of Catherine II was firmly established by the well-known painting "Catherine astride the white horse *Diamond*" by the court painter Stephano Torelli, a professor of the Academy of Arts who lived in Saint Petersburg from 1762 to 1784. The artist portrayed the empress the way she wanted to be portrayed. A self-willed horse turns the head around and foams the furrows. Russia is represented by a female figure; she is kneeling as she places the royal crown on Catherine's head.[25]

---

[25] E. Ia. Dan'ko, "Izobrazitel'noe iskusstvo v poezii Derzhavina," in *XVIII vek*, 2

Catherine's masculine dress was not a simple contribution to the historical episodes of 1762. Torelli, an experienced European artist, depicted Catherine's accession in accordance with the European concept of monarchical power which viewed it as a sacred marriage between king and kingdom.[26] This marriage consisted of a traditionally female nation (the country) and a traditionally male power figure (the king).

Fitting the Empress' Images

By 1766, after the first four years of her reign, Catherine felt a sense of stability and was first able to appreciate the achievements made during her reign. Meanwhile, she saw a keen necessity in creating and establishing her imperial image. Catherine, more than anyone else, perfectly understood all the complexities of her status and all the advantages of a rightly chosen mythology.

Political and ideological challenges provoked the novice Russian female ruler to develop new politico-mythological paradigms of self-representations in order to secure and strengthen her successful but illegitimate accession to the throne. The former German Protestant princess Sophia Augusta Fredericka of Anhalt-Zerbst set out to prove that she was entirely Russian and sincerely devoted to Russian Orthodoxy. She also had to prove that she was absolutely legitimate and even more masculine than her recently deposed, murdered husband, Peter III. She successfully accomplished the first two tasks while still Grand Duchess and wife to the heir apparent. Ekaterina Alekseevna (the name she took on June 28th, 1744, the day she converted to Orthodoxy) quickly learned to speak Russian and familiarized herself perfectly with the ceremonies of the Orthodox Church. She not only became a pedantic observer of the superficial formalities of the Russian religious services and customs, but also skillfully exhibited the Russian qualities of her soul. Her inconsolable grief during the days

---

(Moscow — Leningrad, 1939), 194.

[26] The concept of the ruling as a marriage between the king and his kingdom was a part of the French coronation ceremony: Peter Burke, *The Fabrication of Louis XIV* (New Haven & London, 1998), 128.

of Elizabeth's funeral in the winter of 1761–1762 was etched in the memories of her contemporaries. The French diplomat and political writer Claude Carloman de Rulhière gave an account of those days, adding a sharp commentary on the theatrical nature of Catherine's behavior: "During the obsequies of the late Empress, she gained the hearts of the people, by a rigorous devotion, and a scrupulous fidelity in the observance of the rites of the Greek religion, abounding more with ceremonies than with morality."[27] Pulling off being "exclusively Russian" and "completely Orthodox" was not extremely hard, especially after the irritating and distasteful pro-Prussian habits of Peter the Third, who had worshipped Prussian Emperor Frederick II.

As she wrote in her *Manifesto*, Catherine II came to the throne proclaiming the necessity to defend "an old Russian Orthodoxy" that had been persecuted under Peter III. The manifesto declared that a change in ruler would protect Russians against the planned adoption of a "foreign religious system."[28] Contemporaries testified that Peter III once called for the archbishop Dmitrii Sechenov and forced him to issue a decree stating that all icons be removed from churches (except for icons devoted to Jesus Christ and the Virgin Mary). He also ordered all priests to shave their beards and to exchange their long cassocks for a "foreign type of pastor cloth." Confused Russian clergymen were sure that "the Emperor meant to abolish Russian Orthodoxy in favor of Lutheranism."[29]

In 1762, the Russian poet and playwright Alexander Sumarokov (1717–1777) composed a laudatory inscription for Catherine's portrait (painted by P. Rotary, engraved by Evgraf Chemesov) in which he emphasized the messianic role of the novice Empress who had set out to save Orthodoxy within Russia:

---

[27] Claude Carloman de Rulhière, *The History, or Anecdotes of the Revolution in Russia, in the year 1762*. Transl. from French by M. de Rulhière (London, 1797), 49. Catherine knew about the manuscript, and tried to obtain it. She could only reach a compromise with the writer to permit publishing his book only after her death.

[28] *Put' k tronu. Istoriia dvortsovogo perevorota 28 iunia 1762 goda* (Moscow, 1997), 490.

[29] *Zapiski Andreia Timofeevicga Bolotova 1737–1796*, 1 (Tula, 1988), 332–333.

> She has freed Russian glory from her bonds,
> She has rescued Orthodoxy for her empire,
> She was given the wisdom to govern,
> And the truth to come to the throne.[30]

It was more difficult for her to prove her legitimacy, as she really did not have a legal right to the throne. In 1762, Rostov Archbishop Arsenii Matseevich, one of Catherine's main opponents in the first years of her reign, made an exact count of all the "complications" in the status of the novice Empress. Being prosecuted and exiled, Matseevich testified: "Her Highness is not from our country, she is not versed enough in our Orthodoxy. She should not take the Russian throne. Ivan Antonovich should reign in her stead."[31] He also made suggestions: "It would have been better if she (Catherine. —V. P.) had married him."[32] Catherine attentively studied his statements. The last proposition, to become the spouse of Ivan (VI) Antonovich, a mentally retarded prisoner from the Elizabeth era, was especially impressive. Catherine rather successfully overcame the barrier of her nationality and even of her religious convictions. However, as she understood clearly, her main task was to establish herself as a legitimate Russian Emperor, an heir to Peter the Great. Although it would not be easy, it was an absolute necessity.

The mythology of Empire always makes a distinction between the monarch as a real person and the monarch as a sacred figure, an incarnation of the state's "body." These beliefs would exhibit their resilience for centuries in the European political sphere. The mortal body of a king was thought to contain the immortality of a sacred imperial essence which "never died."[33] Imperial Russia

---

[30] D. A. Rovinskii, *Podrobnyi slovar' russkikh gravirovannykh portretov*, 2 (Saint Petersburg, 1887), 823. Besides A. Sumarokov, M. Lomonosov and E. Dashkova made their inscriptions. See on the history of the inscriptions: V. P. Stepanov, "Zabytye stikhotvoreniia Lomonosova i Sumarokova," in *Russkaia literatura*, 2 (1978), 111—115.

[31] S. M. Soloviev, *Istoriia Rossii s drevneishikh vremen. 1762—1765*, 268—269. See also: V. S. Ikonnikov, "Arsenii Matseevich, mitropolit Rostovskii," in *Russkaia starina* 26 (1879), 190.

[32] N. I. Pavlenko, *Ekaterina Velikaia* (Moscow, 1999), 92.

[33] Richard Jackson, *Vive le roi! A History of the French Coronation from Charles V to*

was no stranger to this concept but did infuse it with certain specific political ideas and poetic metaphors. After the death of Peter the Great, during the reign of his daughter Elizaveta Petrovna, the personality of the first Russian Emperor became an object of the intense mythological elucidation. Mikhail Lomonosov (1711–1765), who had recurrently sung the praises of Elizabeth and her heir and nephew, the future Peter the Third, expounded on mythological role of their God-like predecessor in his *Ode on the Name Day of His Imperial Majesty Grand Prince Fedorovich in 1743* (*Ода на День Тезоименитства Его Императорского Высочества Государя Великого Князя Петра Федоровича в 1743*). Here Lomonosov evokes Peter the Great (comparing the two Peters, grandfather and grandson, was extremely popular at the time):

> He was your God, Russia,
> He took the earthly parts of your body from you,
> When he descended from the mountains <…>[34]

According to Lomonosov, Peter the Great was the God of Russia, an incarnation of God on Russian soil. Thus, medieval Christian theology which depicted an imperial earthly incarnation was transformed into a political concept of an "imperial body" as a symbol of nation or country. Catherine's strategic affinity for Peter I was used to prove her *ideological heritage* from Peter the Great. She tried her hardest to prove that she was Peter's heir not by blood, but by spirit and by the ideological power of reforms which she carried out in Russia. Peter the Great received the status of a Russian Deity (although his opponents viewed him as the opposite, the Antichrist) and his "immortal spirit" descended upon Catherine II.

Vasilii Petrov, in his poetic epistle *To Galaktion Ivanovich Silov* (*Галактиону Ивановичу Силову*, 1772), solemnly summarized Catherine's hereditary "rights":

> Peter's spirit lives in Catherine's body.[35]

Charles X. (Chapel Hill, N.C., 1984); Antoine De Baecque, *The Body Politic. Corporeal Metaphor in Revolutionary France, 1770–1800* (Stanford, 1997).

[34] M. V. Lomonosov, *Polnoe sobranie sochinenii*, 8 (Moscow — Leningrad, 1959), 109.

[35] *Poety XVIII veka*, 1 (Leningrad, 1972), 348.

"Peter's spirit," as Petrov suggests, substitutes for legal or ancestral rights. By adopting "Peter's spirit", Catherine also gains access to his revered, imperial charisma. The Empress, an ardent reader of Diderot and Montesquieu, was attempting to apply an ideological strategy from the Enlightenment onto the feudal, aristocratic political structure of Russia. These new imperial representations assumed that her strategy of personal achievements, intellect, and education should be considered more relevant than blood ties.

The literary reaction to this strategy was quite significant. Lomonosov attempted to apply his experience as a laudatory poet onto this new situation. He wrote two odes: *Ode to the Empress Ekaterina Alekseevna on the Occasion of her Accession on June 28th, 1762* (Ода императрице Екатерине Алексеевне на ее восшествие на престол июня 28 дня 1762) and *Ode to the Empress Ekaterina Alekseevna on New Year's Day 1764* (Ода императрице Екатерине Алексеевне в новый 1764 год). In the first ode (which was written literally during Catherine's coup d'état in 1762), Lomonosov, obviously failing to comply with Catherine's new strategy, portrayed her as Elizabeth reborn:

> Listen, all limits of the world,
> And know what God can do!
> Elizabeth has risen for our sakes,
> Church and Palace are triumphant.[36]

The metaphor could not have pleased Catherine, who did not want to be associated with Elizabeth's character traits, especially her gentleness, Lomonosov's favorite epithet when describing her. Catherine's intentions were not simply to reign like gentle Elizabeth, but to govern as a strong and powerful Emperor. For Catherine, a capricious and weak-willed woman who had shifted the day-to-day affairs of ruling into the hands of her minister or any other

---

[36] M. V. Lomonosov, *Polnoe sobranie sochinenii*, 8, 772. See on the difficult relationships between Lomonosov and Catherine II: S. N. Chernov, "Lomonosov v odakh 1762 g.," in *XVIII vek*, I (Moscow — Leningrad, 1935), 178—180; Elena Pogosian, *Vostorg russkoi ody i reshenie temy poeta v russkom panegirike 1730-1762 gg.* (Tartu, 1997), 107—123.

person nearby could not be viewed as a good model. During the first years of Catherine's reign, Peter I had become the mythological model for her to follow. Lomonosov came to understand his mistake on a personal level, when, in 1763, Catherine signed the order for his retirement. (She would rescind it a few days later).[37]

In his second ode, Lomonosov completely eliminated all comparisons of Catherine with Elizabeth. Moreover, Catherine II received poetic legitimization from him as a "granddaughter" of Peter the Great:

> Among all the triumphant sounds
> Be sure of my fervor for you,
> Now, I sing the praises of Peter's granddaughter,
> As I sang his daughter's before.[38]

Eventually, Lomonosov abandoned his irritating habit of listing all the achievements of Catherine's female predecessors (Catherine I and Elizabeth), which was perceived as giving political advice on how she should rule. He mentioned only Catherine I, Peter's wife, who had ascended to the throne after him. Briefly, but gracefully, Lomonosov invoked "God's sanction" to explain the miracle of Catherine's accession:

> O, scepter, crown, throne, and palace
> Are given to Catherine again,
> Glorify the second Goddess!
> The First received it from Peter, the second from God![39]

The statement on the strength of her rule, sanctioned by not only Peter the Great but God himself as well opened the door to a poetic legitimization of Catherine's accession. It was no accident

---

[37] Stephen Baehr disregarded, in his book, a rudeness of Lomonosov's comparison: Stephen Lessing Baehr, *The Paradise Myth in Eighteenth-Century Russia. Utopian Patterns in Early Secular Russian Literature and Culture* (Stanford, 1991), 40.

[38] M. V. Lomonosov, *Polnoe sobranie sochinenii*, 8, 789. Entitling Catherine Peter's "granddaughter," Lomonosov underlined his solidarity with the *Manifesto* of 1762 that contained a sentence: "Peter the Great, our gratifying grandfather <...>"(*Put' k tronu*, 493).

[39] M. V. Lomonosov, *Polnoe sobranie sochinenii*, 8, 789.

that soon after this ode was written Lomonosov was promoted to the rank of State Councilor.

Ode on the Occasion of the Magnificent Carousel: Patterns of Competition

On June 16th, 1766, Catherine had a grandiose carousel staged in St. Petersburg. These tournaments became a popular component of a late Medieval and Renaissance courtly life; later, they flourished in European courts as a luxurious Baroque half-theatrical, half-military championship. On June 5-6, 1662, the most famous carousel had given by Louis XIV when five military groups dressed as Romans (leaded by the King), Persians, Turks, Indians, and Native Americans participated in a magnificent performance. On January 2, 1743, the young Queen Maria Theresa of Austria decided to celebrate her victories during the War of Austrian Succession by performing a ladies carousel in her Hofburg Palace in Vienna: she herself was among other participants of this ladies contest. Russian empress Catherine II thoroughly studied their lessons.

In this event in Russia, the four branches of the armed forces (dressed as Slavs, Romans, Indians, and Turks) competed in horsemanship. However, the most impressive part of the feat came when young women from the best families suddenly appeared in ceremonial chariots and proceeded to open the festivities. The "Russian Amazons" were a tremendous success and became the focus of the whole performance.

In the same year, Vasilii Petrov (1736–1799), a humble teacher of poetry, stylistics, and rhetoric from the Slavonic-Greek-Latin Academy, had suddenly come to incredible fame. The Empress Catherine the Great very much appreciated his *Ode on the Occasion of the Magnificent Carousel in Saint Petersburg in 1766 (Ода на великолепный карусель, представленный в Санкт-Петербурге 1766 года)*. The lucky author of the work received a gold snuff-box along with 200 chervonets as a sign of royal favor, gifts quite traditional for the time. Two years later, his exemplary skill in publicizing all the latest trends in Russian imperial policy earned him another promotion. Petrov was appointed personal translator and reader for the Empress's cabinet.

Petrov wrote the *Ode on the Occasion of the Magnificent Carousel*, his print debut, while living in Moscow. He did not witness the impressive ceremony in the capital, getting all his information from an extensive report on the festival published in the *Moscow Gazette* (July 7th, 1766).[40] Nevertheless, Petrov grasped the essence of the events. In his poem, he depicted the appearance of the Amazons in "roaring chariots" as the central event of the carousel. He refers to these Russian young women as "Sparta's maidens," admiring their skills in chasing "wild boars" with "foaming mouths," along the moss. He solemnly predicts that these "Russian daughters" would outdo the men and gain possession of their "laurels."[41]

Consequently, Petrov makes the expected parallel—Russian armed maidens remind him of the legendary Amazons and he immediately projects the Russian festivities onto the ancient model. In his poem, he even evokes Penthecilea, an Amazon queen, who, according to myth, headed the Amazon legion which came to the aid of the Trojans.[42] Her sober appearance allows the poet to imbue the description of the Russian feast with shades of antiquity. Troy would not have been destroyed if "such maidens" had come to its aid. Petrov writes:

> All the Greeks would have perished in Ilion,
> If such maidens had fought them.
> Rivers of blood would have flown to Pont. <…>

---

[40] The detailed account on the carousel was published in *Pribavlenie k Moskovskim vedomostiam* (July 7, 1766). See also: A. K. Ganulich, "Pridvornaia karusel' 1766 goda i ee otrazhenie v literature i iskusstve." In *Ekaterina Velikaia: Epokha Rossiiskoi istorii. Tezisy dokladov* (Saint Petersburg, 1996), 234—237; Anthony Cross, "Professor Thomas Newberry's Letter from St. Petersburg, 1766, on the Grand Carousel and Other Matters." In *Slavonic & East European Review*. 76:3 (1998), 487—493.

[41] *Poety XVIII veka*, 1, 327. See on Petrov's odes in *Russkaia oda. Razvitie odicheskoi formy v XVII—XVIII vekakh* (Saint Petersburg, 2005), 275—308.

[42] Wm. Blake Tyrrell, *Amazons. A Study in Athenian Mythmaking* (Baltimore & London, 1984), 78—81.

> The Trojan kingdom would stand safe,
> And Perham would raise its proud walls.[43]

By focusing the reader's attention on both the Russian and ancient Amazons, Petrov expounded on a notion that was already in the air — the image of Catherine II as an Amazon Queen. Voltaire first developed this metaphor in a letter written on July 24th, 1765 in which he compared the Russian Empress to another Amazon Queen, Phalestris.[44] Voltaire's skillful flattery helped him to clarify a confusing comparison. The legend goes that Phalestris wanted to have a child but, ignoring all ordinary men, finally went to Alexander the Great with a proposal to father her child. In Voltaire's thinking, Catherine was so great that the roles would have been reversed: Alexander the Great would have come to Russia to obtain Catherine's favor.

Petrov had managed to pay an exquisite compliment to Catherine II, who had planned the festival and obviously considered it a very significant political event (she was very much interested in how it was received in Europe). But he had gone even further than the usual panegyrics written by poets of the time. He deftly linked the Empress with the most important imperial myth of all, the one which spoke of the Trojan roots of the best European royal houses.[45] The ancient dynastic myth linking the Amazons, a ruined Troy, the fugitive Aeneas, and eternal Rome came to the surface repeatedly in the European tradition. Virgil's *Aeneid* and other ancient legends (the main sources for this mythology) served as a kind of allegorical genealogy which rendered imperial power sacred.

---

[43] *Poety XVIII veka.* 1, 327.

[44] *Documents of Catherine the Great. The Correspondence with Voltaire and the Instruction of 1767 in the English text of 1768.* Edited by W. F. Reddaway (Cambridge, 1931), 3.

[45] Frances A. Yates. *Astraea. The Imperial Theme in the Sixteenth Century* (London, 1993), 50; Frank Kermode, *The Classic: Literary Images of Permanence and Change* (Cambridge, MA -- London, 1983), 58; Marie Tanner, *The Last Descendant of Aeneas. The Hapsburgs and the Mythic Image of the Emperor* (New Haven — London, 1993), 11–16. See also: G. S. Knabe, *Russkaia antichnost'* (Moscow, 2000).

In Europe, the Amazons always served as a vehicle for the development of a whole series of paradigms of *translatio imperii*. This Latin term refers to the transfer or translation (*translatio*) from one civilization to another. In the Middle Ages, both political and cultural legitimacy were thought to have been passed down from classical antiquity (ancient Greece and Rome) to modern day (i.e. medieval) Europe. Both England and France would later seek to prove their superior claims to cultural and political legitimacy by asserting their direct lineage to the glory that was Rome.

The most important steps in laying claim to the transfer were 1) establishing links with ancient Emperors or heroes (ranging from a direct attempt to create genealogical ties to more symbolic /metaphoric parallels and 2) the translation of the major ancient epics into native languages. The Russian Empress cultivated the allegorical and metaphorical linking of her image to antiquity and ordered Petrov to translate Virgil's *Aeneid*.

According to this myth, the female warriors descended from Area, the god of war, and had established their kingdom on the slopes of the Caucasus, in Thrace,[46] or in Scythia (the latter was regarded as the old territory of the modern Crimea, and Catherine's future appropriation of the legendary place would also be associated with ancient mythology). The most important part of the legend was the story that courageous Amazons managed to send a legion headed by their queen Penthesilea to help the Trojans. The Greeks won, Troy fell, and Achilles killed Penthesilea. However, according to myth and to Virgil's interpretation, Troy was "translated" to Italy (to Latium) by Trojan fugitives guided by Aeneas. The Roman Empire was interpreted as Troy was reborn. Later, European monarchs, one by one, would claim their rights to the noble Trojan lineage. The ideology of *translation imperii* became the most relevant component of imperial strategy (in France, this ideology was taken up by Henry IV and reached its apogee with Louis XIV).[47]

---

[46] According to legends, an Amazon state also took place among Slavs in Bohemia. Their chief Libussa (680–738) "left a posterity which was represented in the proud house of the Hapsburgs" (G. C. Rothery, *The Amazons in Antiquity and Modern Times* (London, 1910), 104.

[47] Frances A. Yates. *Astraea. The Imperial Theme in the Sixteenth Century*, 108–109;

As mentioned before, Catherine paid close attention to the planning of the carousel. She ordered Prince Peter Repnin (the chief planner of the carousel) to study the whole historical background of the carousel while she organized it. Catherine took as her model the most famous of carousels, one conducted in 1662 in Paris by Louis XIV. The carousel demonstrated both the stability of the sovereignty of the Sun-King and its prosperity. The ceremony combined elements of a military parade with a theatrical show and revealed the imperial pretensions of European monarchs who did not hesitate to exercise a demonstrative re-feudalization in order to reach their goals.[48]

Nevertheless, a very pragmatic political reason lay behind the feudal endeavor organized by the educated reader of Voltaire and Montesquieu. Beginning with Peter the Great, Russian rulers had tried to force France to accept their use of the title of Emperor. Not until 1745 did Louis XV grant this honor to Elizabeth, a great admirer of France. After her death, however, the title of Emperor was quickly taken away from the next Russian tsar, Catherine's husband, Peter III. Soon after, Catherine II received a refusal from the French royal house to recognize her with the title of Empress. The carousel of 1766 staked a strong claim for *translatio imperii* on Russian soil. At the same time, it represented a political challenge to Louis XV, who Catherine believed had ruined the splendor of his predecessor. The relationship between Louis XV and Catherine was a fairly cold one, seeing that the French court had not supported Catherine in her struggle for the throne during the dramatic events of June 1762. Catherine, according to testimonies from contemporaries, despised Louis XV but worshipped Louis XIV.[49]

The same challenge to Louis XIV resounded in Voltaire's poem of 1766 entitled *Galimatias Pindarique. Sur un carrousel donné par l' impératrice de Russie* (*A Pindaric Nonsense on the occasion of the Carousel given by the Russian Empress*) in which the writer praised

---

Marie Tanner, *The Last Descendant of Aeneas. The Hapsburgs and the Mythic Image of the Emperor*, 11–16.

[48] Frances A. Yates. *Astraea. The Imperial Theme in the Sixteenth Century*, 108–109.

[49] K. I. Lin', "Portret Ekateriny II," in *Ekaterina II i ee okruzhenie* (Moscow, 1996), 394 -- 395; P. P. Cherkasov, *Ekaterina II i Liudovik XVI* (Moscow, 2001).

Catherine and her carousel while condemning the rule of the current king of France:

> Glory lives, in our days,
> In the Empire of an Amazon <...>[50]

Starting in 1763, the beginning of their epistolary relationship, Voltaire began constantly comparing Catherine II with an Amazon Queen and assigning all the glory of the Roman Empire to his royal pen-pal.

It is significant that Petrov, who most likely did not know of Voltaire's ode, also included in his own poem an extensive description of the Amazons, the defenders of Troy. Catherine II greatly appreciated Petrov's allegory. By this time, she had already been skillfully playing up the role of an "Amazon on the throne" for several years. The Amazon myth would soon become one of the most important components of her image as well as a frequent target in anti-Catherine satires and lampoons.[51] Moreover, the Amazon myth would become a part of the Imperial ceremony.

Catherine II was extraordinarily pleased by Petrov's rhetorical stance (also taking part in the carousel were Roman troops headed by her favorite, Grigorii Orlov). The amateur ode-writer had definitely given shape to ideas which were maturing in the Empress's mind. Furthermore, a few years later, Petrov, on Catherine's urging, started to translate Virgil's *Aeneid*, in part as a response to the urgent need to create a Russian version of the Imperial myth. It was also significant that Grigorii Potemkin, while organizing Catherine's trip to the Crimea in 1787, arranged a troop of Amazons as a part of the main ceremony. Potemkin's courier was sent to the Balaklava Greek regiment to select beautiful women from among the local Greek population.[52]

---

[50] *Oeuvres complètes de Voltaire*, 8 (Paris, 1877), 487.

[51] See, for example, a political caricature, which was made by a British satirist in October of 1787. Catherine was pictured as an Amazon, and the inscription said: "The Christian Amazon, with her Invincible Target." On this topic see John T. Alexander, *Catherine the Great. Life and Legend* (New York — Oxford, 1989), 265–266.

[52] In the Balaklava Greek regiment, among relatives of the officers, one

Catherine II made adroit use of the masquerades thrown by her female predecessors. Petrov did as well. In his *Ode on the Occasion of the Carousel* he used the achievements of two poets who had already praised the Amazon-like qualities of Empress Elizabeth of Russia. In 1766, Petrov relied heavily on Mikhail Lomonosov's poem *Inscription to the Brass and Mounted Statue of Her Imperial Majesty Empress Elizabeth Petrovna in Amazon Dress* (Надпись на конное, литое из меди изображение ее Императорского Величества Государыни Императрицы Елисаветы Петровны в амазонском уборе; written between 1751 and 1757) for his descriptions of the Amazons. Lomonosov had already created a strong complimentary metaphor—that Troy would have been saved if the "Queen Amazon" (Elizabeth) had lived in that fabled time. He also suggested that Ilion would have been saved if she had come to its defense. The god Apollo even admired Elizabeth's beauty, declaring:

> "My and Neptune's town would still stand safe,
> If to defend Priam's scepter and throne,
> The queen Amazon like this one had come.
> The crafty Greeks would never have succeeded
>   in their endeavor.
> Elizabeth would have put them down in an hour."[53]

Petrov, an ardent admirer of Lomonosov's poetry, was surely familiar with his *Inscription*, published in the poet's *Selected Works in verse and prose* in 1757. Vasilii Petrov came of age as a poet against the background of this collection, the most famous of its time. More than likely, Catherine II also remembered Lomonosov's verses, which had been composed on the occasion of a court ceremony during which Elizabeth was given a mounted statue as a gift. Catherine, a Grand Duchess at the time, often took part in court festivities. After

---

hundred ladies were chosen and dressed up in Amazon costumes; see the description of the episode in *Moskvitianin* 1 (1844), 266 -- 268. The Austrian diplomat Prince de Ligne wrote about a battalion of two hundred beautiful women and girls, armed and donned in Amazon clothes, who came to meet Catherine's procession just "in curiosity" (Prince de Ligne, *Lettres à la Marquise de Coigny*, 77—78). See also: A. M. Panchenko, "Potemkinskie derevni kak kul'turnyi mif," in *XVIII vek*, 14 (Leningrad, 1983), 96.

[53] M. V. Lomonosov, *Polnoe sobranie sochinenii*, 8, 640.

Catherine became Empress, she engaged her predecessor, who had also enjoyed donning masculine costumes and riding on horseback, in a kind of competition.

Another author, whose descriptions of Elizabeth apparently had an influence on Vasilii Petrov, was Alexander Petrovich Sumarokov, a rival of long-standing of Lomonosov's. In his *Ode on Her Imperial Highness's Birthday Celebrated on December 18th, 1755 (Ода Ее Императорскому Величеству в день Ее Высочайшего рождения торжествуемого 1755 года декабря 18 дня)*, Sumarokov portrayed Elizabeth on a hunt:

> With a fierce and gaping mouth,
> A wild beast runs from the woods,
> A brave maiden chases him,
> Diana's or Peter's daughter,
> She is shining with her beauty
> And bravely shoots her arrows.[54]

Sumarokov's poem, which depicted Elizabeth the huntress, with its picturesque descriptions of her chasing after a "wild beast", made quite an impression on Petrov. In his first ode, Petrov introduced several similar motifs concerning the Russian Amazons. By 1766, as Catherine was molding her image, the ode, with its fervent military spirit and focus on the beauty and courage of the Amazons, served as a fruitful method for referencing the legendary days of June 1762 when she had bravely marched ahead of the regiments in masculine dress.

Catherine as Augustus

Both Russian and European poets competed in their odes and songs in imbuing Catherine's image with features and attributes of ancient Rome. Case in point, the Italian poet Michelangelo Gianetti (1744–1796), who, in his *Song to Her Imperial Majesty Catherine II (Песнь Ее Императорскому Величеству Екатерине II)*, translated by Ippolit Bogdanovich in 1770, compared the Empress to renowned

---

[54] A. P. Sumarokov, *Polnoe sobranie vsekh sochinenii v stikhakh i prose*, II (Moscow, 1781), 17.

Roman Emperors and emphasized the masculine spirit of her rule. The poem pleased Catherine immensely, and the fortunate translator was later given an audience with the Empress. The poem declared:

> Now a happy Neva is more glorious than Thibris.
> Rome was triumphant in giving laws to the world,
> With all the honor of Titus, Trojan, and even Scipio,
> A successful chief of an invincible army
> That bravely conquered African forces:
> All the glory of all the heroes presented by Rome,
> All the glory of those men embodied in you.[55]

The poet implied the most favorable of contexts for Catherine: the recent wars with the Ottoman Empire needed to be associated with the Roman Empire and its conquests. *Translatio imperii* presumed that a new country would claim to be the strongest among all others. Under Catherine's rule, Russia, with its constant wars with the Islamic world, attempted to "translate" the medieval chivalrous tradition of wars against "barbarian hordes." Titus's conquest of Jerusalem and Scipio's destruction of Carthage served as models for the new Empire. Finally Russia had taken the lead in the noble competition for the glory of a newly acclaimed Empire ahead of the two other great European powers, France and Austria.

It must be noted that the use of a masculine title for a female ruler was common in Byzantium. For example, the Byzantine empress Irina (ruled 797-802) held the title of "empress" while sharing power with her son, Constantine. However, as soon as she became the sole ruler, she was given the title of "emperor."[56] Maria, Queen of Hungary (1370-1395), held the title of "rex" (Latin for "king"). The Hungarians also attached the same title to the Austrian queen Maria Theresa.[57]

Virgil's *Aeneid*, the cornerstone of imperial mythology, became vitally important for all imperial "descendants of Aeneas"

---

[55] I. F. Bogdanovich, *Sochineniia*, I (Saint Petersburg, 1848), 260.
[56] B. A. Uspensky, *Tsar' i patriarch v Rossii. Vizantiiskaia model' i ee russkoe pereosmyslenie* (Moscow, 1998), 171.
[57] Ibid.

in Europe.⁵⁸ The extended heroic poem reconstructed the legendary genealogy of the Roman dynasty of "Julus." Aeneas, who brought the Trojan Penates to Latium, was the father of Ascanius. The latter, in turn, founded Alba Longa. The ruler of this city, Numa, left a great many progeny, including the legendary Romulus, the founder of Rome. The complex genealogy was based on Ascanius's second name — Julus.

Later, thanks to Virgil, Julius Caesar would come to incredible fame. In the *Aeneid*, the poet portrayed him as the product of Julus Ascanius's "seeds.". A tricky linguistic play with the similarity of the two names, Julus and Julius, was taken for granted. The dynastic mythology confirmed the noble roots of Caesar's adopted son, the emperor Octavian Augustus. As a result, the ruling emperor and Virgil's patron were given divine provenance; his direct ancestor Aeneas was thought to be the son of Venus and the famous hero Anchises. The *Aeneid* is full of political allusions, especially the fourth and sixth cantos, which Virgil read to Augustus and which are mostly concerned with a prophecy about a great and victorious empire.⁵⁹ An open panegyric to Augustus became not only the main source of future political mythology, but also set the tone for European court ceremonies, art works, and laudatory poetry.

Translatio imperii in Russia also followed these patterns.⁶⁰ In terms of the legitimization and sanctification of Catherine's power in the early stages of her rule, Petrov's "translation" endeavor became the single most important ideological event. In 1769, Catherine II

---

⁵⁸ Roy Strong, *The Cult of Elizabeth: Elizabethan portraiture and pageantry* (London, 1977); Frances A Yates, *Astraea. The Imperial Theme in the Sixteenth Century*; Marie Tanner, *The Last Descendant of Aeneas. The Hapsburgs and the Mythic Image of the Emperor*.

⁵⁹ Frank Kermode, *The Classic: Literary Images of Permanence and Change*, 51.

⁶⁰ Already Ivan IV the Terrible linked his genealogy with the Roman dynasty: he cultivated the idea of the generation of Russian tzars from Prus, the mythic brother of Augustus (Iu. Lotman, B. A. Uspenskii, "Otzvuki kontseptsii "Moskva — tretii Rim" v ideologii Petra Pervogo: K probleme srednevekovoi traditsii v kul'ture barokko," in Iu. M. Lotman, *Istoriia i tipologiia russkoi kul'tury* (St. Peterburg, 2002, 350); G. S. Knabe, *Russkaia antichnost,'* 71). The concept of Moscow as the third Rome became very popular in Russian ideology.

ordered Petrov to translate the *Aeneid* into Russian and then closely followed Petrov's progress. Like Virgil, who had read fragments of the poem to Emperor Augustus, his most prominent patron, in Russia Petrov was instructed to read his translations to Catherine. Catherine clearly designed the reception of the translation of the *Aeneid* according to the lofty model of literary patronage: Augustus / Virgil—Catherine / Petrov. Virgil's epic poem, despite the hermetic nature of some of the cantos, contained a sufficient number of political allusions to receive Augustus's approval. The first canto translated by Petrov in 1770, according to the nature of the genre, also included some allusions to recent political events and demonstrated the strategy of current Russian political mythology.

Petrov even played on one of Catherine's German maiden names, Sophia *Augusta* Fredericka, in the dedication to the first canto of his poem:

> Imitating Maron's lofty musings,
> Ardent in a diligence which overwhelms me,
> I would strive to show the entire World
> How much greater than Augustus is your mother,
>
> Augusta.[61]

Petrov greatly expanded the links between Augustus and Catherine as he wrote the ode. The wars with Turkey provided a perfect opportunity. In 1769-1770, Vasilii Maikov (1728—1778) also used them in his odes when he praised the military deeds of Russian troops in the first war with Turkey. In his *Ode to Catherine the Second on the Occasions of the Victory over the Turks near the Dnestr River (Ода Императрице Екатерине Второй на победу, одержанную над турками при Днестре)* of 1769, Maikov wrote:

> A happy age has returned to us,
> Like in Augustus's days.[62]

---

[61] *Enei. Geroicheskaia poema Publiia Vergiliia Marona*. Perevedena s latinskago Vasil'em Petrovym, 1 (Saint Petersburg, 1770), 1.
[62] Vasilii Maikov, *Izbrannye proizvedeniia* (Moscow — Leningrad, 1966), 209.

In his 1770 *Ode to Triumphant Russian Weaponry (Ода победоносному российскому оружию)*, he confidently declared:

> Oh, Augustus, your power is over.
> Catherine has come to the throne
> To rule the whole universe. [63]

The Russian Empress was obviously searching for an appropriate ideological rationale for her political strategy. The classic Virgilian paradigm looked quite attractive: Aeneas was the father of the Empire, and Emperor Augustus had established the Golden Age, the peak of prosperity, for the Roman Empire. In the Russian context, Peter the Great became the founder, while Catherine II acquired the characteristics of Augustus. She also claimed to have brought a Golden Age to Russia. Catherine the Great attempted to associate herself with the classical masculine models of imperial power by engaging in broad legislative activity and promoting extensive expansionist policies in foreign affairs.

At the beginning of 1770, Petrov published the first canto of his *Enei (Aeneus)*. The Empress expressed her highest approval the same year in her *Antidote* published in French in Amsterdam and devoted to the polemics with Abbé Chappe d'Autéroche. Catherine proclaimed in no uncertain terms: "Especially in recent times, when literature, arts, and science have been especially protected, dozens of books, in the original or in translation, are published every week. Among our young authors, there is V. P. Petrov, the librarian of the Empress's own library, and we cannot pass over his name in silence. The poetic power of the young man already approaches Lomonosov's greatness. In addition, he has greater harmony; his style is full of eloquence and grace. Without mentioning his other works, it is necessary to recognize his verse translation in the *Aeneid*, the first canto of which has just been published. This translation will immortalize him."[64] Russian readers could not doubt that the first canto of the *Aeneid* (*Enei* was its title in Petrov's

---

[63] Ibid, 222.

[64] *Sochineniia imperatritsy Ekateriny II na osnovanii podlinnykh rukopisei s ob"iasnitel'nymi primechaniiami akademika A. N. Pypina* (Saint Petersburg, 1901), 256.

version) would serve as political propaganda of sorts to glorify the Empress. The cover of the book was embossed with Catherine's monogram.

Catherine as Dido

Scholars have linked Petrov's success in praising Catherine in his *Enei* with his identifying of her with Dido. The comparison with Dido already pleased another female ruler — Maria Theresa of Austria, who enjoyed very much the opera *Dido* performed by her court composer Niccolo Jommelli in 1748.

Catherine II had even more justifications for comparisons to Dido: both were female monarchs; both were foreigners who had arrived from abroad and strengthened their countries by expansionism and the enlightenment of the people.[65] In 1778, as Petrov was in the midst of his translations of the next cantos of the *Aeneid*, Catherine II was being embellished as Dido on the cameos of a dinner set made by the Sevres Porcelain Factory. The set (currently in the Hermitage) was a gift to Catherine from Prince Grigorii Potemkin.[66] However, it was not the love story (important for Potemkin) that drew the attention of the exceptionally insightful Russian poet and translator, but Dido's political strategies.

Remarkably, Petrov portrayed Dido, who forgot about her deceased husband and fell in love with Aeneas, extremely sympathetically. Petrov emphasized particular episodes in the Phoenician princess's life. She fled her homeland of Tyre after her brother murdered her husband and usurped the throne; thereafter, she successfully founded the new city-state of Carthage. Clearly, the fate of the Carthaginian Queen would have implications for eighteenth-century Russia. The classical imperial paradigm was destined to serve as a constant model for political comparisons and allegories in Russia. In this case, readers could easily detect

---

[65] Andrew Kahn, "Reading of Imperial Rome from Lomonosov to Pushkin", in *The Slavic Review*, 52:4 (1993), 752–756.

[66] I. V. Riazantsev, "Ekaterina v zerkale antichnoi mifilogii," in *Russkaia kul'tura poslednei treti XVIII veka — vremeni Ekateriny Vtoroi* (Moscow, 1997), 140.

the similarities between Dido's life and Catherine's political maneuverings.

For example, Dido cautiously explains to the stranger Aeneas and his allies that her constant efforts to increase the defense and security of Carthage stem from her swift and unstable ascension to the throne in an alien country.[67] The goddess Venus completes the story by relating all the previous misfortunes which have befallen Dido. First, there was her brother Pygmalion's unjust accession to the throne. A tyrannical, vicious person, Pygmalion ignored all the customs (including religious ones) of the country. Petrov described him as the negative protagonist from the classical canon: "Tyrant, monster, the embodiment of all evil."[68] Pygmalion murders Dido's husband inside the temple, near the altar, during a religious ceremony. He then does not even accord the victim a proper burial. Russian readers could easily make the connection between Dido's persecutor, a barbaric, uneducated dictator who flouts laws and religious customs, and Peter III. At the time of the ode's publication, the judgments on Peter III from the second (so-called "extended") *Manifesto* (published July 6th, 1762) on the occasion of Catherine's accession were still fresh in the Russian readers' memory. Peter III was described according to the classical canon as a despot obsessed with indecent desires and passions:

> "The despotism of a Ruler who wields absolute power and who is the kind of person unbridled by kind and philanthropic qualities is an evil which can lead to fatal consequences. Thus, our fatherland ran into trouble when an Emperor-Tyrant who was slave to his passions, came to the throne. Such a personality did not allow him to think of the good of the country which he ruled."[69]

Readers could also recall passages from the *Manifesto* concerning Peter's disrespect towards Elizabeth on the occasion of her funeral:

---

[67] *Enei. Geroicheskaia poema Publiia Vergiliia Marona. Perevedena s latinskago Vasil'em Petrovym*, 1, 32.

[68] Ibid., 20.

[69] *Put' k tronu*, 491–492.

> "He ungraciously spoke about Her (Empress Elizabeth. — V. P.) body. With none of our sense of kinship or sincere concern <...>, he did not accord this great, generous Empress the funeral she deserved <...>"[70]

The second *Manifesto* also noted that there was a real threat that Catherine would be murdered on the eve of the revolt of 1762. There was another notable detail in Petrov's *Enei* which drew readers' attention — Dido's secret escape from Tyre, which corresponded with the first stage in Catherine's coup, her secret trip from Peterhof to St. Petersburg.[71] Dido's escape from Tyre and her ascension to the throne also corresponded with the events of Catherine's coup.[72]

The paradigm of city-state building in barbaric locales (Carthage and Saint Petersburg) was a significant one. It connected Dido (and, at the same time, Catherine II) with the myth of a creator of civilization. By the chain of allusions to Russian events, Petrov applied Virgil's tradition of city building to Catherine, who then acquired the features of a "cultural hero," a founder of a new civilization.

In his translation of Virgil's *Aeneid*, Petrov found the appropriate material with which to develop the previously approved Amazonian metaphors. The female ruler Dido, despite all her "feminine" qualities, such as her desperate love for Aeneas, was given masculine features. She was portrayed as a strong and powerful autocrat capable of governing barbaric inhabitants, and her image was enriched by Amazonian motifs. In his first canto of Virgil's translation, Petrov saturated the text with images of the female warriors. Moreover, he depicted Virgil's heroines using formulas taken from his *Ode on the Occasion of the Magnificent Carousel*. We see Venus, disguised as an Amazon, and her female companions, described as "Sparta's brave maidens."[73] The phrase

---

[70] Ibid, 492.
[71] *Enei. Geroicheskaia poema Publiia Vergiliia Marona. Perevedena s latinskago Vasil'em Petrovym.* 1, 20.
[72] Ibid, 22.
[73] Ibid, 20.

corresponded with a very well-known line from his *Carousel* ode addressed to the female participants in Catherine's event: "Are they brave Sparta's maidens?"[74] The Amazons, astride strong-willed horses, with their curls streaming in the wind all look the same in Petrov's translation, and thus, all bore close a close resemblance to Catherine's image in Torelli's painting.

In his *Enei*, Petrov consciously emphasized the effects of female masculinity by multiplying the Amazon images and using his own clichés, which, in turn, corresponded with Lomonosov's and Sumarokov's odes to the Empress Elizabeth. Petrov skillfully manipulated the reader's perceptions by constantly returning to the Amazon theme. As a result, a comprehensive image of one brave female ruler was formed. It was no accident that Petrov called Dido "tsarina," incorporating the Russian term into his Latin translation. In fact, the design of Petrov's book as a whole was to include multiple references to Catherine's involvement. The translator even added a poetic dedication to Catherine to the book.

Catherine, however, found only the first canto of the poem, which gave a detailed account of Dido's ascension to the throne and her glamorous years as ruler of a newly established kingdom, to be of use. Petrov's translation of the last cantos appeared only in 1781–1786. Between the first canto (1770) and the last ones, there were many changes in both political and literary trends. The new cantos, which came out in the mid-1780s, excited neither readers nor the empress, who had already adjusted her image and charged the poets of a new generation with its depiction. But in 1770, when Petrov's *Enei* came out, the situation was quite different. Petrov had translated not just a poem; he had made an enormous contribution to Catherine's sanctification in the most suitable of forms. He had "translated" glory, ambition, and success along the lines of the classical model to the Russian throne. By translating Virgil into Russian, the poet had symbolically postulated the paradigms of a Russian *translatio imperii*.

---

[74] *Poety XVIII veka.* I, 327.

Confirming the Amazon Image

Catherine played up her female-male image until the very end of her reign. Masculine dress became her clothing of choice for public appearances and military ceremonies. Her son's teacher, Semen Poroshin, gave an account in his diary of her appearance on April 8th, 1765, when she took part in Easter festivities: "Her Highness visited a public comedy performance today; she was on horseback wearing the military uniform of a horse guardsman. She was donating money."[75] The next day, she visited a suburban tavern in a different uniform: "Her Highness was wearing the uniform of an infantry guardsman today; she went to the 'Three Hands' and had dinner there."[76] She also attended military training in June 1765 near Krasnoe Selo "on horseback, wearing a horse-guardsman's uniform."[77]

This image turned out to be a consistent poetic trope in all ode writing of the time. It reflected the episode from Catherine's coup of 1762 when she had ridden ahead of the army bound for Peterhof dressed as a man. Vasilii Maikov, in his *Ode on the Occasion of the Election of Delegates for a Committee for a New Code in 1767* (Ода на случай избрания депутатов для сочинения проекта Нового Уложения 1767 года), included the same poetic motifs which referred to the event:

> A woman, dressed as a brave man,
> Overflowing with heroic spirit,
> Rushes ahead of defiant combat
> To fight and win all army around;
> Her horse turns and whirls
> And kicks up the sand
> Making clouds of dust
> Peter was great and glorious,
> When he smashed the heads of the
> Reckless Swedes in the battle of Poltava. [78]

---

[75] *Russkii Arkhiv*, 7 (1869), 16.
[76] Ibid.
[77] Ibid, 46.
[78] Vasilii Maikov, *Izbrannye proizvedeniia*, 199.

The competition over Amazon images would continue for the following decades and would establish a ritual for the representation of the empress in poetry. Later, Gavrila Derzhavin (1743—1816), in his extended poem would deem the Amazon image the most appropriate for the empress:

> Dress her beauty in golden armor,
> And put her in masculine attire
> Her helmet with feathers will shine,
> Zephyrs will stream through her locks;
> Her horse will turn its head around
> Stormy foaming his furrows.
> The grey-haired North will be amazed
> And let her possess him <...> [79]

In his *Explanations of the Works*, Derzhavin connected this fragment from his poem to the events of 1762: "This is a picture of the Empress coming to the throne when, dressed as a warrior, sword in hand, she rode ahead of the guards on a brave white horse."[80] In addition, Derzhavin's poem depicted Russian as an allegorical figure of "the grey-haired North," that is, as a male figure in the cold, northern part of the world. After his ode *Felitsa* (Фелица, 1782), Derzhavin tried to revive metaphors of royal representation. The poem *The Picture of Felitsa* included newly invented devices for projecting the empress's image. He associated Russia with a male, not a female, figure. Derzhavin's male "grey-haired North," who bowed before the beautiful horsewoman (and asked her to possess him) represented a chivalrous inversion of traditional gender roles. The poet clearly identified himself with the "grey-haired North," a gallant metaphor (with obvious erotic connotations) of the newly Westernized Russia under Catherine's rule.

During the last years of her rule, as tired of political connotations as she was of cross-dressing, Catherine returned to her early habits: she brought back the masquerade performances

---

[79] *Sochineniia Derzhavina. S ob"iasnitel'nymi primechaniiami Ia. Grota*, 1 (Saint Petersburg 1868), 191.
[80] Ibid, 204.

of Elizabeth's era. In the late 1780s, Catherine got involved with the court theater *Hermitage* where foreign diplomats and her closest circle of friends also participated. The participants, the Empress included, wrote scenarios full of allusions to court life, all in French. Catherine's admirer, the quick-witted Count Ségure, composed *Crispin Duegne*, which addressed the fashionable topic of cross-dressing.[81] Crispin, acting according to his master's plan, disguises himself as a woman and serves as Henriette's *duegne* to help his master court the young heroine. Performances of the comedy were met with tremendous success.

In 1790, Catherine held a court masquerade with traditional cross-dressing. In October, 1790, Alexander Khrapovitskii, her secretary, made note of the occasion in his diary: "I was told in secret that there would be a surprise at the Hermitage; according to the plan, the men should dress as women and the women as men."[82] The era of Empress Elizabeth, who adored masquerades, had faded into the past and become a historic tradition which no longer threatened Catherine' rule and seemed ripe for imitation. Catherine had laid out a plan for the masquerade. She made a detailed account of the number of people to be invited and the items to be prepared. In addition, she described the main scenario for the approaching performance:

> It occurred to me that we could organize a very amazing thing. We should arrange a ball in the Hermitage Palace, like in the old times, but with fewer people, and more distinguished guests. <...> The ladies should wear modest attire, without farthingales and elaborate headdress. <...> After a few dances, the Marshal of the Court will escort the Grand Duchess, in the company of a violinist, through all the rooms and into the large hall near the theater. The curtains in this hall should be down, especially at the entrance, so that what is to happen will be hidden from view. Four boutiques with masquerade costumes should be placed inside, two for women's clothes, two for men's. French actors will play the roles of merchants;

---

[81] *Théâtre de l'Hermitage de Catherine II, impératrice de Russie, composé par cette princess, par plusieurs personnes de sa societé intime, et par quelques ministres etrange* (Paris, 1799), 1, 49—88.

[82] A. V. Khrapovitskii, *Pamiatnye zapiski* (Moscow, 1862), 233.

they will sell, on credit, women's dresses to men, and men's clothing to women. There must be signboards above the boutiques which read: *Men's Goods* for the women's dresses and *Ladies' Wares* for the men's. <...>[83]

The empress and her ninety-four guests participated in the ceremony: the clothing was historical, further confusing and complicating the distinction between male and female. More than likely, the costumes did not make the participants look ugly or uncomfortable — a new kind of cross-dressing which excluded the sadistic subtext of the gender play at work under Elizabeth. Khrapovitskii described the events: "There was a dinner in the Hermitage. After that, we opened the boutiques, donned our dresses, and the masquerade began; all the guests were very happy."[84]

The masquerade had been designed as a theatrical performance: professional actors joined the courtiers, and all participants performed according to Catherine's scenario. The cross-dressing took place in a room near the Hermitage's theater. The empress used her authority to transform the guests (among them was Grand Prince Pavel Petrovich) into obedient actors performing their roles. However, the theatrical character of the event overshadowed any political meaning. The masquerade was supposed to allude to Elizabeth's era, but also to outshine it. Well-organized and pre-arranged, the masquerade was to demonstrate the excellence, style, and assurance of the court and sovereign's power. The reference to Egypt was to demonstrate both the civilized and fashionable attitudes of the royal court. Born of masquerade amusements, Catherine's political strategy of gender inversion had once again returned to its roots and become a court performance played out on the stage of the imperial theater.

---

[83] *Zapiski Imperatritsy Ekateriny Vtoroi* (Saint Petersburg, 1907), 668.
[84] A. V. Khrapovitskii, *Pamiatnye zapiski*, 234.

Chapter Two

Astraea's Coming to the Russian Throne

Among the most consistent titles which the Russian lyrical canon associated with Catherine II (along with Minerva, Pallad, or Semiramid) was the title of Astraea. This particular title seemed to be an additional rhetorical cliché, and scholars did not distinguish it from other flattering allegoric names.[1] Thus, for example, Iurii Lotman, who made significant discoveries in the symbolic context of the Russian literature of the eighteenth century, only briefly mentioned the title among others that were similar. Speaking about Catherine's ideological platform and discussing its dubious character, he wrote: "On the one hand, she is "Minerva," "Astraea," and "Goddess-like queen," on the other, she is a *human being* on the throne."[2]

However, the meaning of this poetic acclaim was not limited to a mere laudatory comparison. The title of Astraea implied strong political connotations and played a significant role in transfers of authority during the eighteenth century. The reference to Astraea always evoked a whole set of corresponding mythological motifs. This title retained its close connection with the myth throughout several Russian monarchs' reigns. It enabled the name of Astraea

---

[1] Stephen Baehr brought in some examples of Astraea's metaphors while investigating Paradise's topics in Eighteen century Russian culture: Stephen L. Baehr, *The Paradise Myth*, 38 -- 40. For some political connotations of the metaphors, see Richard S. Wortman, *Scenarios of Power: Myth and Ceremony in Russian Monarchy*, 1, *From Peter the Great to the Death of Nicolas I* (Princeton, 1995), 84—109.

[2] Iu. M. Lotman, "Ocherki po istorii russkoi kul'tury XVIII—nachala XIX veka," in *Iz istorii russkoi kul'tury. IV (XVIII—naschalo XIX veka)* (Moscow, 2001), 57.

not only to be mechanically reproduced in laudatory poetry, but also to exert its influence upon the Russian political context.

According to Greek mythology, Astraea was the virgin-goddess, and daughter of Zeus and Themed. During the wars of the Titans, Astraea became Zeus's ally and was often pictured as a two-winged maid who carries Zeus's thunderbolts in her arms. She was also considered the goddess of justice who dwelt amongst mankind during Saturn's Golden Age. After she was driven from the earth by the disturbances of the Iron Age, Zeus placed her amongst the stars as the constellation Virgo.[3] The paradigms of Astraea's flight from the sinful earth and ascent to heaven became very popular in European poetry and art.

One of the first to interpret the imagery of Astraea was the Roman poet Ovid. In the first book of his *Metamorphoses*, Ovid presents a very impressive description of the four cosmic cycles which succeed each other in a regressive manner. The first cycle is, as Ovid writes, the Golden Age of Saturn's kingdom, which signifies a constant blessing of human triumphs, an eternal spring, peace, and the absence of labor. It is followed by the Silver and Copper Ages, in which mankind becomes acquainted with the changing of the seasons and the necessity of work. Finally, the Iron Age establishes the kingdom of evil and brings injustice, war, and human vices. People occupy themselves with amassing possessions and murder. As a result, the Virgin Astraea, the last of the "immortals," leaves the earth.[4]

Nevertheless, one of the main sources of the Astraea myth in European poetry is Virgil's *Fourth Eclogue* (39—41 BCE).[5] Virgil's poem contains a Messianic prophecy that suggests the ending of the old world and the immanent coming of the kingdom of Saturn, a return of the Golden Age on earth. The poet's descriptions of the Golden Age were later considered archetypal for poetry and art. European artists and poets especially appreciated Virgil's prediction

---

[3] Ovid, *Metamorphoses*, 1, 149 -- 150.

[4] Ibid, 1, 150.

[5] For a detailed discussion of Virgil's *Forth Eclogue*, see Jerome Carcopino, *Virgile et le mystère de la IV eclogue* (Paris, 1993).

of the emergence of a new generation of people, poetry lovers, who would come to establish their rule. According to the *Fourth Eclogue*, the Virgin earth will bear fruit without any toil. Humankind will come to know Virtue and Justice: the poem implies the idea of Justice and the Prosperity of the Roman Empire under the Emperor Augustus's rule. As the final sign of the Golden Age, the Virgin Astraea will descend to earth and bring forth her child — a sacred baby boy:[6]

> Now is come the last age of the Cumaean prophecy: the great cycle of periods is born anew. Now returns the Maid, returns the reign of Saturn: now from high heaven a new generation comes down. Yet do thou at that boy's birth, in whom the iron race shall begin to cease, and the golden to arise over all the world <...>.[7]

The poem, especially its conclusion, in which Virgil depicts the Mother taking care of her baby boy, anticipates the Christian tradition in portraying the Virgin Mary and her sacred baby boy; though, according to his time, Virgil displays his icon in an Epicurean frame:

> Begin, O little boy, to know and smile upon thy mother, thy mother on whom ten months have brought weary longings. Begin, O little boy: of them who have not smiled on a parent, never was one honoured at a god's board or on a goddess' couch.[8]

Meanwhile, mythology and poetry tightly interlaced with politics in the Roman poetry of the time of the emperor Augustus. Most of all, Virgil, in his *Fourth Eclogue* and his epic poem the *Aeneid*, develops the concept of Rome as a return of the Golden Age. The Roman Empire under Augustus, with the Pax Romana and the flourishing of the country, acquires the features of a universal model for subsequent imperial mythologies.

---

[6] Frances A. Yates, *Astraea. The Imperial Theme in the Sixteen Century*, 38. Frank Kermode, *The Classic. Literary Images of Permanence and Change*, 56–61; Stephen L. Baehr. *The Paradise Myth in Eighteenth-Century Russia*, 7.

[7] *Virgil's Works: The Aeneid, Eclogues, Georgics*. Transl. by J. W. Mackail (New York, 1934), 275.

[8] Ibid, 276.

In European history, Dante made the first and most emphatic turn toward political interpretations of Virgil's *Fourth Eclogue*. In his politico-theological manifesto *Monarchy*, he links Virgil's poetical speculations to his own program. His concept entails the idea of a strong and absolute emperor who suppresses the power of the Church and establishes a sacred empire. Dante associates Virgil's Golden Age with the most successful periods of such an empire.[9] After Dante, Astraea became a symbol of the sacred empire for generations of European poets. The Astraea myth as depicted in paintings, royal processions, acclamatory odes and sculptural ornaments was always a part of the court ceremony.[10] Astraea increasingly lost her cosmic connotations; instead, she acquired the clarity of a political symbol. The Italian poet Ariosto pays tribute to the Astraea metaphors in *The Frenzy of Orlando* (1516). In his epic poem, he proclaims King Charles V a future world ruler who would establish the Golden Age and promote the return of Astraea.[11]

The cult of Astraea reached its peak in the English poetry of the sixteenth century during the reign of Queen Elizabeth I. Mary Sidney Herbert, the Countess of Pembroke, in her *Dialogue Between Two Shepherds, Thenot and Piers, in Praise of Astraea* (1590), Sir John Davies in his *Hymns of Astraea* (1599), and Edmund Spenser in his allegorical epic poem *The Faerie Queen* (1590-96), addressed to Elizabeth I, all treat the theme of Astraea as a proclamation of the Golden Age in England and for England.[12] Their political and theological speculations, converted into poetical myth, elaborate the concept of a national imperialism (the country as the world) and religious independence from the Pope's power. Eventually, the Elizabethans glorified the advantages of Protestant England, their victories over the Spanish Armada, and even the triumphs of their

---

[9] Dante, *Monarchy*, I, XI.

[10] Roy Strong, *The Cult of Elizabeth: Elizabethan portraiture and pageantry*; Frances A Yates, *Astraea. The Imperial Theme in the Sixteenth Century*; Marie Tanner, *The Last Descendant of Aeneas*.

[11] Marie Tanner, *The Last Descendant of Aeneas*, 113.

[12] *The Collected Works of Mary Sidney Herbert, Countess of Pembroke*, 1 (Oxford, 1998), 83–84.

laws, which they considered to be the fairest in the world.¹³ Later, John Dryden in his *Astraea Redux* (1660) applies Astraea symbolism to his political forebodings.

The same metaphors played a significant role in changes of power in France. Each newly crowned French monarch associated his ascension to the throne with a new return of the times of Astraea. The concept of Astraea's return strengthened the French monarchy in general by implying the idea of the continuity of royal power, which emerged anew after the death of the king, like the phoenix from the ashes, with the proclamation of the new ruler. In 1632 the novel *Astraea* by Honoré d'Urfé was published and achieved tremendous popularity. At the beginning of the 1640s, the French royal family commissioned Salvator Rosa to paint *A Return of Astraea*. The painting praises the end of the Thirty Years' War and the return of the peaceful Golden Age ushered in by the regent Anne of Austria (1573–1598) and her young son, the future Louis XIV.

In 1722, on the occasion of Louis XV's ascension to the throne, the royal court participated in a ceremony embellished with inscriptions and slogans taken from Virgil's *Fourth Eclogue*: Astraea descends from heaven in order to glorify the strength and prosperity of the French nation under a new monarch.¹⁴

The Russian Astraea and Questions of Succession to the Throne

In Russia, the appearance of the Astraea paradigm served as a hallmark of the Russian court's adaptation to the European imperial tradition. The youthful Russian empire strove to inherit this Roman link and place Russian rulers among the most distinctive "descendants" of the Roman emperors.

In eighteenth-century Russia, with a sequence of women rulers and juvenile heirs, metaphors from the *Fourth Eclogue* became very popular in poetry, from Mikhail Lomonosov and Alexander

---

[13] Frances A Yates, *Astraea. The Imperial Theme in the Sixteenth Century*, 30–65.

[14] Richard A. Jackson, *Vive le roi! A History of the French Coronation from Charles V to Charles X*, 183–184.

Sumarokov to Nikolai Karamzin. These metaphors were especially far removed, however, from utopian notions of paradise on earth.[15] The problem of succession to the throne became a focus of Astraea's myth in its Russian version. The Russian government of the eighteenth century regularly faced a political situation which involved a recurrent gender distribution: a strong woman would assume the throne on behalf of a juvenile, who, while incapable of ruling, was the legitimate male heir. The paradigms of Virgil's poem — the relationship between Astraea and her baby boy — corresponded very well to Russian political models. The Astraea myth served as a vehicle for different political parties struggling for power.

The question of succession to the throne was not strictly codified and remained quite complicated at the beginning of the eighteenth century. In 1722, Peter I ordered the publication of *A Code on the Succession to the Throne,* which abolished the old tradition of transfers of power in Russia. According to the established procedure, the eldest son (in the case of the absence of a male heir, the eldest grandson) should assume the throne after the death of a tsar. In his new *Code,* Peter I called the practice "an unfair custom" and proclaimed complete freedom in choosing a new heir in accordance with the "benefits" of the state.[16] In 1724, his wife Catherine I had been crowned empress: Peter I personally put the crown on her head. This event opened doors to arbitrary changes of authority as well as to the subsequent series of "palace revolutions."

Lomonosov was the first Russian poet to employ Astraea metaphors in his poetry. In August 1741, just after his return from his studies in Germany, the young poet composed an *Ode on a bright ceremony of the birthday of his Highness Ivan the Third, Russian Emperor and Autocrat, written on 12 August 1741 by the blissful Russia* (Ода, которую в торжественный праздник высокого рождения Великого Государя Иоанна Третьего, Императора и Самодержца Всероссийского, 1741 года, августа 12 дня веселящаяся Россия

---

[15] Stephen L. Baehr, *The Paradise Myth in Eighteenth-Century Russia,* 38—39.

[16] On the details of the succession, see M. Zyzykin, *Tsarskaia vlast' i zakon o prestolonasledii v Rossii* (Sophia, 1924); E. V. Anisimov, *Rossiia bez Petra: 1725—1740* (Saint Petersburg, 1994).

произносит). Lomonosov wrote this ode during the short rule of Anna Leopol'dovna, the niece of the former Russian ruler Anna Ioannovna and mother of the one-year old monarch Ivan (Ioann) Antonovich. Anna Leopol'dovna was the temporary regent of Russia in 1740—1741 while the real heir was still a baby boy.

Like in Virgil's eclogue, Lomonosov, a great admirer and translator of Latin poetry, endows his mother/son picture with the Golden Age's formulas: rivers and waters become warm and blissful, as "the Golden Age begins anew."[17] The poet describes Anna Leopol'dovna as the Goddess of the North who rules over a large country:

> Hope, Light, Protection, Goddess
> Of the fifth part of the whole world,
>   Great Princess of the North,
>   Your hand wisely governs
>   Over the twenty different peoples,
> And the other hand carries the monarch <...>[18]

Lomonosov depicts the Empress in a very significant pose: she governs with one hand and carries her baby boy, the true monarch, in the other. Lomonosov always uses this model for his portrayals of Astraea.

Meanwhile, poet's poetic paradise turned into a real nightmare: Peter I's daughter, Elizabeth, soon deposed both heroes of the poem from the throne, and banned any mention of them. Ivan Antonovich (who was the only legitimate male heir to the Russian throne at that time) spent the rest of his life imprisoned, far away from the capital. Lomonosov never included this poem in any *Collections* of his works. From the beginning, baby boys were considered hostile to a real female power in eighteenth century Russia.

The Empress Elizabeth of Russia also was often associated with Astraea, with a few particular nuances. Because of her name and marital status (Elizaveta Petrovna was not married), poets and courtiers linked her to Elizabeth I of England, and, by extension, to the Maid Astraea. The comparison of Russian and English queens

---

[17] M. V. Lomonosov, *Polnoe sobranie sochinenii*, 8, 34.
[18] Ibid, 41.

became the topic of an ode written by Gottlob Friedrich Wilhelm Junker (1703—1746), a German poet who held a university post in Russia. He composed this poem on the occasion of Elizabeth's coronation in April 1742. Lomonosov, who had to translate the ode from German into Russian, does not miss the comparison:

> You seem alike in all Elizabeth of England <...>[19]

Elizabeth is clearly identified as Astraea in the opera *The Gratitude of Titus* by Pietro Metastasio, translated from Italian into Russian by Ivan Merkuriev and performed during the same coronation festivities of 1742. By the end of this court performance, Astraea had descended from heaven holding a shield adorned with Elizabeth's name. [20]

Lomonosov soon became a constant singer of a beautiful Russian Empress Elizabeth. He also employs the Astraea mythology in his *Ode on the Birthday and Arrival from Holstein of his Highness Grand Prince Petr Fedorovich, February 10, 1742* (Ода на прибытие из Голстинии и на день рождения Его Императорского Высочества Государя Великого князя Петра Федоровича 1742 года февраля 10 дня). The era's political events gave ample reasons for Virgil's paradigms and Astraea mythology to appear in Lomonosov's ode. Just after assuming power, Elizaveta Petrovna, who had no children, hastened to resolve the question of her successor in order to prevent an illegitimate *coup d'état* in the future. On November 28, 1741, three days after her ascension, she issued a manifesto on the succession to the Russian throne. The next day she invited her nephew, the young prince Petr Fedorovich, to Saint Petersburg. Petr Fedorovich was a grandson of Peter the Great (his mother, Anna, was the sister of Elizabeth). Lomonosov wrote this ode during the period from the appearance of the manifesto to the arrival of the prince in the capital. In light of the situation, the poet created an allegorical icon to use as the focus of his lyric descriptions. He depicts Elizabeth as the Maid who carries Petr Fedorovich, the sacred Boy, in her arms:

---

[19] Ibid, 76.

[20] *Teatral'naia zhizn' Rossii v epokhu Elizavety Petrovny*, 2, 54—55. Ivan Merkuriev, the translator of the Office of Foreign Affairs, took over such an important task instead of Lomonosov.

> I see the Maid standing in sun,
> Holding the Boy by her arm,
> Governing Northern countries.
> Decorated all over by stars,
> She sends thunderbolts down,
> Chasing evils and troubles.[21]

Here Lomonosov employs Biblical metaphors referring to the twelfth chapter of Revelations: "Now a great sign appeared in heaven: a woman clothed with the sun, with the moon under her feet, and on her head a garland of twelve stars" (12:1). She gave birth to "a male Child who was to rule all nations with a rod of iron" (12:5). However, following the Baroque poetic tradition, Lomonosov combines Biblical citations with pagan metaphors. His Maid chases evil with thunderbolts (Astraea was often portrayed with thunderbolts in her hands in antiquity). Lomonosov's description aimed to sanction Elizabeth's power and to support her efforts in strengthening the throne through the rightful choice of a future heir — a sacred baby boy, Petr Fedorovich.

The rise of Astraea mythology came with Catherine's appearance in the political arena. In September 1754, Catherine, who was at that time the Grand Duchess through her marriage to Petr Fedorovich, gave birth to a new potential heir, Pavel. The event mobilized the formation of a new political opposition to Elizabeth's rule. By that time, Elizabeth had lost popularity among different political circles of Russian society, from high-ranking courtiers to guardsmen. The former began to worship the young, smart, and beautiful Grand Duchess Ekaterina Alekseevna and her baby boy, Pavel Petrovich.

Alexander Sumarokov clearly expresses the new hopes of the opposition in his prose *Speech (Слово)*, written on the occasion of Pavel's birth on September 20, 1754. While using Biblical quotations to praise the blessed mother and son, Sumarokov concludes his *Speech* with references to Virgil and the Astraea metaphors: "I see now the gates of the Athenian temple opened, and the daughter of

---

[21] M. V. Lomonosov, *Polnoe sobranie sochinenii*, 8, 66.

Saturn's son comes to meet you (Pavel. — *V. P.*) <...>. The blessed wisdom and innocence of the Golden Age come together: Astraea descends to earth from heaven.'[22] Playing with a complicated system of references, the author describes the "Roman decline" before Christ's coming in harsh terms. He denounces the cult of luxury and hypocrisy and complains about the decaying state of the sciences. This depiction obviously targets the last years of Elizabeth's rule: Sumarokov skillfully encrypts his sharp criticism in a laudatory form. The reader could easily recognize an implicit denunciation of Elizabeth's age decorated in Roman features. Using Astraea symbolism, the opposition made the first steps in revealing a new potential leader: Pavel Petrovich.

Catherine's coming to the throne provoked a tremendous increase of the use of Virgil's metaphors. Thus, for example, A. P. Sumarokov immediately links Catherine to Astraea in his *Ode to Her Highness Empress Catherine the Second on the occasion of Her ascension, on June 28, 1762 (Ода Государыне Императрице Екатерине Второй на восшествие ее на престол 1762 года июня 28 дня)*, written right after the revolt, whose impressions were still fresh in his mind:

> You will be an explicit Justice,
> Always welcome for charity,
> A widow will not be in misery
> As well as poor or orphaned,
> The pride will not be flourishing,
> A cry of poverty will not be heard,
> Tears of persecuted will not appear,
> A truthful man will not be troubled in courts,
> Labours will not attract the bribery,
> Astraea will descend from heaven.[23]

Sumarokov's panegyric verses express a clear social and political program, which transformed the ode into an instructional guide for a novice empress. The extended ode, as Grigorii Gukovskii pointed out, comments on the second government's *Manifesto*

---

[22] A. P. Sumarokov, *Polnoe Sobranie vsekh sochinenii v stikhakh i proze*, II, 288.
[23] Ibid, 47.

of 1762²⁴ and contains a very significant reference to the son of Catherine-Astraea:

> God, protect Her and Her Baby-Boy,
> Whom she has brought up,
> By God's grace we passed over
> A terrible ditch trenched for us. ²⁵

The end of Sumarokov's ode not only corresponds to Virgil's *Fourth Eclogue* (as well as to Christian symbolism), but also evidently articulates the position of certain political circles with which Sumarokov entirely agreed. Specifically, it was the program of Nikita Panin's political camp, which sought to limit Catherine's power through the brave "salvation" of a "Baby-boy" Pavel Petrovich, the legal heir to the throne after Peter III. Panin and Sumarokov, as well as their allies, politically interpreted the metaphysics of Astraea; using such allegories, they elaborated the concept of Catherine's regency (while Pavel was young) and Panin's real leadership.²⁶ Notably, Stephano Torelli's portrait of Catherine, commissioned on the occasion of her coronation in 1762, corresponded fairly well to this particular time in which Catherine was stressing her sacred role as her son's savior. Torelli depicts her standing before a table with a small portrait of Pavel in front of her. Later, when the concept of Catherine's regency ceased to be relevant, the image of Pavel vanished from all copies of Torelli's painting.²⁷

Virgil's *Eclogue* became especially popular when the so-called "public opinion" awaited the resolution of Pavel's destiny and the determination of the status of his mother Catherine. Thus,

---

²⁴ G. A. Gukovskii, *Ocherki po istorii russkoi literatury XVIII veka: Dvorianskaia fronda v literature 1750-kh—1760-kh godov* (Moscow — Leningrad, 1936), 165.

²⁵ A. P. Sumarokov, *Polnoe Sobranie vsekh sochinenii v stikhakh i proze*, II, 50.

²⁶ Varvara Golovina, Catherine's maid of honor, in her Memoirs, formulated a typical opinion of society circles on Nikita Panin's objectives: "Being Paul's mentor, yet in the time of Catherine's regency, he hoped to take the reins of government in his hand, but his aspirations failed. Catherine's energy in seizing power deceived his ambition, and he refused to forget it all his life" (V. N. Golovina, *Istoriia zhizni blagorodnoi zhenshchiny*. (Moscow, 1996, 113.)

²⁷ On a description of the portrait, see D. A. Rovinskii, *Podrobnyi slovar' russkikh gravirovannykh portretov.*, II, 784.

for example, Lomonosov also refers to Virgil in his two odes to Catherine. In his first ode on the occasion of her ascension, he proclaims:

> And you, our beloved Baby-boy,
> Rescued from powerful hands,
> Live a blessed life,
> Amongst sciences.
> Our dear Pavel, grow up,
> Take relief in a mother's arms
> And forget former troubles.
> She will calm down all storms,
> She, with her charity and diligence, will arrange
> A gorgeous paradise for you and us.[28]

The "gorgeous paradise" serves as a synonym of Virgil's "Golden Age." In his ode to Catherine on the New Year of 1764, Lomonosov suggests an allegorical figure of Russia, which looks at a baby boy in Catherine's arms and pronounces:

> "O you, a flourishing delight,
> O fulfillment of my wishes.
> Pallas gave birth to you for me
> To continue our Golden days;
> O fruit of the Divine blood,
> Grow up, strengthen in her love,
> Look at her accomplishments,
> Her ability to carry a scepter with joy,
> To guard her and my glory.
> Follow her models..."[29]

Here Lomonosov makes references to Virgil's *Fourth Eclogue* more bluntly: he mentions the divine birth of a baby boy as well as the "Golden days" that herald his arrival. The old ode-maker, however, could not refrain from a small alteration of the canon in order to add more flattery to Catherine II. In contradistinction to Virgil, the divine Baby Boy came not to begin but to *continue* the "Golden days" which, according to Lomonosov's

---

[28] M. V. Lomonosov, *Izbrannye proizvedeniia*, 175.
[29] Ibid, 183.

complimentary version, were already successfully inaugurated by Catherine.

In addition to legacy implications, Astraea's myth began to acquire a social paradigm that was not as common in European poetry. Russian poetry of the so-called "gentry opposition" (Gukovskii's term), especially Sumarokov's odes and choruses, connect Astraea's mythology to an entire program of social reforms. Astraea's coming should bring social balance, justice in law-courts, and the extinction of corruption and vices. Sumarokov's odes present a rather detailed concept of an enlightenment of Russia under the rule of Catherine-Astraea. In his *Ode to the Empress Catherine the Second on her Name Day, 24 November 1762* (Ода Государыне Императрице Екатерине Второй на день ее Тезоименитства 1762 года ноября 24 дня), the poet declares:

> Generosity protects her! (Russia. — V. P.)
> Astraea, in her previous beauty,
> Descended from Heaven,
> And returned on earth over again.
>   Hence the Fortune renews
>   Peace and Silence,
>   Restores Golden days,
>   Throws evil down the hell.
>   Laws became stronger,
>   Thieves got troubles.
>   Corruption will disappear;
>   Justice is shining in its purple;
>   Guilt, not rule scares:
>   Innocent does not have fear <...>
>   Naked truth will not be ashamed,
>   But flourish in its natural beauty,
>   Ignorance, with its wild impudence,
>   Will not be respected.
>   Peoples will love study,
>   They will take pleasure in
>   Only fair deeds.
>   Russians will gain profits,
>   And enjoy living here,
>   Following the Empress' example <...>.[30]

---

[30] A. P. Sumarokov, *Polnoe sobranie vsekh sochinenii v stikhakh i prose*, II, 52—53.

Sumarokov deliberately centers his poem on Catherine's image and anticipations of her reforms. The poet eliminates any provocative depictions of a baby boy in order to emphasize the necessity and the importance of his social program. Instead, he gives the prophetic functions of Virgil's Cumaean Cybil to Peter I, who predicts the emergence of Catherine-Astraea in the middle of the eighteenth century.

Sumarokov writes:

> Covering the earth by a crimson light,
> The Fate reveals the miracles:
> The Sky is open, I see a Hero,
> Who has ascended to the Heaven.
> The Great Russian Ruler,
> Creator of the city on Neva,
> He reads Fate's annals there.
> Goddess exposes him a mystery,
> The Monarch, with excitement,
> Discloses a secret to our lands
> In the middle of the 18th century,
> Russia will meet an Angel,
>> Which will take the throne
>> Disguised as a beautiful Woman,
>> Which will be glorified all around.
>> Her deeds will reach the Heaven,
>> Her name will be Catherine.
>> The Universe will be known:
> God has placed an Angel on our throne.[31]

The appearance of the "shade" of the late Peter I was not Sumarokov's invention. He borrowed this device from Lomonosov, who often implies in his odes this kind of ancient poetic mechanics with the opening of windows and doors in the sky in order to see dead heroes or gods.

Astraea symbolism turned out to be a key vehicle for Catherine's representation in Sumarokov's poetry. Sometimes, Astraea mythology became a useful narrative platform on which to

---

[31] Ibid.

perform poetic experiments. Hence, applying Astraea's paradigms, Sumarokov composed his trochaic dithyramb *To the Empress Catherine the Second on her Name day of November 24 1763 (Государыне Императрице Екатерине Второй на День ее Тезоименитства ноября 24 дня 1763 года)*:

> Witness, Russians, your happiness,
> Better than in Astraea's age <…>.[32]

In his ode *On the First Day of 1764 (На первый День 1764 года)* Sumarokov considers a legendary prehistory of Astraea's ascent:

> Truth was in troubles so far,
> Hell has erupted poison:
> Astraea ascended to Heaven,
> Depriving the universe of all delights.[33]

Then, the poet unveils the story of Astraea's return to the earth. Science and the Muses provided for it: they were the best support for emperors. According to Sumarokov, only poets and scholars would allow Russia to achieve prosperity and progress, as in the Roman Empire under Augustus.

At the beginning of 1764, Sumarokov expected to be selected by the authorities as the new leading poet of Russia. He hoped to be chosen for a close collaboration with the Russian throne: he dreamed of assuming the place of "a new Virgil" at the court of Catherine, who he viewed as "a new Augustus." He mentioned Rome and Augustus in apparent expectation of being appointed the lyric deputy of the enlightened Empress. However, the court did not welcome him, and all his efforts failed. Soon after, Vasilii Petrov, the leader of an opposite political and poetic camp, was chosen to play the role of Virgil and to translate into Russian the most relevant imperial narrative — the epic poem the *Aeneid*.

Another poet in Sumarokov's circle, Vasilii Maikov, also develops Astraea's myth in his odes. In accordance with Sumarokov's program, he presents the Empress as the ideological heir of Peter I.

---

[32] A. P. Sumarokov, *Polnoe sobranie vsekh sochinenii v stikhakh i prose*, II, 64.
[33] Ibid, 67.

In his *Ode on the Ascension and the Nameday of Her Highness*, in 1762 (Ода по восшествии Ея Величества на Всероссийский престол, на день Тезоименитства Ея 1762 года), he depicts Peter I descending from Heaven and authorizing Catherine's right to rule based not on blood, but on her achievements and talents. The concept of Astraea-Catherine's future social reforms follows Sumarokov's patterns:

> "My wisdom embodies in her,
> She knows how to govern a scepter,
> She will give you a fair trial,
> She will complete my laws,
> She will extinguish rude customs,
> She will strike down her enemies."[34]

It was significant that Maikov, elaborating pro-Sumarokov "lessons to the tsar" (introducing a similar program of social reforms), always sensed a link between Astraea mythology and the question of the heir to the Russian throne.

Hence, in his Ode on a New Year of 1763 (Ода на новый 1763 год), Maikov begins with the common flattering depiction of Catherine's ascension as the return of the Golden Age ("all men feel the Golden time"[35]). Then, the poet makes a sudden chronological shift, rather unusual for complimentary odes, to the beginning of the seventeenth century, the quite unpopular epoch when two pretenders to the Russian throne plunged the country into chaos which resulted in foreign intervention. First Maikov recalls Boris Godunov, who, according to legends, ordered the murder of the true heir, the young boy Dimitrii. Afterwards, the poet evokes "a false tsar" Dimitrii (Samozvanets), who claimed the Russian throne under the name of a miraculously survived Dimitrii. Maikov, however, focuses his poetic attention not on their illegitimate ascension to the throne, but instead only on their tyrannical exercise of power. Because of their despotism, both were unlawful usurpers of the throne:

---

[34] Vasilii Maikov, *Izbrannye proizvedeniia*, 188.
[35] Ibid, 192.

> Oh, fear! Oh, sorrow! Oh, deep blows!
> Tyrants govern over the Russians <…>.[36]

A new leader, Mikhail Romanov, the first representative of a future dynasty, eventually brought peace and stability to Russia. He was not a legal heir: he took the throne by necessity and the people's choice. Meanwhile, Maikov completely approves such changes in succession: Romanov was not a tyrant; he governed in accordance with Russia's needs. Thus, a historical precedent allows the poet to explain and sanction the illegitimate nature of Catherine's ascension. Maikov is ready to accept a sudden change of the ruler when he is not a tyrant and acts for the sake of his country.

Maikov describes Russia's joyful festivities in celebrating Catherine's attainment of the throne against the dangerous background of the events of the previous century. The killing of the heir and the subsequent rule of imposters was a very sensitive topic. Maikov introduced this theme for obvious political reasons; it also served as a lesson for Catherine's future kingship. Panin and his political allies stood behind Maikov's concepts and reinforced — using literary means — that only a fair rule justifies an illegitimate ascension to the throne. Not surprisingly, Maikov concludes his ode by referring to Pavel and the next transfer of power to him:

> We are blessed to have her (Catherine. — V. P.)
> Like we were before, with Elizabeth.
> We are cheerful and hopeful to see
> How Pavel will captivate minds.
> Russians are pleased all around,
>   They are looking forward to seeing
>   Mother's wisdom in his eyes.
>   We only want him to show
>   A magnitude of his great grand-father
>   To an entire world.[37]

---

[36] Ibid, 193.
[37] Ibid, 194.

Mikhail Kheraskov (1733–1807), the poet and director of the Moscow University publishing house, was the most cautious poet in Sumarokov's circle to implement Astraea symbolism in his works. Starting in 1762, he became very close to the political alliance of Nikita Panin and Ekaterina Dashkova. He shared their hopes that Catherine's rule would bring about social and political reforms, and, most importantly for him, having already been influenced by freemasonry, a moral enlightenment. He also composed an ode employing Virgil's metaphors, but which represents the roles of the Maid and her sacred Baby-boy in a quite original way. In his *Ode on the Highest Birthday of Her Imperial Majesty, 1763 (Ода на день высочайшего рождения Ее Императорского Величества, 1763 года)*, he draws upon Catherine's humble childhood in her native German town of Zerbst. Astraea appears in the sky above the town and predicts the birth of a "baby," which is the future Catherine II. Kheraskov writes:

> Up above Zerbst, I see a clear dim,
> That has been descended by the Creator.
> It embraces an image of a fine Goddess,
> This holds a scepter and crown.
> Her loud voice repeats:
> "A baby will be born in the world
> To take over this sacred scepter,
> To bring light to a northern country,
> To crown a head and glorify people,
> And to enchant hearts of all nationals".[38]

The concept of "the savior of the son" the future Emperor, played a role during the revolt and the first few years thereafter. Meanwhile, however, this concept became inappropriate for the triumphant Empress Catherine II. Using political means, Catherine adroitly out-maneuvered the so-called "Panin opposition," which had been organized to increase her son Pavel's role in government affairs. At the same time, influenced more by ideological than aesthetic purposes, she rejected the image of Astraea that Sumarokov's odes persistently attached to her.

---

[38] Mikhail Keraskov, *Izbrannye sochinenia* (Leningrad, 1961), 62.

The conflict between Catherine and Sumarokov's group existed all throughout her reign. In particular, Catherine was apparently irritated by a public masquerade entitled *Triumphant Minerva* (Торжествующая Минерва; January 30—February 2, 1763) that was organized in Moscow as a part of the celebration of her official coronation. Sumarokov and his allies Mikhail Kheraskov and Fedor Volkov (1729—1763), the actor and head of Elizabeth's court theater, were appointed to design a procession, as well as to produce verse slogans and ritual choruses. Chariots of Saturn and Astraea, the last procession of the masquerade, obviously symbolized the coming Golden Age of Catherine's rule. Sumarokov composed his official *Chorus to the Golden Age* (Хор ко златому веку), in which he included some eloquent formulas of Astraea's return to Russia:

> Blessed times have arrived,
> Gleams of truth are chining,
> Listen, a whole Universe!
> Astraea is on earth,
> Astraea has returned to our Russian lands,
> Astraea reigns.
> A generous Fate said:
> Do arrive to Russia a most desirable Golden Age.
> Streams of Russian rivers,
> To neighbors' surprise,
> Carry honey and milk.[39]

The solemn Astraea is juxtaposed to other Baroque allegories and emblems. Most carnival masques emblematized vices or bad habits that were supposed to be eradicated by a new ruler. Meanwhile, there was an obvious mistake (probably made deliberately by one of the scenario's authors) in the order of the masquerade's episodes; specifically, Astraea's chariots ambiguously succeeded a procession entitled "The chariot of a Depraved Venus." [40] Besides the strange and provoking conflation of one of Catherine's most popular poetical titles (Astraea) and the unofficial

---

[39] A. P. Sumarokov, *Polnoe sobranie vsekh sochinenii v stikhakh i proze*. VIII, 363.

[40] G. A. Gukovski, *Ocherki po istorii russkoi literatury XVIII veka. Dvorianskaia fronda v literature 1750-1760-kh godov*, 178.

public opinion about her personal life (Depraved Venus), there was another offensive point. The focus on the contents of Virgil's *Fourth Eclogue*, depicted in the final scene of the masquerade, acquired connotations unpleasant for the Empress in the Russian context. The virgin Astraea, an allegory of Justice and Prosperity, could not abolish the legal rights of the Baby-Boy who symbolized the coming of the Golden Age.

In addition to the panegyric chorus to Astraea, Sumarokov composed a carnivalesque *Chorus to the Perverted World (Хор ко превратному свету)* in honor of the occasion. The poem, which was immediately forbidden from being performed, contained thought-provoking content which slung arrows at very sensitive social and political issues. After the ban, Sumarokov wrote *Another Chorus to the Perverted World (Другой хор ко превратному свету)*, a short version of his first extended poem.[41] The poet eliminated critical utterances of a titmouse which, after having returned from abroad, made sarcastic comparisons between life and customs there and in Russia. Instead, Sumarokov depicted a barking dog and replaced the original words with lines that include the repetition "ham, ham, ham."[42] The substitution sounded even more provocative than the original version. Readers and spectators could easily grasp the meaning of such a substitution. Revealing his disillusionment, Sumarokov composed a fable entitled *Two Cooks (Два повара)* in 1765 and published it in pamphlet form. The poem is a harsh satire on incompetent political advisers who cannot prepare any dishes and leave their patron without dinner. Ridiculing Catherine's government, Sumarokov deliberately invokes Golden Age metaphors:

> Oh Golden Days!
> Minerva will change everything,

---

[41] On the authorship of the first chorus, see P. N. Berkov, "Khor ko prevratnomu svetu i ego avtor," in *XVIII vek*. 1 (Moscow-Leningrad, 1935), 181–202; Gr. Gukovskii, "O 'Khore ko prevratnomu svetu. Otvet P. N. Berkovu." Ibid, 203–217; Elena Pogosian, "Momus i Prevratnyi svet v maskarade Torzhestvuiushchaia Minerva", in *I vremia i mesto. Istoriko-filologicheskii sbornik k shestidesiatiletiiu A. L. Ospovata* (Moscow, 2008), 55–71.

[42] A. P. Sumarokov, *Izbrannye stikhotvoreniia*, 279.

> Since she rules Russia now.
> My gloomy mind waits for her shining,
> But my lyre jingles a little fable. <...>[43]

In such a context, Astraea symbolism acquires mock overtones that would become more and more dangerous. Not accidentally, Sumarokov's pamphlet was confiscated and destroyed, while Catherine called the author "a burning mind which began losing sense."[44]

Imperial Paradigm of Astraea

Not by accident, the "pocket bard" Petrov, who was always aware of the ideological needs of the royal court, only sporadically employs Astraea symbolism in his poetry, and rarely in a specific military context. Notably, Petrov uses Astraea comparisons while praising Count Aleksei Grigor'evich Orlov (1737–1808; brother of Catherine's favorite Grigorii Orlov) who was appointed commander-in-chief of the Russian fleet sent against the Turks. When in 1770 Aleksei Orlov successfully defeated the Turkish navy at Chesma, Petrov wrote, in his ode:

> We will erect a marble pillar to the sky,
> Mediterranean waters will pay up all our profits,
> All trophies, which we conquered near Khios.
> That will be a sign of our victory between waves
> > To honor you, Orlov,
> > The assistant of Astraea![45]

Then, in his ode *On the Victories of the Russian Army* (На победы Российского воинства), written in 1771 on the occasion of the successful seizure of the Zhurzhi fortress by troops under the command of P. A. Rumiantsev (1725–1796), Petrov again recalls Astraea:

---

[43] Ibid, 218.
[44] G. A. Gukovskii, *Ocherki po istorii russkoi literatury XVIII veka. Dvorianskaia fronda v literature 1750–1760-kh godov*, 182.
[45] V. Petrov, *Sochineniia*, I (Saint Petersburg, 1782), 58.

> Astraea's revenge has prevailed over the midnight country,
> She turned Moldavia's mountains into her trophies;
> Being Astraea's and Providence's weapon,
> Rumiantsev brought his thunder upon Danube's shores <...>
> Astraea and our duty forces us forward,
> Catherine's voice is the justly Heaven's call.[46]

Astraea's militaristic coloring did not contradict the tradition of European interpretations of Virgil's myth. Moreover, Petrov, an anglophile, was perfectly familiar with the imperialistic and expansionist connotations of Astraea's paradigm in lyric songs to Queen Elizabeth I of England.[47] The colonialist sound of Petrov's military odes belonged to the British tradition that turned the Golden Age myth into a political strategy — the Golden Age of England.[48] The poet craftily adapted Astraea's metaphors to the needs of the political propaganda of Russian military expansionism.

Early works by Gavrila Derzhavin also reflect the imperial paradigms of Astraea. The young Derzhavin, in terms of his political program, found himself very close to the British laudatory tradition of praising the queen. In his first odes to Catherine II, Derzhavin describes the empress as she sets off for her first trip to the Volga River in 1767. He portrays her as a powerful sovereign who strengthens borders, enlightens barbarians, and unites all conquered subjects. In his poem *To the Masquerade Given to the Empress in Kazan' where Nagaian Tartars and All Other Nationalities Danced and Played on their Instruments* (На маскарад, бывший перед Императрицей в Казани, где Нагайцы и прочие народы плясали и играли на своих инструментах; 1767), Derzhavin declares:

> We decently call you Minerva,
> As we look at your wise laws.
> We decently call you Astraea:
> We live the Golden days under your scepter.
> We truly have Orpheus' age with you:
> Mountains and forests get assembly around you.

---

[46] Ibid, 205, 224.

[47] On Vasilii Petrov's trip to England, see Antony G. Cross, "Vasilii Petrov v Anglii (1772—1774)", in *XVIII vek*, XI (Leningrad, 1976), 229—246.

[48] Frances A. Yates. *Astraea. The Imperial Theme in the Sixteenth Century*, 39.

As you appear, the feast and triumph take place,
Youth and elderly, all society rejoices,
Wild steppe inhabitants come to you
And dance and play harmonious music.
Russia! Praise your sovereign:
Yet she conquered barbarian hearts.[49]

The young Derzhavin included Astraea's metaphors in his earliest *Ode to Catherine II (Ода Екатерине II)*, written in 1767 and first published by Iakov Grot one century later. The poet follows Virgil's patterns and describes the Golden Age in Russia under Catherine II, who brings forth justice and prosperity. Yet Derzhavin implements the motif of the salvation of Astaea's baby boy: all of Russia is "rescued" in the end by Catherine's "arrows of law."[50] The young and rather humble poet displayed a strong solidarity with the Empress against Sumarokov and Panin's opposition. He even expressed his skepticism toward Sumarokov's lyrics and Panin's ideology. In 1768, Derzhavin composed two epigrams, *A Signboard (Вывеска)* and *To the Magpie in Defense of the Cuckoos (На сороку в защищение кукушек)*. The latter paraphrases Sumarokov's epigram *To the Cuckoos in Moscow (На кукушек в Москве)*. Derzhavin ridicules Sumarokov and praises Diana (Catherine) and her "courageous Eagle" (Aleksei Orlov).[51] Mocking Sumarokov and singing the praises of Catherine's "eagles" (all four Orlov brothers), the young poet established himself on the current literary scene, and at the same time, entered the court's struggle.

The Baby Boy Pavel I and his Protectors

Catherine's imperial policy resulted in a perverted relationship between herself and her son. In order to guard and strengthen her status, Catherine had to cease being a mother. Many memoirists and historians have written about the very difficult relations between her and Pavel, as well as Pavel's hatred toward his mother,

---

[49] *Sochineniia Derzhavina. S ob''iasnitel'nymi primechaniiami Ia. Grota.* III, 183–184.
[50] Ibid, 186.
[51] Ibid, 190.

the usurper of the throne. Virgil's baby boy must be overlooked forever.

Catherine's gentleman of the bedchamber, F. N. Golitsyn, writes in his memoirs: "The Empress did not treat him (Pavel. — V. P.) as she should have; he did not participate in government matters. She did not consider him a true heir. <...> She made it a rule to keep all power in her hands."[52]

In 1771, Pavel Petrovich was seventeen years old. His official mentor was Nikita Panin, who had been appointed by Catherine at the beginning of her rule. According to circulating gossip, Catherine signed a statement in favor of Pavel's inauguration when he came of age right after she assumed the throne. Considering the situation, Pavel's biographer N. K. Shilder writes: "Pavel's supporters made the false assumption that afterward the Grand Prince would take an active part in ruling and that Catherine would resign or at least waive her power in favor of her son. It was rather peculiar to ascribe such intentions to the empress who said, 'I want to govern alone and let Europe know it!'<...>. Besides, <...> there was not any law to determine the age of majority for an heir apparent at that time."[53]

Instead of coming to the throne, Pavel fell ill by the end of the summer of 1771. The public was seriously troubled by some rumors about the declaration of a new successor (A. G. Bobrinskii, Catherine's illegitimate son by Grigorii Orlov) in the case of Pavel's death.[54] It was a big relief for Nikita Panin and the opposition when Pavel recovered. Denis Fonvizin, one of the leaders of the opposition and Panin's secretary, composed the *Speech on the recovery of the Heir Grand Prince Pavel Petrovich in 1771 (Слово на выздоровление Е. И. Величества Государя Цесаревича и Великого Князя Павла Петровича в 1771 году)*. Vasilii Maikov also responded to the event: he wrote *Ode on the recovery of the Grand Prince and the Heir of the Russian Throne (Ода на выздоровление Цесаревича и Великого Князя Павла Петровича, наследника престола Российского)*. The titles sounded

---

[52] *Zolotoi vek Ekateriny Velikoi: Vospominaniia* (Moscow, 1996), 278—279.

[53] N. K. Shil'der, *Imperator Pavel Pervyi: Istoriko-biograficheskii ocherk* (Saint Petersburg, 1901), 77.

[54] *Zolotoi vek Ekateriny Velikoi: Vospominaniia*, 301; D. Kobeko, *Tsesarevich Pavel Petrovich (1754—1796): Istoricheskoe issledovanie* (Saint Petersburg, 1882), 66.

rather provocative (it emphasized Pavel's right to inherit the throne) and clearly expressed the opinions of Panin's entire group.

That same year, Sumarokov composed a furious anti-Catherine poem entitled *Ode to His Highness Pavel Petrovich on his Nameday of June 29 of 1771 (Ода Государю Цесаревичу Павлу Петровичу в день ег Тезоименитства июня 29 числа 1771 года)*. He barely mentions the victories of the Russian military over the Ottoman Porte — instead, he states that he does not want to celebrate military triumphs; the real subject of his praise is Pavel:

> I put aside the victory,
> I don't praise Russia by it,
> Instead, I want to chant you <...>[55]

He emphasizes the masculine character of Pavel's education in a circle of "the most wise and chosen men" under the leadership of Panin, "the Mentor." He opposes an idealized brotherhood (meaning Panin's group as well as Masonic circles) to a female rule that usurped the throne of a legal masculine heir and the true descendant of Peter the Great. Sumarokov refers to the empress only to underline her most important role — to be a mother to her son, a legal heir to the throne:

> Great Catherine!
> To bring such Son,
> Russia thanks you.[56]

Sumarokov focuses his ode on Pavel and his circle; he refers to Catherine only as Pavel's mother, and he does not even mention the Orlov brothers, notably excluding Aleksei, the hero of the Turkish war as well as of Petrov's odes at that time. Sumarokov's silence on this subject was especially noticeable in comparison with the torrents of flattery to Catherine and all the Orlovs in Petrov's poetry (*On the War with the Turks*, 1769; *On the Seizure of Khotin*, 1769; *On the Seizure of Yassy*, 1769; *On the Victory of the Russian Navy over the Turks*, 1770; *On Naval Victories*, 1770; *On the Arrival of Count Aleksei Grigorievich Orlov from the Archipelago to Saint Petersburg*, 1771.)

---

[55] A. P. Sumarokov, *Polnoe sobranie vsekh sochinenii v stikhakh i proze*, II, 118.
[56] Ibid, 119.

Sumarokov completely rejected Petrov's "pro-British" imperialist variant of the Astraea tradition. Instead, he remained faithful to his Russian mythology of Astraea that proved relevant only as a political question of the succession of the throne or as an allegorical list of impatiently anticipated social reforms. Disillusioned in both of his prospects, Sumarokov began to revise some of his early odes to Catherine. In 1774, he republished his ode to Catherine of 1762 (*Ode to the Empress Catherine the Second on her Name Day, 24 November 1762.*) Keeping the main image of Catherine as Astraea, Sumarokov removed most of the important passages concerning social issues. The goal of such deletions suggested that an anticipated "naked truth" did not appear and that the desired "laws" were not enacted in Russia under Catherine. The 1774 version contained only signs of Astraea's mythology while the contents (the program) were eliminated. Given the situation, the abridged ode sounded like a reproach to the empress who did not fulfill her early role as Astraea, the Goddess of Justice and Truth. The mythology of Astraea became more and more dangerous.

Notably, Vasilii Petrov, always very perceptive to any changes in Catherine's imperial strategy, suddenly employed Astraea's metaphors later in his *Ode to the Birth of the Grand Prince Aleksandr Pavlovich* (Ода на рождение Великого князя Александра Павловича) in 1777 (Aleksandr Pavlovich was Catherine's grandson who, according to Catherine's wishes, should be her successor instead of Pavel).[57] Petrov shrewdly excluded Pavel from all his Virgilian paraphrases and transposed Astraea's metaphors onto a new Baby Boy in the Russian royal family:

> Even he is a baby, he is God <...>[58]

Astraea's mythology turned out to be irrelevant and even perilous for the Russian Empress. According to her decree, allusions to Roman classical mythology must be free of any mystical and/or Messianic undertones that prophesy the unpleasant coming of

---

[57] A. V. Khrapovitskii, Catherine's secretary, testified that the empress attentively studied the rules of succession in recent history (A. V. Khrapovitskii, *Pamiatnye zapiski*, 37–38.)

[58] V. Petrov, *Sochineniia*, I, 157.

a Divine Baby boy. Rejecting dangerous forebodings, she sought a cold and rational pragmatism, slightly flavored with an ancient aroma. In this way, Catherine's imperial strategy represented the ideology of her political symbolism.

The Masonic paradigm of the Astraea myth

Astraea symbolism proved to be exceptionally popular in Russian Masonic circles. The Masons wrote about the Goddess with a warm respect, having been attracted to her by a combination of her esoteric and even cosmic traits, as well as the moral and ethical implications of her image. In interpreting the myth, they pointed out that the moral corruption of mankind had been the reason for Astraea's departure from the earth. The Masons held the conviction that the lost Paradise could be reached only by the ethical renovation of humankind's sinful nature.

The Masons read the myth through the lens of their own program, which suggested how to attain a higher degree of self-awareness, self-perfection, and self-transformation. They presumed that Astraea's descent back to the earth would be a sign that the difficult, mysterious task of acquiring the highest wisdom and moral resurrection was completed.

Already in the 1770s—1780s, there were three Masonic lodges named after Astraea. The first was established in Saint Petersburg in 1775; the second one was opened in Moscow in 1783 at the latest;[59] the third one appeared in Riga in 1785—1787. Later, the Grand Lodge of Astraea was opened in 1814 and became the dominant force in the history of the Russian Freemasonry movement.

The Masons not only expressed their highest respect for Astraea, but they also portrayed her as their mystic protector.[60] At the same time, they could not and did not want to avoid the

---

[59] G. V. Vernadskii, *Russkoe masonstvo v tsarstvovanie Ekateriny II* (Petrograd, 1917), 11, 55.

[60] Some Masonic verses contained direct addressing Catherine II. On this topic, see A. V. Pozdneev, "Rannie masonskie pesni," in *Scando Slavica*, 8 (1962), 60.

political applications of their mythmaking. First, they began with the association of Astraea and Catherine II.

Such comparisons appeared as early as the 1760s. For example, in 1762, Mikhail Kheraskov, the editor of A Valuable Amusement (Полезное увеселение), published, although anonymously, his poem entitled A Letter to Myself (Письмо к самому себе) in the magazine's May issue. Though he was to become one of Russia's most prominent Masons, Kheraskov was not yet registered as an official member of a lodge; however, the poem clearly reveals his pro-Mason sympathies. He gives a detailed account of Astraea's myth:

> The Silver Age instilled the first ferocity in us,
> The Iron Age completed this disaster <...>
> Astraea and our serenity went away to Heaven <...>[61]

Meanwhile, Kheraskov embellishes his picture with some contemporary allusions: he includes some eloquent political hints pertaining to the modern rule of Peter III, as well as presents an allegorical narrative of events that occured during a short and troublesome period of his inconsistent and violent reign. While depicting all of these misfortunes and worries, he concludes with an energetic appeal to Astraea:

> To you, Astraea, I send up my voice,
> I am ardent to bring about your age.[62]

The poem came out on the eve of Catherine's coup d'état in June of 1762. It reflects the gloomy atmosphere of the last months before Peter's dethronement and even implies a veiled appeal to Catherine-Astraea to bring about the Golden Age. Soon after, Kheraskov became involved in the preparations for Catherine's coronation ceremony and her famous courtly masquerade *A Triumphant Minerva*.

At first, Catherine expressed tolerance for Russian Freemasonry. Almost all the members of her inner circle belonged

---

[61] *Poleznoe uveselenie*, V (1762), 224.
[62] Ibid.

to Freemasonry: I. P. Elagin, Z. G. Chernyshev, A. I. Bibikov, N. V. Repnin, A. S. Stroganov, A. V. Khrapovitskii. One of the Masons' songs justly claimed that the winged Maid Astraea lived among them.⁶³ In the 1770s, the Masons attempted to involve Catherine in their activities. She ironically confessed to Grimm that she attentively read the literature offered by the various groups of Masons:

> "In order to satisfy the curiosity of one sick person, I began reading all manner of Mason silliness and absurdity; since I had reason to tease many of them every day, the members of the Freemasonry, vying with one another without intermission, made me acquainted with their beliefs, hoping to seduce me to their side. All the mustard sellers brought me the freshest mustard from countries and lodges far and wide <...> One who does good for the good of all has no need for vows, eccentricities, or absurd and strange dress."⁶⁴

Since that time, Catherine's political struggle with Freemasonry began, later resulting in several imprisonments and banishments, the retirement of several politicians and courtiers, as well as some secret police trials.⁶⁵ The first steps in her struggle had a purely literary form. In 1780, her sharp parody of Masonic rituals appeared under the title *A mystery of some anti-absurd society, discovered by one unbeliever* (Тайна противо-нелепого общества, открытая непричастным оному). She explains her motives in a letter to Grimm:

> "You know, Freemasonry numbers among mankind's greatest errors. I had the patience to read books and manuscripts, all the boring absurdities which preoccupy them. I came to the conclusion, to my disgust, that human beings do not become more educated or reasonable, no matter how deeply you ridicule them. <...> This is what the heroes of our age occupy themselves with; Prince Ferdinand is their

---

[63] Stephen Lessing Baehr, *The Paradise Myth in Eighteenth-Century Russia*, 234.

[64] "Pis'ma Ekateriny Vtoroi k baronu Grimmu," in *Russkii arkhiv*, 3 (1878), 62.

[65] A. N. Pypin, *Russkoe masonstvo XVIII i pervoi chetverti XIX veka* (Petrograd, 1916) (chapter XI.)

chief, and Voltaire belongs to them. How can they restrain from laughter when they meet each other!"[66]

In 1785—1786, Catherine published, as well as staged at the Hermitage Theater, her three comedies against Freemasonry — *The Deceiver (Обманщик)*, *The Deceived (Обольщенный)*, and *The Siberian Shaman (Шаман Сибирский)*. There, she harshly ridiculed their mysticism, their eccentricity, and the deceptive nature of their program. She portrayed Masons as simple charlatans who were preoccupied with no more than intrigues and acquiring money.[67] The empress did not stress the distinctions between the different Masonic movements — the Rosicrucians, the Illuminati, and the Martinists; she found them all to be worthy of her mockery. [68] However, after a few years, she changed her tactics, switching from enlightened ridicule to political persecution. The empress gradually grew angry with their internationalism, active propaganda, and involvement with charitable institutions. In some ways, the Freemason brotherhood acted as a replacement for the monarchy's power and threatened its sacred status. A parallel political power with its own government connections, moral influence, and high social profile put the existing authority at risk. As head of the Russian Orthodox Church, Catherine could not abide the increasing spiritual and even economic influence of Masonic propaganda and print media.

The main cause of such a shift, however, was her son Pavel Petrovich's conversion to Freemasonry. According to some scholars, he joined the Masons during one of his three trips abroad — he visited Vienna in 1772, Berlin in 1776, and toured Europe in 1781—1782. Meanwhile, the most realistic version dated his initiation to 1777, when King Gustav III of Sweden, a prominent Mason,

---

[66] "Pis'ma Ekateriny Vtoroi k baronu Grimmu", 61—62.

[67] A. Semeka, *Russkie rozenkreitsery i sochineniia imperatritsy Ekateriny II protiv masonstva* (Saint Petersburg, 1902); Lurana Donnels O'Malley, *The Dramatic Works of Catherine the Great. Theater and Politics in Eighteenth Century Russia* (Burlington, 2006).

[68] Raffaella Faggionato, *A Rosicrucian Utopia in Eighteenth-Century Russia. The Masonic Circle of N. I. Novikov* (Dordrecht, 2005), 190.

visited Saint Petersburg. Nikita Panin, according to this version, made all possible efforts to involve Pavel in the Swedish system of Freemasonry and arranged the secret initiation ritual in the house of Senator Ivan Petrovich Elagin.[69] A Masonic song of the eighteenth century, distributed in manuscript form, praised Panin for this deed and glorified the rising of the star (another of Astraea's metaphors) which signified the coming of the Golden Age. The Russian Masons began to associate Astraea not with Catherine, but with Pavel, the future Emperor. Disillusioned with Catherine, they put all their hopes in Pavel's ascension to the throne. As they believed, Pavel would bring an era of justice and prosperity to Russia. In the art collection of P. I. Shchukin, there were two portraits of Pavel in which he is ornamented with Masonic regalia and the image of Astraea.[70]

In 1784 *The Freemasonry Magazine (Магазин свободно-каменщический)* published a song most probably written by the well-known Mason Ivan Lopukhin. The song contains a direct appeal to Pavel:

> With you will reign
> Bliss, Truth, Peace!
> Neither the poor nor the orphaned
> Will fear the throne.
> Decorated by the crown,
> You will be our father.[71]

Meanwhile, by the mid-1780s, Freemasonry's popularity and power reached its peak in Europe. In 1786, after the death of Frederick the Great, his nephew and heir Frederick William II, also a Mason, came to the Prussian throne. The example of the two royal Masons — Frederick and Gustav III — influenced the Russian Masons and severely frightened Catherine II.[72] She made

---

[69] *Minuvshie gody*, 2 (1908), 71; E. S. Shumigorskii, "Imperator Pavel i masonstvo," in *Masonstvo v ego proshlom i nastoiashchem*, 2 (Moscow, 1991), 141–142.

[70] Tira Sokolovskaia, "Dva portreta Imperatora Pavla s masonskimi emblemam," in *Russkaia starina*, 10 (1908), 90.

[71] E. S. Shumigorskii, "Imperator Pavel i masonstvo," 143.

[72] M. Longinov, *Novikov i moskovskie martinisty* (Saint Petersburg, 2000), 296.

all efforts possible to isolate Pavel from Masonic influence. She sent away all of his inappropriate acquaintances. As soon as Pavel returned from his European tour in 1782, she banished his close friend A. B. Kurakin, who had been accompanying the Grand Duke abroad, to his village near Saratov. Nikita Panin was removed from his mentorship position, and he died in 1783. The authorities put the Moscow Masonic groups under surveillance, and, after some inquiries, forbade their publishing and charitable activities. Nikolai Novikov's Publishers was closed, and in 1791 Novikov himself, the most active and financially independent Mason, was sent to prison and then exiled. Even earlier, the Saint Petersburg Mason circles were disbanded: most of the prominent Masons found themselves retired or banished to their country estates. The winged Maid Astraea had apparently left the Russian lands.

Astraea's Final Appearance

After Catherine's death, the two subsequent successors to the Russian throne — Pavel I in 1796 and Alexander I in 1801 — clearly demonstrated the power of the Astraea mythology repeatedly to reemerge in the odic genre, as well as the close links between Astraea symbolism and politics.

At first, Pavel's coming to the throne produced a wave of enthusiastic political expectations. In November 1796, Nikolai Karamzin composed the *Ode on the occasion of the oath of allegiance of the residents of Moscow to His Imperial Highness Pavel the First, Autocrat of all of Russia* (*Ода на случай присяги московских жителей Его Императорскому Величеству Павлу Первому, Самодержцу Всероссийскому*), in which he paints a traditional portrait of the Golden Age and Astraea's arrival:

Astraea's age flows for us.[73]

He praises Pavel I as the direct heir to Peter I; he briefly mentions Catherine by making some critical allusions:

---

[73] N. M. Karamzin, *Polnoe sobranie stikhotvorenii* (Moscow — Leningrad, 1966), 189.

> He (Pavel. — V. P.) was destined long ago
> To inherit Minerva's crown.⁷⁴

These lines imply a reproach to Catherine for postponing Pavel's right to succession. Karamzin exhibits his firm solidarity with Panin's circle, which attempted to introduce political reforms and endorse Pavel as their architect. In 1791–1792, while publishing the magazine *The Moscow Journal (Московский Журнал)*, Karamzin failed to engage the imperial authority in a productive dialogue. He was not welcomed by Catherine, who could not forget his involvement in masonry, his closeness to Nikolai Novikov, or his compassion for the exiled masons. Despite Karamzin's break with masonry in 1789, the imperial authority continued to harbor suspicions about his activities, such as his trip abroad in 1789 and his travels around revolutionary France. Apparently, Karamzin was not able to find his political footing in the latter years of Catherine II's reign. He thus placed all his hopes in the new emperor.

Karamzin's enthusiasm for Pavel's ascension was as fervent as it was short. The poet endows the new emperor with all of Astraea's attributes: he calls him a defender of justice and peace and a patron of the arts. Following the canon, Karamzin writes:

> He (Pavel-V.P) holds Themis's scales:
> I am not afraid of powerful ones <…>
> He brought Truth to the throne,
> The Law made peace with Conscience <…>
> Rejoice! Much welcomed Pavel!
> He is a patron of Science and Art <…>
> He came to defeat all adversaries,
> He will usher in a universal peace. ⁷⁵

Karamzin's negative perception of Catherine's reign forced him to reinterpret Astraea's entire mythology, as well as a corresponding arsenal of metaphors. The poet omits any panegyrics to Catherine, and instead, links Pavel directly to Peter I. He purifies his ode from any pagan references, as well as from the Baroque mixture of

---

[74] Ibid, 185.
[75] Ibid, 186-187.

Christian and classical images. Karamzin combines the two names of Peter and Pavel to give his ode a purely symbolic meaning: he endows Pavel's reign not only with the charismatic legacy of his great grandfather, but with the Christian holiness of the apostle Paul:

> Peter the First was the beginning of everything;
> Pavel brought the illumination of happiness
> To the Russian people.
> Forever, forever inseparable,
> Forever will be sacred and blessed
> The two names of these sovereigns!
> The church worships these names together,
> Russia glorifies them both;
> You are more precious to us,
> Peter was great; you bring joy to our hearts.[76]

Similar motifs appear in Pavel Golenishchev-Kutuzov's *Ode on the joyful day of Pavel's ascension to the Russian throne* (1796):

> In *Pavel* the new *Peter* is born![77]

Pavel I immediately accepted his role as Peter's direct blood heir and started to reformulate the political mythology of Catherine's age. Thus, in particular, he organized a symbolic reburial of Peter III and Catherine II. Both coffins were interred together in the Winter Palace; then, they laid the imperial crown on the coffin of Peter III and the so-called "small" imperial crown on Catherine's. In addition to such a vengeful procedure, Pavel ordered the aged Count Aleksei Orlov (one of the suspected murderers of Peter III) to lead the funeral procession from the Palace to the Peter and Paul Cathedral. There, they removed the crown from Catherine's coffin. This most fantastic ceremony — symbolically — dethroned Catherine, stressing her "dependent" role as the wife of Peter III, and established Pavel's hereditary rights as the true son of his murdered father. History was

---

[76] Ibid.

[77] Pavel Golenishchev-Kutuzov, *Oda na vseradostnyi den' vosshestviia na Vserossiiskii prestol Pavla I* (Moscow, 1796), 3.

re-played, and the current order was structured so as to eliminate any gossip about Pavel's "illegitimacy."[78]

Pavel's first steps, meanwhile, inspired enthusiasm among contemporaries who appreciated his peaceful strategy and compassion towards the dissidents of Catherine's time. Without delay, the poets of the day invoked Astraea and metaphors of the Golden Age.

The young student Vasilii Zhukovskii dedicated his early poem *Ode: The Prosperity of Russia is arranged by her great Sovereign Pavel the First* (*Ода: Благоденствие России, устрояемое Великим Ея самодержцем Павлом Первым*; 1797) to Pavel. This ode, written in the Moscow University Gentry Pension, glorifies a restoration of peace and the coming of Astraea. According to Zhukovskii, who attentively studied Lomonosov and Derzhavin, Pavel established "a Golden silence" and stopped history from regressing, that is; a return to the "Copper Age" of wars: "The cannons closed their copper mouths."[79]

In 1801 Astraea's image reemerged — for a moment — in the laudatory poetry written to commemorate Alexander I's taking the throne. In his poem *On the solemn coronation of his Highness Alexander I, Sovereign of Russia* (*На торжественное коронование Его Императорского Величества Александра I, Самодержца Всероссийского*), Karamzin focuses on an idyllic landscape of the Golden Age, mastering the description of country life. He saturates the landscape of a frozen Paradise with emotional language and sentimental lamentations. His political allusions acquired a new individual tone, quite unfamiliar to the odic genre. The laudatory ode gained a humanistic touch:

> We have Astraea! I exclaim,
> Or the Age of Saturn is reborn!
> I heed Clio's answer:
> "It is a man who accepts the throne!" <...>[80]

---

[78] Richard S. Wortman, *Scenarios of Power: Myth and Ceremony in Russian Monarchy*, 1, 173.

[79] V. A. Zhukovskii, *Polnoe sobranie sochinenii i pisem*, 1 (Moscow, 1999), 21.

[80] N. M. Karamzin, *Polnoe sobranie stikhotvorenii*, 268.

In depicting a human monarch, Karamzin refers to Derzhavin's ode *On the birth in the North of a Royal Scion (На рождение в Севере порфирородного отрока)*, written in 1777 and dedicated to the birth of Catherine's beloved grandson Alexander. There, Derzhavin dares to give political lessons to a newborn baby boy, the future emperor Alexander I.

> Be the master of your passions,
> Be a man on the throne![81]

Derzhavin repeats his dream about having a human being as a ruler while depicting Catherine's image in his poem *A Portrait of Felitsa* (1789):

> A happy and blessed people
> Will name her the Great,
> Will present the sacred titles to her,
> But she will reply: "I am only a human being."[82]

Karamzin recalls Derzhavin's lessons and presents them to a novice monarch. In his poem, as in his ode *To His Imperial Majesty Alexander I, the Russian Sovereign, on his ascension* (1801), Karamzin returns to the classical paradigms of Astraea's myth. Not by accident, he employs Astraea symbolism to link Alexander I to his grandmother Catherine II. In connecting both emperors, he was simply following the letter of the law. Alexander I himself, in his *Manifesto* issued on March 12 (24), 1801, promised to rule according to his grandmother's behest. Karamzin writes:

> You shine like an Angel,
> With beauty and generosity.
> In the first speech, you promise
> The return of the Golden Age of Catherine.[83]

However, despite the Pindaric intonation and enthusiasm, Karamzin could not hide his irritation: in his heart, he always

---

[81] *Sochineniia Derzhavina*, 1, 51.
[82] Ibid, 199.
[83] N. M. Karamzin, *Polnoe sobranie stikhotvorenii*, 261.

associated the age of Catherine II with debauchery, favoritism, and corruption of the law. Astraea — as a symbol of the corrupted imperial power — lost its appeal tremendously by the end of the eighteenth century and provoked Karamzin to write bitter and sarcastic verses. In 1802, he composed his *Hymn to Fools (Гимн глупцам)*, in which he scornfully deconstructs the everlasting beliefs in the coming Golden Age:

> When was man blissful?
> In the past, without thinking,
> He lived by his stomach.
> For fools there was always Astraea,
> And the Golden Age did not pass away.[84]

Karamzin clearly treats Astraea as a false tale that masked the political games of the Epicurean age of Catherine II, praised and sanctified by Derzhavin in his "gastronomic" odes to Felitsa. Singing his sarcastic farewell to Catherine's time, as well as to the past century, Karamzin invalidates the Astraea mythology, labels its believers fools, and detaches his poetic strategy from the old imperial symbolism.

---

[84] Ibid, 289.

Chapter Three

CATHERINE THE HEALER

The eighteenth century, in European history, marked its coming by a universal fall of belief in the magic qualities of the King's power — in the miraculous strength of the King's touch, which could "heal" maladies. In European courts, it became completely out of fashion for the king to put his mighty hands upon the purulent boils of scrofulous peasants, to distribute curative paper seals or to hang a remedial coin around the neck of an invalid. In 1714, after the death of Queen Anne, the old ritual of royal healing was abolished in Great Britain. Real politics (together with the rise of Parliament's influence) ousted supernatural demonstrations of power. In France, the process of desacralization of the monarch's magical power was belated, despite philosophers' ridicule of the ritual and even in spite of the extreme depravity of King Louis XV. Contemporaries mocked the fact that the king's mistresses died of scrofula even though the King had "touched" them. In 1774, after a habitual visit to Trianon to meet a sixteen-year-old girl, sent by the Countess du Barry, Louis XV caught smallpox and rapidly perished. In three days, the young mistress who had infected him with the fatal illness also died. The death of the French monarch provoked Catherine II to make a sarcastic remark that was in clear reference to her recent and courageous inoculation. She wrote to her friend and constant correspondent Friedrich Melchior, baron von Grimm on 19 June 1774: "The French King ought to be ashamed of dying from smallpox in the 18th century."[1]

---

[1] *Sbornik imperatorskogo russkogo istoricheskogo obshchestva*, 13: 408. In his article *On*

European monarchs not only were unable to maintain their reputations as "chief surgeons" of the nation, but most often they themselves fell victim to the very epidemics that ravaged the common people. A deadly outbreak of smallpox proved to be a true peril of the eighteenth century, as the fatal illness attended almost all European royal houses. In 1711, Joseph I, the Habsburg Emperor, died from smallpox. A few days earlier, the son and heir of Louis XIV had passed away from the same cause. In 1724, smallpox took the life of the king of Spain — Louis I.[2]

This awful disease made a significant impact on the complicated affairs of the Russian court. In 1730, the fourteen-year-old tsar Peter II, the grandson of Peter I, died from smallpox, which he had caught from his fiancée Catherine Dolgorukaia. Elizaveta Petrovna grieved for the rest of her life over her fiancée Karl August of Holstein-Gottorp, who had gone to Russia to marry her while still a princess and died before the wedding. Her nephew Peter III, a few weeks before the arrival of his future wife Catherine II, fell sick with smallpox. He survived, but was so blemished that Elizaveta Petrovna prearranged his first meeting with his German bride in a darkish room.

In the 1760s, smallpox was raging all across Europe. Especially often smallpox attended the Austrian court. Maria Theresa's son, the future Joseph II, lost his pregnant wife Isabella. In 1767 Joseph's sister and second wife both succumbed to smallpox. Maria Theresa also contracted the disease, but survived only by miracle.

To put an end to this ever-present threat, Catherine II resorted to the most advanced method against such a deadly disease and authorized vaccinations that would inoculate patients with material taken from a person infected with smallpox. She announced that she would be the first to prove the effectiveness of the procedure to the courtiers who vigorously opposed such an endeavor. In France at

---

the Death of Louis XV and on Fate (*De la mort de Louis XV et de la fatalité*, 1774) Voltaire juxtaposed an "unenlightened" French king to Catherine II who had completed a deed worthy of a cultural hero (*Oeuvres complète de Voltaire*, 29) (Paris, 1879), 300.

[2] Donald R. Hopkins, *Princes and Peasants. Smallpox in History* (Chicago and London, 1983), 54.

that time, the procedure of inoculation was forbidden as antithetical to the religious perception of Providence.

Later, after a quick recovery, Catherine II, wrote a letter to Frederick II, an adversary of inoculation, which gave a detailed account of the causes that had forced her to receive the vaccination:

> "Since childhood, I was accustomed to fear smallpox; when I grew up, I made an enormous effort to eliminate my fear; at every paltry bout of sickness I suspected smallpox. Last Spring, when a violent outbreak of the disease swept away everybody, I had to move from one place to another; and for five months, I was expelled from the city, as I did not wish to put my son and myself at risk. I was so stricken and frustrated with the vile circumstances that I thought it would be a weakness not to change them. I was advised to let my son be immunized. I answered that it would be a shame if I did not start with myself; how could I launch inoculation without setting a convincing example? I began studying the subject in order to select the least risky course of action. I had to make a choice: to remain in real threat all my life along with thousands of other people, or to be exposed to a considerably lesser danger and to save many lives. I thought that in choosing the latter I had made the most right decision."[3]

The letter sounded like a page from an Enlightenment novel which narrated a story of the victory of reason, human bravery, and knowledge over fear, sickness, and prejudice. Meanwhile, Catherine's courage reflects not only her personal qualities, but most of all, a savvy political strategy containing both secular and sacred features.

First, the Russian empress was not the first sovereign who became vaccinated against smallpox. In 1768, a few months prior, the vaccination had been performed in the royal family of Habsburg in Vienna. The success of the experiment inspired Catherine to follow the European model. Second, her resolution to receive inoculation before her son Pavel did not exemplify merely a mother's care. Immunization, especially in the case of failure, could incite rumors

---

[3] *Sbornik imperatorskogo russkogo istoricheskogo obshchestva*, 2: 295; S. M. Soloviev, *Istoriia Rossii s drevneishikh vremen*, 28 (Moscow 2002), 364.

about the illegitimate poisoning of the heir to the throne, as the people's prejudice against inoculation was very strong. Many years before, the death from smallpox of Peter II had ignited such gossip and provoked a fierce struggle between political groups. Third, the prospect of war against Turkey, which was viewed as the permanent source of epidemics in Europe, spurred Catherine to accept immunization.

However, Catherine made every effort to transform the very pragmatic procedure of inoculation into a solemn and even sacred act of healing and rescue of her fatherland from a pernicious threat. The whole endeavor was explicitly designed to gain considerable "symbolic capital" that endowed her political image with mythological and religious attributes.

On October 12th, 1768, the British physician Thomas Dimsdale inoculated Catherine with tissue taken from a recovered boy by the name of Alexander Markov.[4] After a few weeks of seclusion in Tsarskoe Selo, during which time Catherine developed a mild case of smallpox, she returned to Saint Petersburg completely recovered. At this time, her own "smallpox substance" has been used to inoculate Pavel. The second inoculation, which took place on November 10th, 1768, was successful. Catherine awarded Dimsdale a Baron title, and granted him a permanent post as her physician-in-ordinary with a pension of 500 pounds.[5] Alexander Markov

---

[4] John T. Alexander, *Catherine the Great. Life and Legend* (New York & Oxford, UK, 1989), 143–148; R. P. Bartlett, "Russia in the Eighteenth Century European Adoption of Inoculation for Smallpox", in *Russia and the World of the Eighteenth Century* (Columbus, OH, 1988), 193–213.

[5] Catherine arranged Dimsdale's secured departure in case of a failure resulting in her death: "When Dr. Dimsdale inoculated Catherine the Second for the small-pox, that princess, — who, whatever might be the vices of her moral character, possessed a very enlarged and magnanimous mind, took precautions for securing his personal safety in case of her death. Finding herself much indisposed on a particular day, she sent for Dimsdale, whom she had already remunerated in a manner becoming so great a sovereign. "I experience," said she, "certain sensations which render me apprehensive for my life. My subjects would, I fear, hold you accountable for any accident that might befall me. I have therefore stationed a yacht in the Gulf of Finland, on board of which you will embark as soon as I am no more; and whose commander, in consequence of my orders, will convey you out of all danger." This anecdote, so honourable to the empress, I heard from one

received the respectful title of nobleman as well as an addition to his last name: Markov-Ospennyi (Markov of the Smallpox). In memory of the event, the famous craftsman I. T. Ivanov engraved a medal showing the empress leading Pavel by the hand, alongside a figure of a woman with a bowed head (symbolizing a grateful Russia) and two children holding their arms out towards the empress. The medal also depicted a cathedral, and, by the bottom steps, there was a destroyed "hydra of prejudices." The inscription underneath announced: "She has set an example. 12 October 1768."

First of all, the image of the empress as a savior of the nation involved biblical paradigms. On 22 November the Senate, the deputies of the Legislative Commission, and ministers gathered in the Kazan Cathedral where, after the liturgy, there was announced a Senate decree to establish a state holy day on 21 November. Then, while already located in a palace, Count Kirill Razumovskii gave a speech in which he also relied on Biblical associations of Catherine: "Now all ages and both sexes embrace your feet and praise in you the image of our God the healer <...>"[6]

Answering to the solemn speeches of the Senators who welcomed the empress's recovery and return to the palace, Catherine declared:

> "My goal was, by setting an example, to save from death my loyal subjects who, not knowing the goodness of such a procedure, remained in fear and danger. I had accomplished, in part, my obligation, since, according to the Gospel, the good shepherd lays down his life for the sheep."[7]

Catherine stressed the messianic feature of this event when she participated in ceremonies organized for the Russian public. On that day, churches performed liturgies and hierarchs pronounced celebratory sermons while bells chimed all around the city. On 28 November 1768 the ballet *Triumphant Minerva, or a Defeated*

---

of Dimsdale's sons, above forty years ago." (Sir Nathaniel William Wraxall, *Posthumous memoirs of my own life*, III (London 1836), 199.

[6] S. M. Soloviev, *Istoriia Rossii s drevneishikh vremen*, 28, 365.

[7] Ibid. Catherine referred to the particular lines of the Gospel (Gospel of John 10: 14–15).

Prejudice by the Italian ballet master in the Russian service D. M. G. Angiolini (1731–1803) was performed at the Saint Petersburg court theater. The spectacle, designed as a choreographic ode, presented Chimeras (Smallpox) eating children and, afterwards a distressed Ruthenia (Russia.) The latter found herself safe and sound with the help of brave Minerva (Catherine II) and her son Alcid (Paul). The baroque allegories, however, co-existed with biblical connotations in fawning praise of Catherine's deed.

Vasilii Ruban, the poet and Senate translator, greeted the event by composing his *Ode to the Joyful Celebration of the great deed of inoculation successfully committed by her Imperial Highness and his Imperial Excellence to the happiness of Russia, 22 November 1768*. In his poem, Ruban implied a biblical reference to the verses of Numbers about Moses and the image of a serpent: many Israelites died after having been bitten by the desert's serpents, and, as a result, the people of Israel began to revolt against God and their leader Moses. Then, Moses, "endowed with wisdom" and "chosen by God," placed a bronze serpent on the tree and asked his people to look up at the serpent's image to be healed.[8]

This miraculous salvation from poisoned snakes with the help of an image of a bronze serpent served as a rhetorical vehicle to demonstrate the power of faith. Having rejected God and doubted his power, the sinful men were rescued from death by a metonymical action: Moses used a harmless sign of serpents instead of their real poison. The allegory overall was supposed to demonstrate the power of Christ who provided Moses with such a magical tool.

Ruban's complimentary poem established a link between Moses's serpent, an embodiment of Christ, and Catherine, the healer of her nation:

> Now Catherine, we see in you
> The image of our salvation <...>[9]

---

[8] Numbers, 2:4–9.

[9] Vasilii Ruban, *Oda na den' vseradostneishego torzhestva na predpriniatyi i blagopoluchno sovershivshiisia k neopisannomu schastiiu vseia Rossii, Eia imperatorskogo velichestva i Ego imperatoeskago vysochestva v privitii ospy, 22 noiabria 1768 goda*, 2–3.

The metaphor of Moses's serpent became a general frame for the concept of any antidote, and henceforth, as Ruban attempted to present, signified Catherine's inoculation. In a sequence of Baroque analogies, the poem involved the association of Catherine with both Moses and Christ. In his courteous adulation, Ruban plainly called Catherine "an earthly God."

Similar metaphors appeared in poems written by Vasilii Maikov, who was in charge of composing a whole scenario for a theatrical performance devoted to Catherine's inoculation and recovery and performed on the court stage. In his *Sonnet on the Day of Celebration of a Happy Recovery from Inoculation* (Сонет ко дню празднования о благополучном выздоровлении от прививныя оспы), Maikov shows Catherine as "our Savior and our Deity" and praises the empress who had rescued Russia already for the second time:

> She has changed our terrible existence;
> She saved our whole Russia twice,
> She overthrew vice and hydra to hell.[10]

Hence, the successful inoculation, the victory over the "hydra," once more legitimized Catherine's accession to the throne (Maikov's mention of the "vice" referred to the reign of Peter III). Catherine's primary concern of receiving inoculation before her son also strengthened her claim to power. Her revolt of 1762 was executed under the motto of saving the nation and rescuing her son and heir from the tyrant Peter III. As before, in 1768, the empress strove to emphasize her salutary mission toward her son, the country, and the throne. At the same time, this medical endeavor gained political significance as a clear proof of Catherine's pro-western orientation: medical metaphors in Russia were always associated with a foreign, western course, and sometimes included diabolic links.[11] Not by accident, Mikhail Kheraskov, in his ode *On a successful and joyful recovery of Her Imperial Majesty from smallpox inoculation* (На благополучное и всерадостное освобождение Ея Императорского

---

[10] *Sochineniia i perevody Vasiliia Ivanovicha Maikova* (Saint Petersburg, 1867), 55.

[11] For an overview of the materials concerning Peter I and his medical experiments, see: K. A. Bogdanov, *Vrachi, patsienty, chitateli: patograficheskie teksty russkoi kul'tury XVIII–XIX vekov* (Moscow, 2005), 39–78.

Величества от прививания оспы, 1768) interprets Catherine's deed as a political (and even legislative) decontamination from poisoning.

Catherine apparently welcomed the use of biblical metaphors in constructing her image, addressing them especially to her Russian audience. Moreover, she strengthened the sacred connotations of her deed when she began to distribute her own smallpox "material" (a part of the empress's body!) to subsequent patients. Among the recipients of the empress's "body" were approximately 140 persons, all belonging to the Russian aristocracy.

The success of the procedure overwhelmed society, and inoculation became a fashion. The elite rushed to accept Catherine's "body," and even those who had survived natural smallpox strove to take part in such an incredible endeavor. In giving her "smallpox material" to the nation, Catherine cultivated an association with Christ at the Last Supper: "And when He had taken some bread and given thanks, He broke it and gave it to them, saying, "This is My body which is given for you; do this in remembrance of Me."[12]

Catherine's reply to the hierarchs' speeches when she modestly compared herself to a "kind shepherd" was not a mere aside. The empress used every possible occasion to imbue her grand gestures with greater symbolic power.

Not surprisingly, the empress tried hard to spread the news about her recent "healing actions" among her foreign counterparts. She informed the Russian ambassador in London, Count I. G. Chernyshev, on 17 November 1768:

> "Now we have only two subjects to discuss, first, the war, and second, inoculation. Starting with me and my son who is also recovering, there is not any famous house where one cannot find several inoculated persons; many regret that they had natural smallpox and cannot participate in the latest fashion. Count G. G. Orlov, Prince K. G. Razumovskii, and numerous others handed themselves over to Mr. Dimsdale; even such beauties as Princesses Shcherbatova and Trubetskaia, Elizaveta Alekseevna Stroganova, as well as many other people who had refused to accept the operation. What an outcome of setting the example! Three months ago

---

[12] Luke, 22: 19, 20.

nobody wanted to hear about that, and now they consider it their salvation."[13]

Working on the scenario for a theatrical performance in honor of Catherine the healer, Maikov crafted a Prologue in five parts entitled *A Triumphant Parnassus (Торжествующий Парнасс)*. It appears that the title corresponded with another notable performance, the famous *Triumphant Minerva,* which took place in Moscow in January of 1763 to venerate Catherine's accession. Maikov, one of the authors of the libretto of *Triumphant Minerva,* staged his new theatrical production of 1768 using a similar technique that epitomized the aesthetics of Baroque court festivities.

The setting of his Prologue was supposed to represent Parnassus, while background decorations depicted Saint Petersburg "in doom and darkness."[14] Smallpox appeared in the form of a venomous dragon:

> Thrown out into the world,
> The monster from Hell,
> Emerges in the sky and leaves a gloomy trace,
> Parents and children are trembling.
> The dragon flies and whirls the air.
> He poisons everybody with his gasp,
> Smashes all down in rage,
> Without pity for age or person,
> Slays youth, babies, maids,
> Scorns brave warriors,
> Strikes and tramples upon their corpses <...>[15]

Catherine, "Russian Pallas," engages in a struggle with the monster and defeats him:

> A trembling dragon
> Felled by the Goddess.

---

[13] A. V. Bekasova, "Istoriia o tom, kak privivali ospu Rossiiskomu dvoru," in *Ekaterina Velikaia: epokha rossiiskoi istorii. Tezisy dokladov* (Saint Petersburg, 1996), 21.

[14] *Sochineniia i perevody Vasiliia Ivanovicha Maikova,* 494.

[15] Ibid, 495.

> She extracted his deadly sting,
> And she reduced
> Threat and fear to ashes.[16]

Catherine's combat with the dragon refers by now not to biblical text, but to mythology. Maikov establishes a link between the empress's victory over smallpox and the second labor of Hercules who had to kill the Lernean Hydra. The latter, according to legends, was so venomous that she killed men with her breath. The poet lays emphasis on the secular outcome of Catherine's deed. He praises Catherine not as a miraculous healer, but as an enlightened monarch who helped her nation to surmount the darkness of fear and prejudges.

Undoubtedly, a single association with Hercules implied very important political connotations. The European court culture had already elaborated a metaphoric system of comparison of monarchs with Hercules.[17] In the sixteenth century, the image of Henry IV as Hercules appeared on coins, triumphant arches and courtly decorations.[18] One of the most popular mythological subjects was the second labor of Hercules, and hence it became quite traditional to bestow thoroughly modern virtues upon the Greek hero. Renaissance and later Baroque writers epitomized Hercules as a wise ruler, strong in reason, not merely in body, the one who triumphed over the adversary forces of darkness and ignorance. Victories over chthonic monsters enabled the humanistic tradition to epitomize Hercules as a cultural hero, to link him with arts and laws.[19] Russian Baroque writers perfectly acquired the tradition, and yet, in early panegyrics, they repeatedly called Peter the Great a "new Hercules."[20]

Laudatory verses in the Prologue, written by Maikov, continued the tradition of endowing the empress with characteristics

---

[16] Ibid, 496.

[17] M. R. Yung, *Hercule dans la littérature française du XVI siècle* (Geneva, 1966).

[18] Corrado Vivanti, "Henry IV, the Gallic Hercules," in *Journal of the Warburg and Courtauld Institute*, 30 (1967), 176–197.

[19] Ibid, 184–185.

[20] *Panegiricheskaia literature petrovsogo vremeni* (Moscow, 1979), 136.

of the mythological hero, and, simultaneously, with an authoritative emblem of power. It was no accident that right after the depiction of her victory over the "dragon," Maikov brought in a cheerful forecast of Catherine's inevitable triumph over the Turks (by the end of 1768, Russia had become engaged in a military campaign against the Ottoman Porte). In his quite pompous ending, made out of the poetic matrix of the military ode, Maikov applies the well-played metaphor of the conquered dragon to military paradigms; soon the image of Turkey as a terrible dragon would stream out of Russian poetry. The brass jaws of this dragon, as Maikov puts it, will be "pierced and burned" by Catherine's "lightning," and enemies will stop fighting against Russia:

> Asia will lose its futile hopes
> To wage war against Russian Pallas,
> Who will turn the cities to ashes.
> The Turks will learn how to respect Russia;
> No one will dare to fight back against the country
> Protected by Heaven! [21]

In his poem *A Picture of Felitsa* (1789), Derzhavin gives instruction to a new artist, a "new Raphael," on how to depict the empress; he focuses upon the most significant episodes of her reign, including inoculation. The poet suggests portraying Catherine as Felitsa who has drunk some "poison" in order to rescue her people:

> To save the health of her world,
> She drinks poison without fear;
> Her vigor strikes malicious Death
> That turns away his lackluster eyes <…>
> All of a sudden, millions of children
> Raise their arms toward Heaven <…>
> Their parents declare: "We witness in Felitsa
> Your image, o God!" [22]

At the same time she was emphasizing the sacred meaning of inoculation to her Russian audience, Catherine enveloped her story

---

[21] *Sochineniia i perevody Vasiliia Ivanovicha Maikova*, 496.
[22] *Sochineniia Derzhavina*, I, 199.

into quite a secular form for her foreign correspondents. Moreover, she even treated the "sacred" deed of inoculation with irony while she described her condition in a letter to Voltaire on 17 December 1768:

> "I forgot to tell you that I supplemented the small amount or complete lack of medicine that is given during the inoculation with three or four excellent patent remedies, which I recommend every man of good sense not to neglect in similar circumstances: namely to have someone read to one L'Ecossaise, Candide, L'Ingénue, L'Homme aux quarante écus, and La Princesse de Babylone. It is impossible to feel the least bit ill after that."[23]

This statement reveals more about her philosophy. As a participant in an international community of liberal minds, the so-called "republic of letters," Catherine radically adjusted her image of a sacred healer. From now on, not she, but the works of the enlightened deist "healed" the empress from a deadly disease. In this scenario, Voltaire's texts stood in for curative paper seals, while the process of reading them served as a kind of magic act. She prided herself on being a brave and rational personality who set an example that was followed not only by her courtiers, but also by clerics. She concluded her letter to Voltaire:

> "As for news from here, let me tell you, Sir, that everyone wants to be inoculated: a bishop is going to have it done, and more people have been inoculated here in one month than in eight at Vienna."[24]

In his turn, Voltaire praises Catherine for her open-mindedness and blames the French for conservatism in medical thought (only in 1769 had the practice of inoculation been officially accepted in France, but it remained extremely unpopular). Voltaire wrote to Catherine on 26 February 1769:

---

[23] *Voltaire and Catherine the Great. Selected Correspondence* (Cambridge, UK, 1974), 54.
[24] Ibid.

"Oh, Madam, what a lesson your Majesty is giving to us petty Frenchmen, to our ridiculous Sorbonne and to the argumentative charlatans in our medical schools! You have been inoculated with less fuss than a nun taking an enema."[25]

Later Voltaire, in his essay *On the death of Louis XV and fate* (*De la mort de Louis XV et de la fatalité*), written in 1774, recalled Catherine's description of her experiment right after composing a prose *Eclogue Funeral* (*Eloge Funèbre*), full of irony and contempt toward the French monarch. Juxtaposing the light-mindedness and calm fatalism of Louis XV to Catherine's rationality, Voltaire praised her eagerness to abandon all prejudices and fears for the sake of enlightenment and progress.[26] Again, inventing the letter from Catherine, Voltaire tried to convince the French to follow her example; he brought "her" words about the ease of inoculation, her scorn towards the worthlessness of all religious discussions surrounding the medical procedure, and her brave commitment to save her nation.[27]

These secular connotations of Catherine's inoculation were bound up with political context and marked her attempt to portray herself as an enlightened ruler to her European audience, a strategy that had become more crucial than ever on the eve of the war with the Ottoman Porte. If biblical associations contributed to traditional representations of the Russian monarch's charisma, secular paradigms of inoculation prompted the view of the Russian sovereign as the most civilized modern leader who strove to overcome the uncivilized tyrants of the East. Catherine's inoculation, on the one hand, demonstrated the "European" qualities of the country (the Russian, as Voltaire put it, even outdid the French). On the other hand, Catherine's brilliant performance proved to be a modernized and enlightened "interception" of the sacred charisma right in time of its decline, if not death, in Europe.

---

[25] Ibid, 56.
[26] *Oeuvres complète de Voltaire*, 29 (Paris, 1879), 301.
[27] Ibid, 302.

Overcoming the Plague

Less than three years later Catherine faced another epidemic invasion, this time the bubonic plague. Since the beginning of the war with the Ottoman Porte in 1769, some incidents of plague had sporadically threatened Russian troops as soon as they reached the southern lands of Moldavia.[28] However, the peak of the disease came in Autumn of 1771, when it struck down about 100,000 inhabitants of Moscow and provoked a plague riot which was tamed, according to the official version, by Grigorii Orlov.

The occurrence of 1770–1771 was not the first outbreak of plague in Moscow. In 1654, in time of Aleksei Mikhailovich, the bubonic plague raged over the capital while the tsar left the devastated city and its population to the care of the icon of Our Lady of Kazan.[29] During the events of 1770–1771, Catherine made every possible effort to stop the infection and to protect her subjects. She actively participated in the meetings of the State Council, analyzed in detail all doctors' recommendations, wrote instructions to officials, and informed her foreign correspondents about the course of her struggle. Moreover, after studying the medical records, she proposed her own "method" to treat the disease by using the "cold regiment," i.e. ice baths or wrappers. Her method proved to be effective in some cases and even came into some medical reviews under her name as *Remedium Antipestilentialae Catharinae Secundae*.[30]

Despite strict quarantine measures and the involvement of the army, Moscow's desperate and superstitious population, influenced by local clergy, fled hospitals, struggled against officials and doctors

---

[28] For a detailed account of the causes of the outbreak of the disease in Moscow, see: John T. Alexander, *Bubonic plague in early modern Russia: public health and urban disaster* (Baltimore, 1980). Moscow's extensive textile industry with its dense worker population and poor housing conditions, the disordered structure of Moscow, and bad environmental settings contributed to the spread of the plague.

[29] A. Brikner, "O chume v Moskve 1771 goda," in *Russkii Vestnik*, 173 (1884), 27.

[30] D. Samoilovich, *Mémoirs sur la peste, qui, en 1771, ravagea l'empire de Russie, surtout Moscou, la capital* (Paris, 1783), 153.

and relied, as in 1654, on the miracle of religious processions and "healing" icons. During the first months of plague, the rich left the city for their country estates, together with the governor of Moscow, Petr Saltykov. Factory workers as well as poor urban inhabitants protested against quarantines and doctors' prescriptions to follow the rules of sanitation, relying instead on "healing" icons and priests who organized religious services and collected money from the desperate population. Memoirs written by Andrei Bolotov give an eloquent and detailed account of first occurrences of plague in Moscow: the educated and perceptive memoirist describes "profit-hungry priests who left their churches and services, gathered there with their lecterns and oversaw not pilgrimages, but a regular marketplace; for everyone, in order to save their own lives, begrudged nothing but gave everything they could, seeking only prayers for their well-being."[31]

Rumor told that the Icon of the Virgin Mary of Bogolyubovo, in Kitai-gorod, not far away from the Kremlin, was especially helpful. For three days (September 15–17 of 1771), angry crowds smashed hospitals and quarantines, killed doctors and soldiers. Eventually, they cruelly slaughtered the Moscow Archbishop Ambrosius, who attempted to stop gatherings near the famous icon in order to prevent circulation of infection.

Catherine described the events to Voltaire in her letter of 17 October 1771 as an illustration of the barbaric nature of the Moscow population that could hardly be cured by the age of Enlightenment:

> "I have a small supplement to the article on *Fanaticism* for you, which would also not be out of place in the article on *Contradictions*, which I read with the utmost satisfaction in *Questions sur l' Encyclopédie*. This is what it is about.
>
> "Disease is rife at Moscow: there is an epidemic of various fevers, which are causing numerous fatalities, despite all the precautions which have been taken. <…> Archbishop Ambrose of Moscow, a man of intelligence and ability learned that vast crowds of people had for several days been gathering before

---

[31] *Zhizn' i prikliucheniia Andreia Bolotova, opisannye samim im dlia svoikh potomkov. 1738–1793*, 3 (Saint Petersburg, 1872), 18.

an image which was supposed to heal the sick — these were in fact dying at the holy Virgin's feet, and that people were bringing large sums of money to this shrine. He therefore had the money taken under his official charge, in order to use it later on in various charitable causes, a financial measure which every bishop is fully entitled to take in his diocese. It is to be supposed that he intended to have the image removed, as has been done more than once, and that the confiscation of the money was the preamble to this. Certainly, this horde of people gathered together during an epidemic could only help it to spread. But note what happened. Some of the rabble began shouting: *The Archbishop is going to steal the holy Virgin's treasure; let us kill him.*" [32]

The most frenzied burst into the Kremlin to search for the Archbishop's residence; they looted and destroyed the Chudov Monastery and got drunk in the cellars (the merchants kept their wines there). Ambrosius left his apartments and found refuge in the Donskoy monastery.

The next day, September 16, insurgents became even more rabid, and the riot expanded its power. The rebels arrived at the Donskoy monastery "from where they dragged this old man, and killed him without mercy."[33] Describing in detail all the occurrences of the riot, Catherine concluded:

> "The famous Eighteenth Century really has something to boast of here! See how far we have progressed! But I do not need to speak to you on this score: you know mankind too well to be surprised at the contradictions and excesses it is capable of."[34]

Not surprisingly, Catherine called her description of the plague riot "a small addition" to Voltaire's article *Fanaticism*, published in his *Philosophical Dictionary* in 1764. Voltaire interpreted fanaticism as an epidemic disease, like plague or smallpox:

---

[32] *Voltaire and Catherine the Great. Selected Correspondence*, 121.
[33] Ibid, 122.
[34] Ibid.

"We understand by fanaticism, at present, a religious madness, gloomy and cruel. It is a malady of the mind, which is taken in the same way as the smallpox."[35] He proclaimed that religion became a "poison" in a fanatic mind, and prescribed the only one curative method: "There is no other remedy for this epidemic malady than that spirit of philosophy, which, extending itself from one to another, at length civilizes and softens the manners of men, and prevents the access of the disease."[36]

While Voltaire rhetorically associated fanaticism with epidemics in his article, in his letters to Catherine he made more definite connections. There, speculating on the topic of the ongoing Russian-Turkish war, he boldly linked the Turks' fanaticism and the plague. Answering Catherine's letter, Voltaire wrote on 12 November 1771:

"No mishap could befall your Imperial Majesty from your brave troops or your sage administration. You could suffer only from the disasters which have always afflicted humanity. The epidemic raging in and around Moscow is the result, it is said, of your very victories. It is rumoured that the contagion spread from the corpses of some Turks around the Black Sea. The plague is all that Mustapha could give; it always rages in his fair land. This was indeed one more reason for all your princely neighbors to join you and exterminate, under your auspices, the two great scourges of the earth — the plague and the Turks."[37]

As he assumed, the Russian empress, in this war, was combating not only her geopolitical enemy, but also a stronghold of barbaric fanatics and diseases. Voltaire seemed intent on keeping to his early pledge to inspire Catherine in her war against the "barbaric tyrant" of the East. It was also quite characteristic that Catherine, in her letters to Voltaire, refused to confirm that she dealt with a plague: she insisted that there were some mortal "fevers" in

---

[35] Voltaire, *A Philosophical Dictionary*, I (London 1843), 480.
[36] Ibid, 481.
[37] *Voltaire and Catherine the Great. Selected Correspondence*, 124.

Moscow. She perfectly understood that a plague, in the cultural perception, was synonymous with barbarism, ignorance, and superstition. An enlightened Minerva of the North could not be associated with a symbolic manifestation of the eastern tyranny.

Meanwhile, if Voltaire linked fanatics, the Ottoman Porte, and plague, Catherine applied Voltaire's paradigm to her own kingdom in order in juxtapose Petersburg and Moscow. Her famous prose sketch *Considerations on Petersburg and Moscow* (Размышления о Петербурге и Москве, written soon after the Moscow plague) provides an image of Moscow as a stronghold of fanaticism, the same as it was described in Voltaire's article. All misfortunes came to Moscow because, for a long time, its inhabitants were widely exposed to "healing icons at every step, churches, priests, monasteries, prayers, beggars, thieves, and useless servants."[38] It created a gloomy atmosphere of fanatic beliefs, ignorance, and superstitions. Eventually, according to Catherine, Moscow became a gigantic village with a vast population of unenlightened masses that ensured chaotic riots and political turmoil. A year later, Catherine mocked Moscow in her comedy *O Time!* (О время! 1772), which contains the eloquent subtitle, "Composed at Iaroslavl' during the plague." The Moscow setting revealed the empress's disdain for the city's customs: the three female characters, Mrs. Devout (Khanzhakhina), Mrs. Gossip (Vestnikova), and Mrs. Strange (Chudikhina) exhibited the cultural qualities that, according to the empress, predestined Moscow's riot.

Catherine did not like Moscow; she was not even enthused by Voltaire's letter praising her as a ruler "who was born to instruct men as well as govern them."[39] Catherine ignored all missionary prospects, and eventually, decided to send Count Grigorii Orlov to Moscow. On 21 September, Catherine issued a Manifesto:

> "Looking at the horrifying events in Moscow in which a great number of people died from infectious diseases, We had intent to rush there in order to fulfill our duty. However, taking into account circumstances of war, our trip could put

---

[38] *Zapiski imperatritsy Ekateriny Vtoroi*, 652.
[39] *Voltaire and Catherine the Great. Selected Correspondence*, 124–125.

important affairs of our Empire out of order. Being unable to go and to share all danger menacing Moscow's inhabitants, We decided to send there a person whom We trust and who would possess all power to arrange necessary measures to rescue people and to provide provisions for them."[40]

She informed Voltaire of Orlov's mission:

"The Grand Master, Count Orlov, asked as a favor to be allowed to go there, to ascertain on the spot what measures would be the most suitable for checking the outbreak. I agreed to this request, such a fine and zealous one on his part, not without feelings of acute anxiety over the risks he would run."[41]

The events were grave, the danger was immense, and rumors circulated that the empress sent her favorite to Moscow in order to finish their relationship, which bored and annoyed her.[42] As usual, Voltaire found a poetic image that became the rhetorical frame for the official perception of Orlov's mission. Voltaire replied to Catherine:

"The Master of the Ordnance, Count Orlov, is a consoling angel; he performed a heroic deed. I can understand that it must have greatly moved your heart, divided as it was between fear and admiration; but you should be less surprised than another: great deeds are part of your style."[43]

As Voltaire prescribed, not Catherine, but Grigorii Orlov became the main focus of the event. Several odes were promptly composed in honor of Orlov's "deed": by S. V. Naryshkin, by P. S. Potemkin, and by Vasilii Maikov. V. G. Ruban also published his *Inscription on the Successful Return of his Excellency Count Grigorii Orlov from Moscow to Saint Petersburg*.[44] Of the list of works on this event, none has achieved more fame than Maikov's ode. Maikov

---

[40] S. Soloviev, *Istoriia Rossii s drevneishikh vremen*, 28, 365.
[41] *Voltaire and Catherine the Great. Selected Correspondence*, 121.
[42] A. Brikner, "O chume v Moskve 1771 goda," 528–529.
[43] *Voltaire and Catherine the Great, Selected Correspondence*, 125.
[44] *Trudoliubivyi muravei*, 20 (1771), 160.

had already manifested great dexterity in courtly adulation, and a thorough knowledge of court politics. The poet equipped his ode with an informative and straightforward title: *A Letter to His Excellence Count G. G. Orlov, on His Departure from Saint Petersburg to Moscow, in the Time of Contagious Disease in Order to Exterminate It*. Maikov (like all other poets) avoided calling the malady a plague, and instead, brought in a more accurate and politically vague definition: "a contagious disease." His title overall introduced the political message and extinguished potential rumors about the motivations for Orlov's trip to Moscow. Most likely, the rumors about the awful relationship between Grigorii Orlov and Catherine had considerable substance, since soon after his triumphant return to Saint Petersburg Orlov would be sent abroad. In June 1772, Orlov would leave Saint Petersburg to conduct diplomatic negotiations with the Turks in Fokshany, in Wallachia. So Maikov's descriptive tone and restrained compliments to Orlov signaled that the poet grasped the court situation and paid tribute to the official form.

The success of Maikov's works on Catherine's triumph over smallpox made his new ode a pattern of poetic mythology around a new epidemic disease. The rise and flourishing of military odes during 1769–1770 also contributed to the elaboration of the solemn ode addressed to a "hero," not only to the sovereign. Such "indirect" glorification of the empress proved to be even more effective at that time. Maikov portrays Orlov as a Roman hero, "enlightened" by "Minerva's "ray," and protected by "her shield."[45] So Orlov turned out to be only Catherine's envoy, and all praise went back to the empress.

The poet depicts Orlov's expedition to Moscow as a kind of mythological procession through dark clouds. The metaphor contained both figurative and real meanings, as many people burned the belongings of infected victims while local medics prompted the burning of some special "healing fumigations" saturated with herbal supplements. Voltaire called Orlov a "consoling angel," but at that time Biblical associations did not work out and could not be introduced. Instead, Maikov implies strict Roman references:

---

[45] Maikov, 104.

besides the already approved and successful Hercules connotations, he refers to the Roman topographical legend about a young Roman hero Marcus Curtius:

> What example can I bring to compare?
> Hardly one seems to be equal to your deed.
> Curtius made his glory in ancient times,
> He jumped into a burning abyss and saved Rome from strife.
> Don't we perceive more glory for you now?
> Moscow confronts worse danger than Rome.[46]

The legend said that a huge burning pit opened in the middle of the Roman Forum, and all efforts to cover it were in vain. The Romans asked the Oracle, which advised them to throw in the most valuable things in their possession. Marcus Curtius interpreted it as his destiny to sacrifice his life (the most precious thing he had) for the sake of his compatriots. Armored and mounted on horseback, he threw himself into the abyss which then closed, leaving only a small lake.

Catherine ordered Etienne-Maurice Falconet and Marie-Anne Collot, his pupil, to fabricate a medal in honor of Orlov's endeavor. Falconet, as usual, invented a very conceptual design combining antiquity and modernity (Collot was supposed to apply a portrait resembling his profile on the medal). However, the empress quickly arranged her own drawing based on the Curtius legend, apparently after being acquainted with Maikov's ode. Moreover, she asked the famous sculptor not to use his own motto for the medal, but to engrave an inscription taken from Maikov's poem: "Moscow is rescued from strife by Orlov": "In Russian the verse is very resonant."[47]

However, the inscription went not onto the medal, but the triumphant arch (made by Antonio Rinaldi) which Catherine ordered to be erected for Orlov's return. The medal engraved by G. Vekhter and P. Utkin displayed, on its front side, the portrait of Grigorii Orlov, decorated by a ribbon which contained (besides an

---

[46] Ibid, 104–105.

[47] *Sbvornik imperatorskogo russkogo istoricheskogo obshchestva*, 17 (Saint Petersburg, 1876), 155–158.

order of Andrew the First Called) a medallion portrait of Catherine II. On its reverse side, Orlov was pictured in Roman dress astride his horse, disguised as Curtius who was galloping in front of the Kremlin. The inscription below said: "Russia possesses such sons'" (according to memoirs, Orlov asked Catherine to change the first version which sounded more "complimentary": "Russia possesses such a son").[48]

The Moscow plague riot hit the highest point of chaotic foment where all institutional power completely failed. Orlov arrived in Moscow as Catherine's special envoy, accompanied by four guard regiments, a whole army of doctors, and equipped with considerable sums of money. His actions, entirely coordinated with Catherine's orders, intended to bring discipline and order to a plague-stricken town plunged into chaos. However, the measures he imposed involved not only the usual models of "discipline and punish" (as it was before in classical examples of plague epidemics),[49] but also the strategy of an enlightened cultural hero. Not incidentally, Maikov in his poem mentioned a "ray of enlightenment" which Orlov had acquired from Catherine-Minerva and brought to Moscow. If the first episodes in Moscow's events of 1771 developed the old paradigms of a medieval-like plague-stricken city (the rich left the city, and the poor revolted against doctors, sanitation measures, and quarantines, as well as relied on religious rituals and healing icons), the last occurrences, which took place already under Orlov's command, involved something new linked with the paradigms of the Enlightenment.

First of all, Count Orlov had, since his arrival on September 26, settled down in the center of Moscow, apparently demonstrating not only his bravery, but a sense of order, responsibility, and commitment to restore the failed order. He immediately embarked on inspecting hospitals and quarantines. Orlov brought to the city a whole army of doctors who were charged with shedding light on the diagnosis. On September 30, he addressed to the Moscow

---

[48] A. Brikner, "O chume v Moskve 1771 goda," 529.

[49] Michel Foucault, *Discipline and Punish: the Birth of the Prison* (New York, 1995), 195–228.

population his statement *On the Plague in Moscow*, which not only declared the proper character of disease, but also proposed a whole plan of action. He ordered that free clothing be distributed as well as money (quite considerable for the time!) to all patients who survived and were discharged from the hospitals: 5 rubles for a single person, 10 rubles for married persons. He also gave money (20 rubles) to the persons who reported concealed cases of disease in houses or alleged sales of the clothing taken from dead people. The measures worked, and the population started to arrive at quarantines and hospitals. The provisions were sent to Moscow, municipal jobs were created, and a variety of public institutions (designed for orphans, the homeless and the sick) were founded. In addition, Orlov ordered that the salaries for doctors and their assistants be doubled. The government granted a huge amount of money (400,000 rubles) for the war on the plague. In three months, the epidemic was practically over.

The plague riot shocked Catherine more than the pestilential threat itself. Her primary concern was based on the assumption that it was a return to the epoch of Peter I; Catherine wrote in September 1771 to Nikita Panin: "Moscow's condition bothers me very much, since, apart from disease and fires, there is too much stupidity. The whole thing smacks of the beard of our ancestors <...>"[50] When the riot was over, she wrote to A. I. Bibikov on 20 October 1771: "We have spent a month in circumstances like those that Peter the Great lived under for thirty years. He broke through all difficulties with glory; we hope to come out of them with honor."[51] The events in Moscow have been interpreted as a return to the beginning of the eighteenth century, to the epoch of Peter's struggle against barbarism, religious fanaticism, and the backwardness of Russia. For a month Catherine found herself in Peter's situation, but the resolution of the crises was achieved by means much more gentle and civilized.

---

[50] S. Soloviev, "Moskva v 1770 i 1771 gg.," in *Russkaia starina*, 17 (1876), 195–196.
[51] *Sbornik imperatorskogo russkogo istoricheskogo obshchestva*, 13: 179–180.

Chapter Four

TOPPLING THE BRONZE HORSEMAN

The concept of the main City as the center of an imperial power and the legend of its founding both played considerable roles in Russian political myths. Saint Petersburg, built by Peter I in 1703, symbolically designated a new period in Russian history: almost immediately, the new capital tended to forge new frontiers in Russian culture. Relocating the capital to the shores of the Neva, in fact, brought the history of the kingdom of Muscovy to a close and ushered in the age of the Russian Empire. Saint Petersburg, as soon as it had risen above its "quagmire of swamps," brutally abolished all Muscovite cultural values, as well as Moscow's legal claim to be the center of power. Moscow had been called a stronghold of schismatic religious beliefs, stagnated cultural tastes, and backward types of everyday life. The new capital declared its pro-Western orientation in this sense, which could be understood as mythological.

The main feature of this orientation, besides superficial and incoherent economic and social reforms, consisted of an appropriation of the Western "imperial idea." At the beginning of the eighteenth century, the nascent Russian capital on the Neva River hastily arrogated traditional symbols and emblems of imperial authority. Rome, the Eternal City, which for subsequent generations embodied the idea of Empire combined with Christianity, became an inexhaustible source of allegories and metaphors for European empires, and finally, for the newborn Russian empire.

Peter I looked upon Rome as the fullest and most permanent expression of the existing doctrine of Empire, and, at the same time, as the perfect pattern of a classical, universal culture that stood for the ideal of unity as opposed to national self-determination on the part of "barbaric" peoples. Peter I not only actively introduced Roman *emblemata* to Russia, but also strove to outdo their grandiosity. Pagan or Christian, these symbols and allegories were often appropriated from discrete historical periods. His main creation, Saint Petersburg, the city of Saint Peter, had clear pretensions to the title of a "new Rome" that would replace a conservative and hated Moscow, as well as dissolve Moscow's earlier claims to be "the third Rome."[1]

In rejecting the old Russian capital, Peter I drew a distinct border between "civilization" and "barbarity." The founding of the city in spite of the obstacles posed by nature and indigenous peoples, as well as the subsequent transfer of the capital to a newly occupied place, clearly manifested the traditional paradigms of *translatio imperii*. Through these means, Russia not only asserted her right to be considered the rising dominion among the old and already decaying empires, but also attempted to secure her status as a sacred charismatic power, the most Christian nation among all others. At the same time, the fact that the city was built on the country's northern frontier clearly indicated the main direction of Russia's geopolitical aspirations.

Meanwhile, at the beginning of the eighteenth century, as the Muscovite kingdom gradually evolved into the Russian Empire, the concept of Saint Petersburg also underwent some considerable changes. Little by little, Saint Petersburg lost its association with Saint Peter, acquiring instead a strong and enduring link to its founder, Peter I. Both his contemporaries and their successors connected the City of Saint Petersburg only to Peter the Great, who, in his turn, began to replace his sacred predecessor. A tremendous sacralization of power and the personality of the emperor paradoxically coincided

---

[1] On the earliest perceptions of the Saint Petersburg's myth, see Iu. M. Lotman, B. A. Uspenskii, "Otzvuki kontseptsii 'Moskva — tretii Rim' v ideologii Petra Pervogo: K probleme srednevekovoi traditsii v kul'ture barokko," in Iu. M. Lotman, *Izbrannye stat'i v trekh tomakh*, III, 201–212; G. V. Vilinbakhov, "Osnovanie Peterburga i imperskaia emblematika," in *Semiotika goroda i gorodskoi kul'tury: Peterburg. Trudy po znakovym sistemam*. XVIII (Tartu, 1984), 46–55; G. Z. Kaganov, *Peterburg v kontekste barokko* (Saint Petersburg, 2001), 155–207.

with a secularization of everyday life and habits. This process was completed in 1721 when Peter officially accepted honorary Roman titles, such as that of "Emperor," "Father of Fatherland" (Pater Patriae), and "The Great" (Maximus). For subsequent generations, in all cultural and literary traditions, the "city of Peter" symbolized a break with the past (that is, with an old and barbaric Muscovite Russia) as well as the westernization of life and thought, constantly associated with Peter the First alone.[2]

Peter accepted the title of Emperor without any "confirmation" of its legitimacy from European powers, the Pope or the Viennese court (the Austrian Emperor held the ancestral title of Emperor of the Holy Roman Empire).[3] Peter's claims purported to make Russia "equal" to the other main Christian powers, and included Peter in the honorable family of Rome's "descendents." This event contained both Christian and pagan elements that referred to the medieval symbolism of the Emperor as a Christian king and to the early Roman meaning of the Emperor as a military chief (thereby linking Peter's title with Russia's success in the Great Northern War in 1721). The controversy surrounding the situation took on some peculiar features when Peter began to be regarded as God by his followers and as the Antichrist by dissident groups.[4] This duality made it possible to praise Peter as the Russian God or another

---

[2] On the main concepts of Saint Petersburg's text and its literary interpretations, see V. N. Toporov, "Peterburg i peterburgskii tekt russkoi literatury: vvedenie v temu," in *Semiotika goroda i gorodskoi kul'tury: Peterburg*, 4–29; Iu. M. Lotman, "Simvolika Peterburga i problemy semiotiki goroda," Ibid, 30–45; A. L. Ospovat, "K preniiam 1830-kh gg. O russkoi stolitse," in *Lotmanoskii sbornik* 1 (Moscow, 1995), 476 -- 487; Evgeniia Kirichenko, "Sviashchennaia toponimika rossiiskikh stolits: vzaimosviaz' i vzaimovliianie," in *Rossia/Russia: Kul'turnye praktiki v ideologicheskoi perspective*, 3 [11](Moscow — Venice, 1999), 20–35.

[3] On a discussion of Peter I's title, see Isabel de Madariaga, "Tsar into emperor: the title of Peter the Great," in Isabel de Madariaga, *Politics and Culture in Eighteenth-Century Russia. Collected Essays* (London and New York, 1998), 15–39; B. A. Uspenskii, *Tsar' i imperator: Pomazanie na tsarstvo i semantika monarshikh titulov* (Moscow, 2000), 79.

[4] E. Shmurlo, *Peter Velikii v otsenke sovremennikov i potomstva*, 1 (Saint Petersburg, 1912), 82–83. See also: *Petr I v russkoi literature XVIII veka. Teksty i kommentarii*. Ed. S. I. Nikolaev (Saint Petersburg, 2006.)

Russian domestic deity. Notably, Mikhail Lomonosov wrote in his inscription to Peter I's monument (designed by Carlo Bartolomeo Rastrelli and cast by Alessandro Martelli in 1745–1746):

> In short, this is Peter, the Father of the Fatherland.
> Russia praises the earthly God,
> And lights as many altars in front of his visage,
> As there are hearts are devoted to him.[5]

Lomonosov's draft of these verses contained a more expressive formula: instead of the "earthly God," the poet called Peter I a "domestic deity" ("domashne bozhestvo").[6] Peter the First still kept his sacred charisma even through the end of Elizabeth's rule. In 1760, Sumarokov could, in his translation into Russian of an inscription to Peter written by Nikolai Motonis in Latin, easily assert:

> You, Peter, accomplished many good deeds,
> If, in ancient times,
> A man like you had appeared,
> Would the people have called you merely the Great?
> You would have been called God.[7]

The cult of Peter I determined the specifics of Saint Petersburg's myth: the initial symbolism of the city that was originally named after the Apostle Peter was replaced by a new mythology of Peter the First. By the end of the century, the city's name and imagery were tightly associated with the Emperor Peter I. The formula "Peter's city" implied not "Christian" connotations, but instead a whole spectrum of secular meanings reflecting Peter's westernization of life and culture.[8] It was significant that, decades after Peter's death, the town continued to be perceived as its founder's posthumous cloister, especially after the erection of a monument to him in 1782.

---

[5] M. V. Lomonosov, *Polnoe sobranie sochinenii*, 8, 284.
[6] Ibid, 285.
[7] A. P. Sumarokov, *Izbrannye proizvedeniia*, 483.
[8] Vera Proskurina, "Ot Afin k Ierusalimu", in *Lotmanovskii sbornik*, 1, 488–502; Andrew Kahn, *Pushkin's The Bronze Horseman* (London, 1998), 89–97.

Already in Catherine II's time, during a break in the Russo-Swedish War, the old enemies of Peter the Great (who had smashed the Swedish army near Poltava in 1709) attempted to take revenge on the Russians by attacking Saint Petersburg, storming the city and toppling the Bronze Horseman. The military campaign of Gustav III had to reverse Peter I's previous deeds and history itself. Russian military intelligence informed Catherine II of Sweden's plans: "<…> Land in Krasnaia Gorka, burn down Kronstadt, go into Petersburg, and topple the statue to Peter I."[9]

Saint Petersburg: "then" and "now"

Catherine's coming to the throne brought about new attitudes in the interpretation of Peter I's image. It also generated a new mythology which was closely connected with the most vital tasks of power. The events forced Catherine II to rely upon the so-called "Peter's behest," but Catherine's belonging to Peter I's ideological lineage was not based on her own voluntary choice: she had been fastened to the Petrine heritage which substituted, to some extent, for the absence of her own dynastic myth.

The events of 1762 made Petrine "links" a kind of religious sanctification; an association with Peter's mythology became more important and more influential than any legal right to the throne. Disregard for Peter's achievements and/or interests could be interpreted as high treason, as in the case of Peter III.

The medal presented to Catherine on the occasion of her ascension to the throne illustrated well the new configurations of the imperial imagination. The reverse side of the medal pictures an allegorical figure which clearly symbolizes Saint Petersburg. "Saint Petersburg" is kneeling, and another figure dressed in a military uniform (most likely, representing the guards) is carefully supporting the shaky "city."[10] An Angel descending from heaven is holding out his hand toward Catherine, and with his head turned

---

[9] A. V. Khrapovitskii, *Pamiatnye zapiski*, 79.
[10] S. N. Isksul', *Rokovye gody Rossii. God 1762. Dokumental'naia khronika* (Saint Petersburg, 2001), 237. The medal was designed by I. G. Vekhter.

toward Saint Petersburg, he pronounces an engraved slogan: "This is your salvation." Allegorically, this scene indicates that Catherine's coming to the throne was not only a successful rescue of the nation, but also a heroic liberation of the Peter's city. The Saint Petersburg myth served as a convenient vehicle to explain and justify the deposition of Peter III, who supposedly made an attempt to revise or even abolish "Peter's deeds."

The Second Manifesto on the occasion of Catherine's ascension directly and openly linked Catherine's revolt to the necessity of the *restoration* of Peter I's deeds that had been neglected during the reign of Peter III. The text written in the name of Catherine declares:

> "<...> He (Peter III. — V. P.) attempted to add insult to injury by corrupting all the things that the Great Monarch and Father of our Fatherland, our blessed and eternally unforgettable Emperor Peter the Great, our most dear grandfather, established and achieved in Russia through his vigilant work during the 30 years of his rule <...>."[11]

The first years of Catherine's sovereignty marked her deepest (yet completely pragmatic) association with the Petrine myth. The appellation of "grandfather" went almost unnoticed: the idea of Catherine's blood relationship was abandoned by G. N. Teplov, the real author of the *Manifesto*. It reflected some uncertainty on the part of the authorities, who could not yet find the right strategy and hastily validated the legality of her ascension. At the same time, the innovative concept that Catherine's ideological heredity had been passed down to her through Peter's ideas and passion for reforms turned out to be extremely popular. A. P. Sumarokov, in his *Ode to the Empress Catherine the Second on the day of her ascension to the throne, on June 28, 1762* describes the empress as Peter reincarnated:

> Mars gets enraged, he throws his sword,
> He yells: I will be defeated!
> Catherine rules,
> Great Peter resurrected.

---

[11] Ibid, 184.

> Pluto shouts: Great Peter
> Arose from his grave, and evil was cast down.[12]

Vasilii Maikov, in his *Ode on the ascension of her highness and on her name day in 1762*, consistently refines the notion that Catherine's exclusive wisdom and skills were characteristics inherited from Peter the First. In Maikov's poem, Peter appears and justifies Catherine's rule on the basis of her knowledge and talents:

> My wisdom lives in her,
> She knows how to wield the scepter <...>.[13]

The Song to Catherine, written by the Italian poet Michelangelo Gianetti (1744–1796) and translated into Russian by Bogdanovich summarizes the initial myth of the relationship between Peter and Catherine, created by poets in the 1760s. He writes:

> The successor to Peter the Great's dominion,
> A true admirer of his glory,
> You carry his labors, you love his law,
> You have his spirit, and you rule like him.
> Your soul inspires my mind henceforth,
> And my verses revert from Peter to Catherine.[14]

Meanwhile, relying upon Peter I, and even publicly declaring complete loyalty to "Peter's behest," Catherine began developing new contours of the Saint Petersburg myth. She was completely satisfied when Vasilii Petrov, following a precedent established by Virgil, formulated new attitudes toward her great predecessor. Peter the First received the status of a great founder, the Aeneas of Saint Petersburg, while the empress was bequeathed the significance of a new Augustus who fulfilled the precursor's deeds and guided his country to prosperity and success.

The concept of *the brilliant accomplishment* of the deeds which Peter I *had begun* became one of the most popular poetic formulas

---

[12] A. P. Sumarokov, *Polnoe sobranie vsekh sochinenii v stikhakh i proze*, II, 45.
[13] Vasilii Maikov, *Izbrannye proizvedeniia*, 188.
[14] I. F. Bogdanovich, *Sochineniia*, I, 258.

in Catherine's time. Thus, Vasilii Maikov applies this formula in his *Ode on the occasion of the election of deputies to the Committee of a New Code in 1767*. Addressing Catherine, Maikov writes:

> The almighty hand of God
> Put you on the throne
> For our happiness and peace
> You have been given a monarch's power:
> To raise and glorify Russia,
> To restore the just courts,
> To finish Peter's deeds.
> Fate took that man away,
> Providence gave us you
> To fulfill his policy.[15]

In 1767, Gavrila Derzhavin wrote the poem *On the presentation of the title of Catherine the Great to her Highness by her deputies* (На поднесение депутатами Ея Величества титла Екатерины Великой):

> Though the whole dazzling world witnessed the glory,
> As Peter's name resounded all over
>   after his victory at Poltava;
> However, not only his military deeds
> Have brought the worship of all;
> But also laws, verdicts, and enlightenment of habits
> Grant him eternal adoration.
> He became great not through his victories;
> But by bringing prosperity to his people.
> Our Highness! You take his reins;
> Call yourself *Great*: what he has begun, you will finish.[16]

In 1767, the Senate and the members of the Commission for the composition of the new Code project decided to grant Catherine with new titles: the Great, the Wise, and the Mother of the Fatherland. She refused to accept them.[17] She obviously was not excited by the simple act of a formal inheritance of Peter's titles.

---

[15] Vasilii Maikov, *Izbrannye proizvedeniia*, 198.
[16] *Sochineniia Derzhavina s ob''iasnitel'nymi primechaniiami Ia. Grota*, III, 188.
[17] *Polnoe Sobranie Zakonov*. Vol. XVIII, # 12, 978.

Meanwhile, this rejection, which was construed as an exhibition of the Empress's modesty, exposed, for the first time, her concealed intention to revise the "symbolic heritage" of Peter the Great. The secretary to Count A. K. Razumovskii informed the exiled Ivan Shuvalov (a former favorite of Elizabeth) of some new trends in political life on August 20, 1767:

> "Last Sunday at the palace we had a reception to honor Her Highness, and there was a procession of deputies who, as said, asked her to accept the titles of the Wise, the Great, and Mother of the Fatherland. Her reply was as decent as our Empress herself: only God is Wise; my progeny will appraise my Greatness; as for the Mother of the Fatherland? I would rather say: I love you and want to be loved."[18]

Publicly, Catherine always stressed absolute respect for Peter I. At the beginning of 1760, she constantly discussed Peter's great achievements in her correspondence with Voltaire in a tone of absolute admiration. She expressed her deep gratitude to Voltaire as he sent her new parts of his *History* of Peter I. She also mentioned that she began to collect all of Peter's memorabilia. In 1763, Catherine explained to Voltaire her decision to refuse the Senate's proposition to erect a monument in her honor, stressing instead the necessity of building a new monument to Peter the First.[19]

Nevertheless, already by the end of 1760 the cultural mythology of Catherine and Peter I's relationship shifted to a new focal point. Catherine's achievements began to be considered more significant than Peter's "deeds."

Catherine II visibly emphasized her deepest respect for Peter I. She liked to openly hold a talisman with Peter's image, and she reproached anyone among her company who dared to criticize her great predecessor.[20] Meanwhile, in her correspondence (in letters to Voltaire and to her personal secretary Ivan Betskoi, founder of many

---

[18] *Sochineniia Derzhavina s ob'iasnitel'nymi primechaniiami Ia. Grota*, III, 188-189 (commentaries by Ia. Grot.)

[19] *Documents of Catherine the Great. The Correspondence with Voltaire & Instruction of 1767 in the English text of 1768.* Ed. by W. F. Reddaway (New York, 1971), 1–32.

[20] Prince de Ligne, *Mémoires et mélanges historique et littéraire*, 2 (Paris, 1827), 360.

charitable institutions and chief of Saint Petersburg's Committee of Buildings), she cautiously showed disapproval for most of Peter's deeds. She blamed him for reforms in church and education; she scorned his poor fleet, and eventually accused him of choosing a false way of westernization in general.[21] Her growing dissatisfaction with Peter's decision to found Petersburg in such an awful location became a leitmotif in her correspondence with Voltaire.

Moreover, by the end of 1760s, Catherine's achievements had shifted to the center of Saint Petersburg's mythology, relegating "Peter's paradigm" to the margins. Peter's deeds began playing the role of respectable historical decorations, a kind of theatrical background for the Empress's cultural presentations. Catherine II turned out to be the only focus of Petersburg's cultural myth.

Voltaire contributed a great deal to this concept. In the 1750s, he was asked by Elizabeth to compose a history of Peter I. His two volume *History of Russia during the reign of Peter the Great* (*Histoire de l'empire de Russie sous Pierre le Grand*), published in 1759–1763, gave a restrained account of Peter's actions, ideology, and reforms. Because he was fulfilling a government contract, Voltaire limited himself to a strictly factual portrait of the activities of the first Russian Emperor, and thus, his account is remarkably free of commentary and interpretation.[22] As soon as Catherine took the throne, Voltaire began to create the image of the "greatest" Catherine against the background of her "great" predecessor. He always put them together, with Peter serving as a great pedestal for Catherine's shining statue.

In his story *The Princess of Babylon* (*La Princess de Babylone*, 1767), Voltaire describes the Cimmerian empire under the rule of a wise and most brilliant "empress" who had fulfilled the great deeds of a previous great "man." The splendor of the capital impressed the traveling Princess of Babylon, who was accompanied by a phoenix:

---

[21] Karen Rasmussen, "Catherine II and the Image of Peter I", in *Slavic Review* 37:1 (1978), 56.

[22] Nicholas V Riazanovsky, *The Image of Peter the Great in Russian History and Thought* (New York-Oxford, 1985), 18–22.

"After a few days journey, they entered a very large city, which has of late been greatly improved by the reigning empress: she herself was not there, but was making a progress through her dominions, on the frontiers of Europe and Asia, in order to judge of their state and condition with her own eyes, to enquire into their grievances, and to provide the proper remedies for them. <...> — How comes it, said he (Phoenix. — V. P.) that such prodigious changes have been brought about in so short a time? Formerly, when I was here, about three hundred years ago, I saw nothing, but savage nature in all her horrors; at present, I perceive industry, arts, splendor, and politeness. — This mighty revolution, replied the Cimmerian, was began by one man, and now carried to perfection by one woman; a woman who is a greater legislator than the Isis of the Egyptians, or the Ceres of the Greeks."[23]

Readers did not have any doubts that Voltaire associated this "empire" with Russia, and he obviously linked the enlightened empress to Catherine, who had fulfilled the reforms of Peter I. In the context of the City paradigm, the formula "then and now" signified the transformation of a wild, barbaric place into a flourishing country. The formula, Virgilian in origin, belongs to a great European and Russian poetic tradition, which Pushkin has explores to the full in his *Bronze Horseman*.[24] This formula has always stood for the great pathos of civilization against nature and barbarism. Voltaire carefully eliminates the clear imperialistic connotations present in Virgil's verses, emphasizing instead the power of knowledge, enlightenment, and the arts. He granted Peter simply the honor of being a "founder," while he endowed Catherine with the much more honorable title of an "enlightener."

In his poetic epistolary of 1771, addressed to Catherine (and translated rather freely by Ippolit Bogdanovich), Voltaire again refined his preliminary concepts. He always made comparisons to Peter I in order to flatter Catherine much more. Here, in particular,

---

[23] Voltaire, *The Princess of Babylon* (London, 1768), 89–91.
[24] L. V. Pumpianskii, "Mednyi vsadnik i poeticheskaia traditsiia XVIII veka," in L. V. Pumpianskii, *Klassicheskaia traditsiia. Sobranie trudov po istorii russkoi literatury* (Moscow, 2000), 163–165.

he points out the military success of her southern strategy. This compliment was made at the expense of Peter I, whose failure in the Pruth campaign of 1711 (during which he barely escaped captivity) was well known. Voltaire writes:

> Where Peter the Great produced men,
> Catherine created heroes,
> Her great spirit, as a mighty god,
> Endows all with good sense and leads in combat.[25]

The subsequent development of Saint Petersburg cultural mythology reduced Peter I's role, while highly elevating Catherine's accomplishments. The mythology of Saint Petersburg began to center on a formula which referred to Augustus's famous declaration that he inherited a Rome of brick but was leaving one of marble.[26]

The theme of Saint Petersburg's architectural excellence acquired political aspects as well. The formula "then and now" distributed Peter's and Catherine's contributions unequally: "then" (Peter's time) corresponded to an initial period of miserable hovels, while "now" (Catherine's time) stood for the beauty of magnificent palaces. The political implications of the comparison of the past and the present gained new power.[27]

Two versions of the first canto of Petrov's translation of Virgil's *Aeneid* clearly reflect a conscious fabrication of this paradigm as well as the gradual development of its political program. Petrov plays all along with the allusive essence of Virgil's epic and skillfully interprets the political strategies of his powerful patron. Significantly, Petrov's translation accents different segments of the same text. In the first version, written in 1770, he implies the theme of the City (Carthage, Dido's kingdom) as a stronghold that

---

[25] I. F. Bogdanovich, *Sochineniia*, 1, 270. See in original text: "Pierre était créateur, il a formé des hommes. / Tu formes des héros <...> / Mais Catherine veille au milieu des conquêtes; / Tous ses jours sont marqués de combats et de fêtes" (Oeuvres complètes de Voltaire, 10. Paris, 1877, 437).

[26] Suetonius, referring to a famous Augustus saying on Rome, wrote that "he had found it built of brick and left it in marble" (Suetonius, *The Lives of the Caesars*) (New York, 2004), 62.

[27] L. V. Pumpianskii, "*Mednyi vsadnik* i poeticheskaia traditsiia XVIII veka," 164.

must protect a newly acquired, precarious throne against enemies and chaotic forces. Petrov did not describe the City's landscape by focusing on formidable or well-built walls. At that time, during the first years of Catherine's rule (and also during her war against the Turks), he underscores the necessity for Catherine's Russia to build up a military fortress that is safe and strong:

> They rush to the nearest hilltop,
> From which they could observe the whole of Carthage.
> Aeneas was astonished to find
> Enormous walls, and gates, and tidy stone towers,
> Where before there were only miserable hovels <...>[28]

In the first version, Carthage symbolizes the triumph of Catherine-Dido over her political enemies. In 1781, Petrov, while preparing a complete edition of the *Aeneid*, rewrote this same fragment. In his version of 1781, Petrov emphasizes the splendor of the city:

> The chief of the Trojans was astonished
>   by the splendor of the city.
> Where there once were woods, mass of buildings stood.
> He observed the beauty of the gates and
>   the elevated towers,
> As well as tidy cobblestone streets.[29]

The first version highlights the beginning of the City's construction as the most important concept. It corresponded to the main paradigm of Russian politics at that time, which was during the beginning of Catherine's legal reforms. Petrov clearly implied the events of Catherine's early legal projects as he writes:

> Looking at the buildings,
> Aeneas uttered: Blessed are the people
>   who are setting up a City.[30]

---

[28] Virgil, *Enei. Geroicheskaia poema*, translated by Vasilii Petrov (Saint Petersburg, 1770), 25.

[29] Virgil, *Enei. Geroicheskaia poema*, translated by Vasilii Petrov (Saint Petersburg, 1781), 28.

[30] Virgil, *Enei. Geroicheskaia poema*, translated by Vasilii Petrov (Saint Petersburg, 1770), 25.

In his version of 1781, Petrov depicts a completely raised City that already reaches the skies.

> Looking at the buildings,
> Aeneas uttered: Blessed are the people
> Whose City reaches the skies. [31]

These two versions of Petrov's translation make a declaration in poetic form of a shift in Saint Petersburg's reception from Catherine's early years to the epoch of her absolute power. Since the beginning of 1780, the splendor of Saint Petersburg became one of the most indicative features of Catherine's rule, and the formula "then and now" began to play an important role in the propagation of her image. This opposition concerns only two figures (Peter I and Catherine II) and does not take into account Elizabeth's time on the throne. Elizabeth's architectural achievements appear to have been "forgotten" by contemporaries. Catherine hated Elizabeth's architectural tastes; soon after her ascension, Catherine began to rebuild the old Baroque palaces; she also frequently expressed her dissatisfaction with Carlo Rastrelli, who symbolized the style of her female predecessor. Catherine's switch from Rastrelli to Etienne Falconet, and then to Quarenghi, embodied not only the change of the general style from Baroque to Neo-Classicism, but also the political strategy to reduce and even eliminate Elizabeth's participation in Saint Petersburg's mythology.

The splendor of Saint Petersburg became a political metaphor that implied the magnitude of Catherine's deeds in service of the state, the success of her victories, and the grandiosity of her cultural achievements. The plan for the city turned out to be an expression of Catherine's politics. Since Peter's monument was erected in 1782, this metaphor became emblematic of Catherine's time. The office of buildings' archival record for August 7, 1782 depicts the dedication of Falconet's monument:

> "The army, as soon as it saw its creator, saluted him by shooting and raising their banners; the ships also raised

---

[31] Virgil, *Enei. Geroicheskaia poema*, translated by Vasilii Petrov (Saint Petersburg, 1781), 29.

their flags; at that moment, the shooting started in both the fortresses and the ships, and then their noise got mixed in with fire, drum-rolls, and military music; it shook the whole city, *which was founded by Peter, and flourished under Catherine.*"[32]

The French diplomat Count Ségure, who spent five years in Russia starting in 1785, actively incorporated the formula "then and now" into his paintings of Saint Petersburg. He wrote:

> "Before her (Catherine's. — V. P.) reign, Saint Petersburg, built in the cold and ice, remained an almost unnoticed, insignificant town in Asia. During her reign Russia became a European country. Saint Petersburg occupied a distinguished place among the capitals of the educated world, and the Russian throne was raised as high as the most powerful and important thrones."[33]

Actually, Catherine's rule marked a time of cultural flourishing in Russia. She ordered the acquisitions of the first large collection of arts for the Hermitage. In 1775–1782, a new building of the Great Hermitage was erected, designed by Iurii Felten. A. F. Kokorinov and J.-B. Vallen de la Motte undertook the building of the Academy of Fine Arts, a great neo-classical edifice; in 1782, its dome was decorated with a statue of the empress (the design was the brainchild of I. P. Prokofiev). The Small Hermitage, the Big Stone Theater, the Hermitage Theater, and the Marble Palace were built in 1768–1785. Many of the empress's suburban palaces underwent reconstruction as well as had new buildings added. According to contemporaries' testimony, Saint Petersburg's architecture created an atmosphere of enormous cultural prosperity. The state-secretary to the empress, A. Gribovskii, writes in his memoirs: "The buildings, which were commissioned by her, made Saint Petersburg the most excellent

---

[32] A. Kaganovich, *Mednyi vsadnik. Istoriia sozdaniia monumenta* (Leningrad, 1975), 163. On the history of the monument see Alexander M. Schenker, *The Bronze Horseman: Falconet's Monument to Peter the Great* (New Haven & London, 2003).

[33] *Ekaterina II i ee okruzhenie*, 148–149.

city in the world. There she collected the finest arts of different genres."[34]

Prince I. M. Dolgorukii, looking at the triumphal flourishing of the capital from the vantage point of the provinces, addresses Fate in his eponymous poem of 1790:

> Look now at the northern capital!
> Crowds of kings, princes, and ambassadors go in and out,
> Since I sent Felitsa to their throne,
> There are now daylight miracles instead of woods.[35]

Inscriptions and Monuments: Asserting the Image

Any new monument that was ostensibly connected to Peter I received an additional meaning under Catherine: contemporaries considered it to be a monument to Catherine as well. In 1768, St. Isaac's Cathedral started to be built according to the design of Antonio Rinaldi. Predating the cathedral, St. Isaac's Church was founded in Peter I's time and opened on May 30, 1707, the Emperor's birthday. The church was named in honor of the saint Isaakii Dalmatskii, on whose name day Peter the First was born. The church had become completely dilapidated by Catherine's time. On May 30, 1768, the cathedral was solemnly reopened.

It was a symbolic action: in place of a small church (as commissioned by Peter I, it had been remolded from an old drawing barn), a grandiose five-dome marble cathedral was erected. Rinaldi preserved. The style of early Petrine architecture in the new structure: the neo-classical cathedral with its three-story tower-like structure maintained a stylistic connection to the old church to St. Isaac. According to the design, St. Isaac's Cathedral should exceed the grandeur of the Peter and Paul Cathedral, the tallest and most significant Saint Petersburg architectural spire. The name "Peter and Paul" invoked a potentially dangerous association for Catherine: any links between her son Paul, that is, Pavel, and Peter I could provoke the burning question of Pavel's legal right to the

---

[34] Adrian Gribovskii, *Zapiski o imperatritse Ekaterine Velikoi* (Moscow, 1864), 40.
[35] I. M. Dolgorukii, *Sochineniia*, 1 (Saint Petersburg, 1849), 229.

Russian throne (see Chapter 3.). The mere conjunction of the names of these two saints (Peter and Paul) could easily incite concern for Pavel Petrovich, Peter's grandson and a legitimate heir, who was denied the throne by his mother. The "neutral" name of St. Isaac respectably commemorated Peter the First, and, at the same time, eliminated politically explosive issues.

In response, A. P. Sumarokov made a poetic inscription devoted to the future cathedral. He also invoked the comparison of Peter I to Catherine II here. Imitating the Baroque style of Lomonosov's early laudatory inscriptions, Sumarokov writes:

> Peter the Great was given to Russia on St. Isaac's day,
> God was generous to the Russian kingdom on that day;
> That was the reason to set up a splendid cathedral,
> Which Catherine had built.[36]

Seemingly, Sumarokov was not satisfied by this poem. At the same time, he composed a second inscription to the cathedral in which, besides suggesting political implications, he tried to find a more appropriate modern language instead of that of the Baroque genre. A refined poetic language allowed the poet to develop a clearer concept of the Peter — Catherine comparison:

> The day to glorify Isaac was established,
> Peter was born on this saint's day:
> The shores of the Neva proclaim it,
> The thunder of bombardment is heard in the air
> Near Peter's walls;
> Wisdom creates a home for God.
> It will shine like a lily of paradise;
> The splendor to this day
> Is given
> By Catherine the Great.[37]

Here two ideas are fused. In this poem, Catherine is called as great as Peter, and she even appears to be more powerful, since she constructed the cathedral to Peter I and brought splendor to

---

[36] A. P. Sumarokov, *Polnoe sobranie sochinenii v stikhakh i proze*, 1, 269.
[37] Ibid, 272.

the country. In 1767, Falconet began to design an equestrian statue to Peter I. The work provoked a new round of discussions on the sensitive topic of the comparison of the two epochs. By the end of September a huge rock, called "the Thunder Rock" by residents of Saint Petersburg, had been delivered to the place of construction. The rock was to serve as the monument's pedestal. Its enormous size, as well as the difficulties involved in transporting it (it was a complicated project to engineer) became a popular topics for cultural reflection.

Vasilii Ruban, Catherine's so-called "pocket poet," solemnly describes this event in his laudatory inscription. The poem praises this gigantic rock as a natural monument "not made by human hands." The inscription was appreciated even by opposing circles of writers and was published in Nikolai Novikov's *Essays for the Historical Dictionary of Russian writers*:

> The Colossus of Rhodes, restrain your proud look.
> Sky-scraping pyramids of the Nile,
> Cease to be called miracles!
> You were built by human hands:
> Here the Russian rock, not by hands made,
> Following God's voice in Catherine's speech,
> Came to Peter's city across the Neva's depths,
> And fell down under the Great Peter's feet.[38]

Work on the monument to Peter I began in 1767. Started in the first years of Catherine's reign, the monument was finished in 1782 as the utmost triumph of her rule. The statue, highly elevated above a rough-hewn rock, symbolized the victory over the old, barbaric pre-Petrine Russia. Falconet was not simply a sculptor; he was a thinker, deeply influenced by the ideas of the Enlightenment. He consciously created an elaborate design, according to which the pedestal had to remain "natural," even "wild."

Falconet refused to follow the well-known classical pattern established by the equestrian statue of Marcus Aurelius.[39] He

---

[38] N. Novikov, *Opyt istoricheskogo slovaria o rossiiskikh pisateliakh* (Saint Petersburg, 1772), 191–192.

[39] H. Dieckmann and J. Seznec, "The Horse of Markus Aurelius. A Controversy between Diderot and Falkonet," in *Journal of the Warburg and Courtauld*

considered a bronze statue to be too old-fashioned, too distant from any ideological expressiveness. In 1770 the sculptor wrote a special work entitled *Comments on the statue of Marcus Aurelius* (*Observations sur la statue de Marc-Aurèle*).

The general design of Peter's monument as the Bronze Horseman, placed on a rock, first came into Falconet's mind in Paris, during his conversations with Denis Diderot. It was Diderot who produced the first draft of Falconet's project. At the beginning of September of 1766, soon after Falconet left for Saint Petersburg, Diderot sent him a letter describing his "vision" for the statue:

> "Sharpen your pencil, take a stick and show them your hero astride, on a fierce horse that ascends a huge rock serving him as a pedestal, and chases away barbarism. Let sparkling water pour out of the clefts of the rock; gather all the streams in a wild, unpolished basin. Serve the common wealth without harming poetry; let me see the Barbarian, with long hair, half weaved in plait, with a body clothed in animal skin; with furious eyes looking ferociously at your hero; at the same time frightened and ready to be crushed by the hooves of his horse. Let the People's Love stand aside, looking at him and thanking him, with arms outstretched toward their leader. Let the Symbol of the Nation be placed on the other side, down on the earth, relaxing and enjoying peace, calm, and security <...>"[40]

Falconet always kept in mind that the first sketch of his monument had been done in Paris, "on the corner of a table" in Diderot's salon. However, the sculptor did not accept the extended project described in his friend's letter. Falconet considered Diderot's project too "allegorical" and "literary." He believed that there was a distinct difference between the symbolisms of bronze and literary images. The sculptor refused to decorate his monument with figures which he found more appropriate for literary expression. The embodiment of ideas and passions in bronze should be more laconic and restrained. He replied to Diderot from Petersburg on February 26, 1767:

Institutes, 15 (1952), 198–228.

[40] Denis Diderot, *Correspondance*, 6 (Paris, 1961), 329.

"The monument will be executed in a simple way. There will be no Barbarian, People's Love, or Symbol of the Nation. Perhaps such figures would insert more poetry into a literary work, but in my business and when you are fifty years old, you need to make things easier if you want to accomplish your work. In addition, Peter the Great himself is the subject and its symbol: it should be shown. Therefore, I decided upon a statue of a hero presented not as a great commander or conqueror, though, undoubtedly, he was that, too. I have to show humanity a much more tremendous image — a figure of his country's founder and benefactor. <...> The tsar does not grasp a scepter in his arms; he holds his beneficent hand over the country which he gallops through. He ascends the rock which serves him as a foundation — an emblem of difficulties that he has overcome. Thus, the hand of the patron, the gallop up the rock is the plot that Peter the Great suggests. Nature and the resistance of his people were his main obstacles; his strength and the firmness of his genius prevailed over them. He has quickly accomplished good deeds that people did not want."[41]

All along, Falconet discussed his perception of Peter I as well as the design of his monument with Catherine II. Their correspondence sheds light on the creation of the monument and the political associations surrounding it. Falconet's approach to Peter's deeds was quite controversial. On June 21, 1767, he wrote to the empress that Peter I guided his country as though it were a "blind and deaf mass" that he sometimes had to strike with his scepter.[42] On the other hand, the sculptor, as a representative of the age of Enlightenment, rushed to justify Peter's oppressive actions on the basis of progress and westernization. Falconet came to the conclusion that he had to reduce all the historical and national connotations inherent in Peter's image and emphasize what he called the "symbolic" essence of his achievements. In his view, Peter should be dressed in a universal "hero's costume," devoid of any reference to time or place.[43] The sculptor disapproved of any

---

[41] Ibid, 7, 33.
[42] *Correspondance de Falconet avec Catherine II. 1767-1778* (Paris, 1921), 18.
[43] Ibid, 8.

suggestions to embellish the Bronze figure with Roman or Russian cloth.[44]

Quite surprisingly, Catherine II, despite the dissent of many loud voices, agreed with Falconet's plans for the monument. Earlier, in 1764, she had already rejected a few proposals for a monument to Peter that had been put forth by the academician Iakov Shtelin. She disliked the idea of a pedestal with bas-reliefs on all four sides which represented the most glorious moments of Peter's reign. The empress also abandoned C. B. Rastrelli's idea of using an old pedestal for the monument. This pompous Baroque monument would also have bas-reliefs that related Peter's triumphs. Evidently, the empress preferred to have a symbol, not a narrative.

Catherine completely shared Falconet's vision, as their correspondence attests. From the beginning stages of the monument's inception, she rejected projects that depicted the key events of Peter I's reign on the pedestal along with the founder himself. She also preferred to imagine a symbolic figure, devoid of any real historical context. At that time, her conviction was that the monument should exemplify some sort of ancient mythological hero or colossus who fundamentally transformed Russian life. She prized Falconet's retrospective utopia which dealt with metaphorical concepts, symbolical visions, and liberated posthumous interpretations. The design of the Bronze Horseman epitomized the emergence of two differently-oriented ideas: the strategy of the Enlightenment (Falconet) and the imperial imagination, based on mythological grounds and mixed with the needs of real-life politics (Catherine). Both interpretations incorporated the following logic: Peter I has tamed chaotic, natural forces (like building Saint Petersburg in an environment characterized by moors, ice, and wild woods), while Catherine is polishing the country, "the rock," further.

The pedestal as a rock also had obvious biblical associations (Mathew, 16:18), which were associated with Peter's name: "Peter" means "stone" in Latin. The Russian religious and

---

[44] Ibid, 129.

rhetorical tradition already had a history of using this metaphor. For example, a famous panegyrist of the Petrine era, Feofan Prokopovich, archbishop of Pskov and Narva, declares in his well-known *Speech on Peter the Great's funeral* on March 8, 1725 that Peter found a Russia that was weak but made it stone, as his name indicated.[45]

This metaphor, which compares monuments to the reigns of emperors, remained in the Russian cultural canon. Later, in 1834, when Alexander's Column had been erected in Saint Petersburg, the poet Vasilii Zhukovskii recalled Falconet's "wild" monument. He wrote in his *Memoir on the Ceremony of August 30, 1834*:

> "On the Neva's shores, there is a wild and shapeless rock, with a colossal horseman on it <...>. From its vantage point, a newly erected colossus is now visible, and the pillar is not wild or built of shapeless stones, like the first one, but well-proportioned, magnificent, adroitly shaped. <...> Russia was a shapeless rock before, but now it is a column, well-proportioned, and unique in its greatness."[46]

Zhukovskii implies here an old paradigm: a "well-proportioned" Alexander's Column became a symbol of the new kingdom of Alexander I that was interpreted against the background of the hulking, uncultivated mass of the Petrine epoch, symbolized by Falconet's Bronze Horseman.

Pygmalion, Galatea, and Catherine-Venus

Contemporaries began to consider Catherine's statue to Peter I, still in progress, to be a monument devoted to both emperors. All throughout his work, Falconet linked both Peter and Catherine to his project; in his letter to Catherine on August 15, 1767, he implies an aphoristic paraphrase of a few aphoristic verses from Horace's ode *I Have Completed a Monument* (Horace, Odes III. 30): "Yes, Madame, as long as a bronze monument ***to Peter I and You*** exists,

---

[45] Feofan Prokopovich, *Sochineniia*, 126.
[46] V. A. Zhukovskii, *Polnoe sobranie sochinenii v 12 tomakh*, X (Saint Petersburg, 1902), 31.

your descendants will read on the pedestal: Falconet has completed this."[47] Horace ensured his immortal glory by composing his poetry that would last longer than any bronze statue. The sculptor, not without a certain curious irony, joined Horace's tradition and projected his immortality upon his own creation. At the same time, he clearly professed the concept of a dual monument, and his sculpture incarnated the current political myth of Peter I, cultivated by Catherine, rather than immortalized him as an historical figure. This sculptural project, as well as its interpretations, generated poetic metaphors that linked the two names together.

The idea of a monument to Catherine, to be erected in close proximity to Peter I's monument, was already in the air. Having been inspired by Catherine's military victories over the Turks, Voltaire, in his letter to the empress on December 3, 1771, suggested that the Russians should place Catherine's statue directly in front of Peter's.[48] He continued to repeat his proposal, even though he knew that Catherine II had refused to have a monument built in her honor. Meanwhile, at the same time, poetry began to play the role of sculpture. Given the situation, the lyrical texts attempted to compensate for the lack of a physical bronze statue by developing the concept of an imaginary monument to Catherine. The praise accorded to Peter's statue in poems, odes, and inscriptions turned into contributions to a kind of lyrical monument to the empress.

In the middle of the 1770s, the young Derzhavin wrote several drafts of his lyric *On the statue of Peter the Great* (*На статую Петра Великого*), thus proving the popularity of this concept; the poet treated Falconet's project as a monument to Catherine's own achievements. Derzhavin writes:

> Catherine erected the statue of him (Peter. — V. P.)
> To make the Russians venerate. This is an image
> of her deeds.[49]

---

[47] *Correspondance de Falconet avec Catherine II*, 21.
[48] *Documents of Catherine the Great. The Correspondence with Voltaire*, 145.
[49] *Sochineniia Derzhavina s ob'iasnitel'nymi primechaniiami Ia. Grota*, III, 250.

In May 1770, a model of Falconet's statue was unveiled at an exhibition at the Academy of Arts in Saint Petersburg. It provoked a wide-spread discussion on the monument and its poetic interpretation as well. Poets composed verses and inscriptions devoted to all the significant episodes of the monument's construction: the completion of Falconet's large bronze model in 1769, its exhibition in 1770, the transportation of the Thunder Rock (for use as the statue's pedestal) from the outskirts of the city to Senate Square, and — finally — the opening of the monument in 1782.

Already in 1769, an anonymous contributor to Catherine's weekly *All Sorts and Sundries* published an inscription, entitled *To the Statue of the Tsar Peter the Great (Ко статуи Государя Петра Великого)*.[50] The author suggested that the situation would have been quite the opposite, that is, such a monument would have been erected in honor of Catherine II by Peter I, had the emperor lived during the present era:

> This bronze presents the face
> Of Peter the Great, father of the Fatherland;
> He founded this city, built fleet and army;
> He elevated Russia with his heroic deeds.
> As a sign of gratitude from all of Russia,
> This image has been erected by Catherine.
> But if Peter were to live now in Russia,
> He would build a more gorgeous statue to Catherine.
> Peter defeated all domestic and foreign enemies,
> Conquered sea and earth,
> He brought glory and wealth to the Russians.
> Peter has given us existence, while Catherine
>   has given us soul. [51]

The author presents a detailed account of Peter's achievements, but all his deeds are supposed to pale before the most significant accomplishment of Catherine. Under her rule, Russian has gotten a "soul," while under Peter she received only physical existence.

---

[50] Sumarokov's authorship was repudiated by Sumarokov's editor N. I. Novikov. On the recent correction by N. D. Kochetkova see *Petr v russkoi literature XVIII veka* (Saint Petersburg, 2006), 414.

[51] A. P. Sumarokov, *Polnoe sobranie vsekh sochinenii v stikhakh i proze*, 1, 266.

This formula comparing the two emperors had appeared before, and the anonymous author most probably relied upon an official and politically engaged opinion. Not accidentally, the formula had first been first introduced in an official speech by Ivan Ivanovich Betskoi, Catherine's closest courtier, politician, and the Director of the Bureau of Buildings (the government organ responsible for the monument).[52] Soon after that, Mikhail Kheraskov composed a lyrical epilogue to his allegorical novel *Numa Pompilius, or Flourishing Rome* (*Нума Помпилий, или Процветающий Рим*). He makes a significant distinction between Peter and Catherine:

> Above all other Sovereigns our Peter the Legislator!
> He works, keeps vigil, and animates Russia,
> He renders a new heaven and a new world <...>
> Then Catherine came, more beautiful than a lily of paradise,
> Flourishing in our eyes, Catherine!
> She has no need for Nymphs or miracles;
> She has not an idle hour,
> She brings charity, peace, enlightenment;
> She writes law which speaks truth <...>
> Let the world share our joy,
> And set her example to all kings.
> I would never disrespect the holy words:
> Peter gave bodies to the Russians, while Catherine
>   gave the soul.[53]

Kheraskov's novel acquainted Russian riders with the story of Numa, Romulus's successor and the second king of Rome. The life of a wise and generous king served as a historical projection of the rule of Catherine, the author of the recently published *Instructions* to the Legislative Commission of 1767. The Romans appreciated Numa's lofty spiritual qualities and elected him in spite of his humble ancestry and poverty. The appointment of the sovereign based on his "achievements" (not on his blood or lineage) corresponded very well with the mythology of Catherine's ascension. The Romans were

---

[52] Ivan Betskoi, in his Senate's speech on 11 August 1767, made a similar comparison: Riasanovsky Nicholas V., *The Image of Peter the Great in Russian History and Thought*, 37.

[53] M. Kheraskov, *Tvoreniia*, XII (Moscow, 1803), 165.

not misguided: Numa's "wisdom" brought prosperity to Rome. Kheraskov's description of an idealized Rome, already influenced by masonry, reflected early Masonic projects of an idyllic Russia under Catherine's rule. In this context, the formula "body — soul" (Peter I — Catherine II) acquired additional connotations. The Masonic circles looked forward to initiating a moral revival in Russia under the enlightened empress. As Kheraskov believed, Catherine had to carry out the sacred mission of spiritualizing or "instilling soul" into the Russian "body," Peter's legacy.

The formula of comparing both kingdoms (and the distribution of Peter I's and Catherine II's roles) relied upon two traditions — Biblical and mythological or pagan. First, it invokes the famous passage from the Genesis: "And the LORD God formed man of the dust of the ground, and breathed into his nostrils the breath of life; and man became a living soul."[54] Second, it refers to the myth of Pygmalion and Galatea, extremely popular at that time, which was well known from Ovid's *Metamorphoses* and from arts.

According to the Greek mythology, Pygmalion, a sculptor in Cyprus, carves a beautiful statue of a woman named Galatea, and then, after he falls in love with her, she comes to life. In and the visual rhetoric of the first quarter of the eighteenth century, the myth served as a vehicle to convey the concept of Peter as the sculptor of a rough and unshaped Russia.[55] Feofan Prokopovich employs this metaphor in his speech on Peter I: "The whole of Russia is your statue, recreated by your great mastery <…>"[56] Many writers, when trying to describe Peter's age, often resorted to sculpture metaphors. Nikolai Karamzin, in his unfinished essay *Thoughts for a Laudatory Speech on Peter I* (Мысли для похвального Слова Петру I; 1798) established a parallel between Peter and Pheidias, the Athenian sculptor, who had built the Temple of Zeus at Olympia. Karamzin writes: "The art of Pheidias can excite us more if we look at an ugly piece of marble: from such a raw material he formed his Jupiter of

---

[54] Genesis 2:7.

[55] V. Iu. Matveev, "K istorii siuzheta *Petr I, vysekaiush'ii statuiu Rossii*," in *Kul'tura i iskusstvo Rossii XVIII v. Novye issledovaniia i materially* (Leningrad, 1981), 26–43; G. Z. Kaganov, *Peterburg v kontekste barokko*, 174–175.

[56] Feofan Prokopovich, *Sochineniia*, 144.

Olympia!"[57] According to Karamzin, Peter I "formed" Russia from a raw and unpolished substance, like God and the famous sculptor simultaneously.

The myth of Pygmalion proved its extreme popularity in Catherine's time. For example, in 1763, Falconet cast his famous sculpture *Pygmalion and Galatea*, and in 1768, he made a gift to the Russian Academy of Arts of François Boucher's painting on the same theme, *Pygmalion and Galatea*. Following the version of the myth in which Venus brings Galatea to life, Boucher places Venus, accompanied by Nymphs and Amours in the center of his work, between the sculptor and his creation. This work of Boucher is referred to in Kheraskov's poem quoted above:

> She has no need for Nymphs or miracles <...>[58]

Kheraskov means that Catherine animates Russia like Venus; but, in distinction to the ancient goddess, the Russian empress can do it alone without help. The Pygmalion plot appeared again in 1776: in September, the Grand Duke Pavel Petrovich married his second wife, Maria Fedorovna. On the occasion of the royal marriage, Vasilii Maikov composed a short piece — "a musical drama in one act," entitled *Pygmalion, or the Strength of Love*, which was performed at the palace.[59] In the mid-1770s, the Russian Academy of Arts commissioned the painter I. A. Akimov to produce a picture on the topic: *Prometheus Makes a Statue by the Order of Minerva*.[60] The plot of the painting (currently held in the Russian Museum in Saint Petersburg) follows the other version of the myth, in which Prometheus forms a man of clay, into whom Pallas Athena (Minerva in Latin) breathes a soul. The interpretation corresponded very well to the tendency, quite popular in the 1770s, to associate Catherine II with Minerva and Peter I — with Prometheus, the symbol of the founder of civilization.

---

[57] N. M. Karamzin, *Izbrannye stat'i i pis'ma* (Moscow, 1982), 159.

[58] M. Kheraskov, *Tvoreniia*, XII, 165.

[59] Vasilii Maikov's drama appeared in 1779.

[60] I. V. Riazantsev, "Ekaterina II v zerkale antichnoi mifologii," in *Russkaia kul'tura poslednei treti XVIII veka — vremeni Ekateriny Vtoroi. Sbornik statei*, 136.

Sculpture as a Political Manifesto

Later, by the time of the opening of the Bronze Horseman, the concept of the imagined monument to Catherine, built by Peter the First, was developed to an extreme. A. S. Khvostov, in his lyric inscription of 1782, not only compared both emperors, but also put Catherine in the first place. Mere chronology did not allow for an inversion of the situation:

> If God, the creator of earthly order, had allowed
> That Catherine should have lived earlier than Peter,
> A miraculous rock, in that case,
> Would now be given the image of Catherine, not Peter.[61]

This mythological concept influenced the choice of inscription made on the granite base of the Falconet's monument: *To Peter the First from Catherine the Second*. This motto was carved out both in Russian and Latin: *Petro Primo Catharina Secunda*. The message, though it looked historically truthful, was absolutely symbolic, as it not only united the two names eternally, but also suggested their equality. The pure symbolism of the inscription was perfectly grasped by contemporaries. Discussing the appropriateness of the phrase in his letter to Catherine II on January 16, 1783, Melchior Grimm made a notice that the motto would look better with omitted numerals: Petro / Catharina.[62] His version made this equation even more clear. Catherine replied to Grimm on March 9, 1783: "Do criticize me: *Petro Primo Catharina Secunda*. I requested this inscription because I wanted people to know that it was me, and not his (Peter's. — V. P.) wife."[63] Several reasons lay behind such a choice. First, she might have truly been afraid to be confused in the future with Catherine I, who reigned in 1725–1727. Catherine II made sarcastic comments on her female predecessor in her essay *The Palace of Chesma*.[64] Second, she definitely liked Falconet's laconic

---

[61] A. L. Ospovat, R. D. Timenchik, *Pechal'nu povest' sokhranit'* (Moscow, 1987), 40.
[62] *Sbornik Imperatorskogo russkogo istoricheskogo obsh'estva* 44 (1885), 310.
[63] "Pis'ma Ekateriny Vtoroi baronu Grimmu", in *Russkii arkhiv* 3 (1878), 88.
[64] *Zapiski imperatritsy Ekateriny Vtoroi* (Saint Petersburg, 1907), 601.

sentence, elegantly ornamented in the Roman style. The sculptor wrote to Catherine on August 14, 1770:

> "I made the short inscription *"Petro Primo Catharina Secunda posuit"* on the base of the statue <...> It is in the best lapidary style, which the ancients successfully used for inscriptions on their monuments."[65]

Meanwhile, this lapidary junction contained political implications. The inscription confirmed and even immortalized the main paradigm of Catherine's legitimacy. It emphasized the concept of the rightness of her succession based not on blood or dynastic ties, but on her achievements and the qualities of her persona. Later, when Pavel Petrovich (Pavel I) came to the Russian throne, he made the monument as well as this inscription the objects of his political revenge. He attempted to rewrite the whole history of the monument to Peter I and to eliminate his mother (as a "usurper") from the Saint Petersburg mythology. In 1800, in the courtyard of his Mikhailovskii Palace, he installed an old monument to Peter by Carlo Bartolomeo Rastrelli. In 1764, Catherine II had rejected this Baroque monument and decided to search for a new sculptor. Consequently, the old statue had been forgotten. Pavel had the monument recovered and a new inscription carved: *To Grandfather from His Grandson*. It was a demonstrative political act which targeted Catherine II and her inscription. Underscoring blood ties and direct male ancestry, Pavel restored the traditional model of the hereditary rights and buried Catherine's concept of her *ideological* link with Peter I. Rastrelli's monument was to cancel out Catherine's monument to Peter and all of her reign as well.

The struggle between the monuments continued on. Dissatisfied with the slow progress being made on his Mikhailovskii Palace (a gloomy unfinished castle instead became his main residence, as well as the place of his horrific death in 1801), Pavel ordered marble to be taken from St. Isaac's Cathedral, which had been under construction since Catherine's time, to speed up the process. Pavel instructed workers to finish the cathedral by laying

---

[65] *Correspondance de Falconet avec Catherine II*, 134.

bricks on the marble foundation. Such a structure, with a marble base and a brick top, inspired an anonymous epigram which associated the two kingdoms — of Catherine's and Pavel's — with the two "layers" of the cathedral:

> The monument matches the two kingdoms:
> A marble ground floor goes to a brick top.[66]

The epigram referred to Catherine's rule as an age of "marble" and ridiculed Pavel's time as much less noble and successful. It also inverted a very popular statement ascribed to Augustus, who said: "I found Rome brick and left it marble."

On August 8, 1782, the day after the statue's unveiling, Catherine described her impressions in a letter to Grimm:

> "Let's say that he (Peter's monument. — V. P.) was rather satisfied with his creation. Being emotional, I did not dare, for a long time, to look at him closely; when I looked around, I saw that everybody was in tears. He faced the side opposite the Black Sea, but the expression on his face proved he did not look at any side. He was rather too far away to speak to me; however, he seemed quite pleased <...>."[67]

The opening ceremony was designed to demonstrate Catherine's triumph: the bronze Peter (with whom the empress had an imagined conversation!) was assumed to be contented by the current condition of the city he founded. The monument was erected in front of the Senate (the symbol of Catherine's successful legislative endeavors), near the Neva river (the shores had recently been covered with granite embankments). In addition, the empress mentioned that Peter's head was not turned toward the Black Sea. The Horseman was turned toward the north as a sign of Peter's most successful political direction. The empress, thought she stressed her "emotional" condition, remained yet very ambitious and competitive toward Peter I. The Black Sea was her monumental achievement, as she had recently defeated the Turks and annexed

---

[66] *Russkaia epigramma vtoroi poloviny XVII–nachala XX v.* (Leningrad, 1975), 189. On different variants of the epigram see V. P. Stepanov, "Ubiistvo Pavla I i vol'naia poeziia", in *Literaturnoe nasledie* (Leningrad, 1975), 78–86.

[67] *Russkii Arkhiv* 3 (1878), 84.

Crimea. She could not restrain herself from underlining her success in the southerly direction, as it looked especially distinguished in comparison to the failure of Peter's army there, most notably in his Pruth campaign of 1711. Not by accident, the opening ceremony included the procession to the Saint Peter and Saint Paul Cathedral, where Catherine's officers proudly put trophies, obtained during the war with the Turks, on Peter's grave.

"He blames our age and praises the past one"

At the beginning of the 1780s, the worship of Catherine II not only totally eclipsed the fading glory of Peter I, but also began to entail some cautious blame towards the emperor. Already in the 1760–1770s, the first signs of aristocratic Slavophilism appeared.[68] Nikita Panin, rejecting the bureaucratic organization of power in Russia, accused Peter I of establishing the system and dreaming of an aristocratic republic.[69] In his project of the Imperial Council, offered to the then novice empress Catherine II, he called all previous ages "barbaric times."[70] Later, Ekaterina Dashkova, evidently influenced by Panin, continued accusing Peter I of despotism and the creation of bureaucracy in Russia as well as expressed her high regard for the pre-Petrine era.[71] In one of his unfinished manuscripts (1782), Mikhail Shcherbatov, the author of a famous book *On the Corruption of Morals in Russia*, severely criticized Peter, arguing that he could have reached the same goals by more humane means, resulting in smaller losses even though it might have taken a longer period of time.

In Vienna in 1780, Dashkova had a private conversation with the Austrian Chancellor Wenzel Anton Count of Kaunitz about Peter I and Catherine II. The contents of this discussion became well-known in Russia, and later, Dashkova gave a detailed account of

---

[68] G. A. Gukovskii, *Ocherki po istorii russkoi literatury XVIII veka*, 225.
[69] V. A. Bil'basov, "Nikita Panin i Mercier de la Rivière, 1762–1767," in *Russkaia starina* 11–12 (1891), 284.
[70] V. O. Kliuchevskii, *Sochineniia*, V (Moscow, 1989), 316.
[71] E. Shmurlo, *Petr Velikii v otsenke sovremennikov i potomstva*, 1, 82–83.

the talk in her memoirs. She rejected the popular European concept that Peter I created Russia and Russians: she insisted that it was a fantasy of Western writers who considered Peter out of context. She also stirred controversy with her remarks that Peter I had annihilated authentic Russian culture and the successful political achievements of his father, "the Quietest" Alexis I of Russia (Aleksei Mikhailovich.) Dashkova's passionate philippics drew a distinction between Catherine's civilized methods of government and Peter's cruelty:

> "Cruel and brutal, he (Peter I. – V. P.) treated all, without distinction, who were subject to his sway, as slaves whom he believed were born to suffer. <...> After setting aside the code of his forefathers, so often changed his own <...> The nobility as well as the slaves were equally the victims of his innovating frenzy <...> And for what? To clear the way for the introduction of a military despotism <...> His vainglorious aiming at the fame of a creator hastened the building of Petersburg by circumstances so little mingled with mercy, that thousands of workmen perished in the marshes. The nobles, too, were compelled to lend their assistance, not only in furnishing a continual succession of laborers to expedite the work without intermission, but also in causing houses to be built for themselves after the emperor's plans <...> Under Catherine, Petersburg had flourished in a fourfold proportion, both as to its extent and the splendor of its imperial palaces and public buildings which owed their origin neither to taxes, nor compulsory measures, nor to oppression of any description."[72]

Dashkova was perfectly aware of Catherine's sensitive attitude toward Peter's glory. The princess's talk in Vienna, in the center of Europe, was calculated to be heard in Saint Petersburg. The half-exiled Dashkova, who had lived for many years abroad, was eager for Catherine to listen to her. In fact, she soon received some quite eloquent hints suggesting that she would be welcomed again at the Russian court. Meanwhile, Dashkova's statements were not a mere

---

[72] *Memoirs of the Princess Dashkova, Lady of Honour to Catherine II, Written by herself*, 1 (London, 1840), 260–262.

expression of her loyalty to Catherine. She sincerely believed that Peter I was evil for Russia: her conviction was not personal but rather socially motivated. It reflected the hidden aristocratic resistance to Peter's reforms that became apparent in Catherine's time and coincided with the empress's own desire to revise Peter's and Saint Petersburg's mythology. Concluding her *Memoirs*, Dashkova writes:

> "Should I live a few years longer, it is my intention to write some anecdotes of Catherine the Second, justly called the Great; to recapitulate her beneficent actions, and to draw a parallel between her and Peter the First, whom some have unjustly ventured to compare with this illustrious empress — one who was much superior and whose reign has rendered Russia a preponderating power <…>"[73]

In 1783, in the magazine *Interlocutor of Lovers of the Russian Word* (1783-1784), edited under the direction of Dashkova (and with the active participation of Catherine II), there was a very significant discussion on Peter I. It began with the publication of an article written by Sergei Petrovich Rumiantsev (1755–1838), a young poet and diplomat, as well as the future minister to Berlin.[74] The essay was entitled *Peter the Great* and attached to Rumiantsev's polemical letter to the author of an anonymous satirical review *Truths and Trifles* (Catherine's authorship was well-known to the public.) Rumiantsev paid an honorable tribute to Peter's deeds, and called Catherine merely "Peter's outgrowth."[75] He also slung some critical arrows toward Peter I's foreign detractors. The young author continued to debate Peter's "cruelty" and to excuse his "unnecessary punishments" which, in Rumiantsev's opinion, should be treated rather as indicative of his firmness and commitment to transform Russia.[76] Rumiantsev also declared that only war and early death prevented Peter from establishing a real civil society in Russia that

---

[73] Ibid, 2, 50 (with my corrections).
[74] "Avtobiografiia grafa S. P. Rumiantseva", in *Russkii arkhiv* 7 (1869), 839–854.
[75] *Sobesednik liubitelei russkogo slova*, VII (1783), 173.
[76] Ibid.

still had not been accomplished.⁷⁷ Moreover, he explicitly held Catherine responsible for the absence of changes in the "conditions of our civic society" since Peter's time.

Rumiantsev's criticisms enraged Catherine, as she considered her reign much more gentle, fair, and civilized than Peter's. After reading the manuscript of Rumiantsev's article, Catherine asked Dashkova to publish it and to provide it with a detailed answer. Rumiantsev recalled later that Catherine was very discontented by his article, thought it did not derail his career.⁷⁸ In the seventh volume of the magazine, Dashkova printed Rumiantsev's essay with some brief comments on the conditions of the civic society in Russia: "Anybody with any sense cannot disbelieve the existence of such a society, and Catherine's immortal deeds clearly prove it."⁷⁹

An extremely intensive correspondence between Dashkova and Catherine concerning Rumiantsev's essay demonstrates that the article on Peter I touched upon very sensitive matters. In her next *Truths and Trifles (Были и небылицы)*, Catherine herself replied with an essay parodying Rumiantsev's "fashionable" and "philosophical" style.⁸⁰ Then, in the eighth issue of the *Interlocutor*, an anonymous article, belonging to Dashkova, came out. It concluded with a poem that consisted of a comparison between the two kingdoms and made unflattering statements about the pre-Catherine era:

> Some people, in old times, went to bed in fear
> Of being accused in the morning for somebody else's faults;
> Meanwhile, sometimes, some people extol the old age,
> And unfairly reproach our new times.
> Though now we can calmly go to sleep,
> Without being afraid of suffering while innocent;
> But if some noble slave, as though he were mad,
> Blames our age and praises the past one,
> Only rascals, wise or dull,
> Can bow and say: O yes, Sir, you are right!⁸¹

---

⁷⁷ Ibid, 175.
⁷⁸ *Russkii arkhiv*, 7 (1869), 850.
⁷⁹ *Sobesednik liubitelei russkogo slova*, VII (1783), 175.
⁸⁰ Ibid, 177–181.
⁸¹ *Rossiia XVIII stoletiia v izdaniiakh Vol'noi russkoi tipografii A. I. Gertsena*

The poem was written a few months after Derzhavin's *Felitsa* (1783) had been published in the first issue of the *Interlocutor*, as a program for shaping the image of Catherine II. Like Derzhavin, Dashkova, in her poem, underlines the liberalization of civic life as Catherine's greatest achievement. In *Felitsa*, Derzhavin employs examples from Anna Ivanovna's rule in order to make his comparison more distinctive. In his next ode, *Reshemyslu* (Решемыслу; 1783), published in the sixth number of the same magazine, Derzhavin also provides a flashback to old times to make Catherine's image more impressive:

> There were the days before,
> When honest people
> Were afeared to stay by the throne.
> They tried to escape the tsar's favorites,
> They could not love those snakes,
> Who sucked their blood<...>[82]

Derzhavin dedicated his ode to Grigorii Potemkin — Reshemysl was Potemkin's name in Catherine's own tale, *Fevei*. Derzhavin was asked to compose an ode on Potemkin by Dashkova, who tried her hardest to create an enlightened image of the empress as a defender of freedom of speech ("svobodoiazychiie").

Right at that time, Dashkova (with the clear support of Catherine, who read all the significant manuscripts submitted for publication in the *Interlocutor*) introduced the concept of the age of Peter I as a repressive time. In the ninth issue, the princess published her article *The Brief Notes of a Peddler*. Ridiculing the stylistic blunders of Rumiantsev's article, she provides quotations from his article that demonstrate (against the will of the author) the oppressive methods of Peter's rule: "You can say that, in all of Peter's deeds, one can feel the brand of his spirit." [83] The word "brand" referred not only to a positive context (an "etching" of Peter's spirit), but to the cruel

---

i N. P. Ogareva. *Spravochnyi tom k Zapiskam E. R. Dashkovoi, Ekateriny II, I. V. Iopukhina* (Moscow, 1992), 132.

[82] *Sochineniia Derzhavina s ob''iasnitel'nymi primechaniiami Ia. Grota*, 1, 119.

[83] E. R. Dashkova, *O smysle slova vospitanie. Sochineniia. Pis'ma. Dokumenty* (Saint Petersburg, 2001), 141.

practice of "branding" criminals sentenced to hard labor. Dashkova attempted to stress the pitiless methods of bringing about reforms under Peter I. Catherine expressed her approval of Dashkova's article. She wrote to the princess:

> "When I was reading *A Peddler*, I could have sworn that it had been written by me, as the author successfully imitated my style. As for polemics, your article is very harsh, but surely fair, and you should beware of his reply."[84]

The dispute over Peter's legacy exhibited a new reality: the Russian gentry, dissatisfied with Catherine's reign, was attempting to remove Peter's mythology from the official propaganda and to present the emperor as an ideological icon of the opposition. In praising Peter I and the modest customs of his court, they blamed the "new times" and Catherine's reign. Thus, in 1782 the comedy *The Minor (Недоросль)*, written by Denis Ivanovich Fonvizin debuted (1744–1792). The playwright shared the views of Panin's circle (he was Nikita Panin's secretary), and the comedy, besides giving a satirical panorama of uncivilized provincial life, concealed some political allusions. The ideological concept of this comedy was revealed in Starodum's monologues. The name of the main protagonist alone — Starodum — indicated his belonging to an old tradition of "thinking." Starodum harshly criticized modern mores and customs for promoting corruption, idleness, intrigues, and dishonest service. He also proclaimed that he had been brought up by his father who received his own strong opinions from Peter's court.[85] Fonvisin, while he portrayed a mythological image of Peter instead of a real one, expressed the views of all the circles of those discontented with Catherine's rule.

---

[84] *Rossiia XVIII stoletiia v izdaniiakh Vol'noi russkoi tipografii A. I. Gertsena i N. P. Ogareva*, 136.

[85] D. I. Fonvizin, *Sobranie sochinenii*, 1 (Moscow, 1959), 129. For a detailed account of polemics around Fonvizin's comedy see V. P. Stepanov, "Polemika vokrug D. I. Fonvizina v period sozdaniia *Nedoroslia*," in *XVIII vek* 15 (Leningrad, 1986), 204–229.

Moving the Capitals

In 1762, after reading Jean d'Alembert's essay on Montesquieu's works (Mélanges de Littérature, d'Histoire et de Philosophie. Nouvelle édition. T. 2, pag. 370 et 371), Catherine II copied out an excerpt on the causes of Rome's decline and fall that impressed her the most; according to French philosophers (d'Alembert was in agreement with Montesquieu at that point), one of the causes consisted of "the transfer of the capital and the division of the empire which first, in the west, was ruined by barbarians, and then, over the course of centuries, gradually weakened in the east, having been under feeble-minded or cruel emperors; it faded without a trace, like rivers do, vanishing in the sand."[86]

A few years later in 1770, this passage influenced Catherine's own essay which was later published under the title *Considerations on Petersburg and Moscow* (Размышления о Петербурге и Москве):

> "In olden times, some people raised their voice in dissent, and still now, though not as caustic, some people say that it was wrong to found Petersburg, to settle the court there, to abandon Moscow. They say, and, in part, it is true, that hundreds of thousands of workers died from scurvy and other illnesses, especially at the beginning; that the provinces were forced to send workers who never returned home; that high prices there, compared to the lower ones in Moscow and other places, ruined the gentry; that the location was not healthy or pleasant, that (besides other reasons) St. Petersburg is less suitable than Moscow as the empire's seat of government. Some presume that the action of Peter the Great was similar to the deeds of Constantine who moved the throne of empire to Byzantium and left Rome; consequently, the Romans did not know what to call their fatherland. They could not see all the things that inspired admiration and enthusiasm in Rome, and their virtues began to decline and eventually, they lost them forever."[87]

---

[86] *Zapiski imperatritsy Ekateriny Vtoroi*, 622.
[87] Ibid, 651.

Usually, scholars interpret Catherine's statement in accordance with the famous Russian juxtaposition: Saint Petersburg versus Moscow. [88] However, the essay is important not only as a declaration of Catherine's attitude toward this specific example, but also because it reveals her attitude toward the act of moving capitals in general.

As Montesquieu wrote in his *Considerations on the Causes of the Greatness of the Romans and Their Decline*, the moving of the throne to the old Greek colony of Byzantium on the Bosphorus and the foundation of a new capital Constantinople (on May 11, 330 they celebrated its official opening) broke the balance of power in the state. Roman laws, customs, even their spirit itself were seriously changed. The proximity to the Asian despotic regimes ruined the rest of their democratic institutions and engendered the cult of the emperor, who became all-powerful. [89] The Senate also moved to the fledgling capital, but, in Byzantium, it began to play a nominal role. Treasures taken from conquered peoples flooded into Constantinople, which became a rich and splendid city, but, as Montesquieu concluded, one that did not have any reason to exist. [90]

In this brilliant book, Montesquieu defines the early Enlightenment's concept of state as an organic unity of climate, location, mores, and customs. From such a point of view, any movement of the capital should be considered an archaic, magically symbolic act that contradicts the new rational approach. In enumerating all the negative consequences of Petersburg's establishment, Catherine II expressed her solidarity with Montesquieu. His book created a political context which allows for a better understanding of Catherine's essay and her critique of Peter's endeavor.

In her piece *The Beginning of Oleg's Reign* (*Начальное управление Олега*; 1787), Catherine relies upon Montesquieu's

---

[88] E. A. Pogosian, "Ot staroi Ladogi do Ekaterinoslava (mesto Moskvy v predstavleniiakh Ekateriny II o stolitse imperii," in *Lotmanovskii sbornik* 2 (Moscow, 1997), 511–522.

[89] Montesquieu, *Considérations sur les causes de la grandeur des romains et de leur decadence* (Paris, 1879), 185.

[90] Ibid, 187.

concept of the "organic" nature of the state. Not by accident, she confessed to having read the French *Encyclopedia* while she worked on her historical drama.[91] Her piece relates to events of the 870s described in the *Primary Chronicle* and is concerned with a conflict between the pagan Prince Oleg (Rurik's son) and Askold, who has accepted baptism. Catherine's interpretation was quite extraordinary. Some Kievan people come to Oleg with a complaint about Askold's behavior:

> "The Kievans sent us to you, our Sovereign, to explain that Prince Askold changed our old customs without informing you; our people suspect that Askold, during his campaign to Constantinople, accepted their beliefs and rituals <...> Since returning to Kiev, he does not attend the sacred hills and temples, he does not conduct funeral feasts, and he apparently scorns our priests."[92]

Catherine stressed the ability of Prince Oleg to find a correct solution (though it contradicted the Chronicle!): he went to Kiev, dethroned Askold, and restored paganism. Oleg considered the change of religion a rude violation of the people's mores and customs. The empress endowed Prince Oleg with some of her own ideas and qualities. The royal author characterizes him as a very wise ruler who began his reign by traveling around the state and establishing new cities. Contemporary readers could easily perceive a reference to Catherine's travels. Her Prince Oleg took part in establishing Moscow (the empress included a good deal of fabrication in her "historical" dramas) where he invited all pagan priests to conduct their usual rituals. He did not interfere in the rituals, though he censured them for harboring excessive superstitious beliefs.

Catherine's critique of Askold, depicted in her piece as a radical reformer who scorned tradition, targets two real reigns and two real rulers. First, it refers to Peter III, her murdered husband, who, as some people believed, had plans to modernize the Russian Orthodox Church or even to replace it with Protestantism. Second,

---

[91] A. V. Khrapovitskii, *Pamiatnye zapiski*, 14.
[92] *Sochineniia imperatritsy Ekateriny II*, 2, 268–269.

it implies some criticism towards Peter I, whose ideological legacy had been recently challenged. [93]

During her trip to the Crimea in 1787, Catherine, besides founding the new town of Ekaterinoslav, discussed the possibility of transferring the capital there.[94] She openly criticized Peter's choice of location for the capital. Visiting Kursk, she uttered: "It is a pity that Petersburg was not built here; in passing these places, you can imagine the times of Vladimir I (Prince Vladimir Sviatoslavovich the Great. — V. P.) who made these lands very populated."[95] A year later, when the war with Sweden broke out and their cannons were heard in Tsarskoe Selo, she complained about the unfortunate placement of Saint Petersburg: "It is true that Peter I built the capital too close."[96]

Peter's strategy compelled him to build the capital close to the northern frontiers, the focus of his politics. Meanwhile, Catherine's strategy to take possession of southern lands forced her to consider the possibility, if only hypothetically, of moving the Russian capital south. Notably, she underscored in her letter to Grimm that the head of the Bronze Horseman was turned to the side *opposite the Black Sea*. She aggressively annexed southern territories (forgetting her literary fantasies about the organic states), and she still cherished the so-called Greek project, hoping to acquire Constantinople (with her grandson Constantine as emperor) as her second capital. [97]

---

[93] A similar double reference to Peter I and Pavel Petrovich was found in Catherine's opera libretto *Fevei*, see Stefano Gardzonio, "Librettistika Ekateriny II i ee gosudarstvenno-natsional'nye predposylki,, in *Rossia/Russia 3 (11). Kul'turnye praktiki v ideologicheskoi perspective. Rossiia, XVIII–nachalo XX veka* (Moscow — Venice, 1999), 87.

[94] A. M. Panchenko, "Potemkinskie derevni kak kul'turnyi mif," in *XVIII vek*, 14 (1983), 101. Catherine II criticized Peter I's choice of a new place for the capital in her letter to Voltaire, see *Documents of Catherine the Great. The Correspondence with Voltaire*, 101.

[95] A. V. Khrapovitskii, *Pamiatnye zapiski*, 28–29.

[96] Ibid, 72.

[97] At the beginning of the 1790s, Platon Zubov, the last Catherine's favorite, worked on some giant (as well as utopian) geo-political projects to extend borders of the Russian Empire and to establish six capitals, such as Saint Petersburg, Moscow, Berlin, Vienna, Constantinople (V. O. Kliuchevskii, *Sochineniia v deviati tomakh*, V, 306).

Given the circumstances, the Saint Petersburg myth served Catherine's *translatio imperii* successfully. Catherine secured her reign by putting her own achievements forward and relegating Peter's figure to the background. First, she made Peter I her ideological ally, thereby taking advantage of his mythological legacy. Then, in constructing a bronze statue to Peter, she deconstructed his sacred stance in the Saint Petersburg myth. Her political strategy as well as her cultural fantasies contributed much to future discussions on the nature of Saint Petersburg and the validity of its building.

Chapter Five

THE WAR IN GREEK GARB

During the time of Catherine II, a military paradigm arose quite naturally in the Russian imperial myth. War is not only a consequence, but also a necessary condition of the empire's existence, as the empire always cherishes the eternal and inextinguishable hope of establishing its supremacy throughout the universe.[1] The redrawing of geographical boundaries, invasion and/or liberation, and the change of regimes and governments proved to be the most effective methods by which to establish the *translatio imperii*. War usually generated a tremendous outburst of mythmaking, and furthermore no wars were launched in the pursuit of purely pragmatic goals.

The empire always demarcates a boundary between "civilization" and "barbarity." In European history the distinction is usually signified a border — geographical as well as cultural — between the West and the East. Social and religious implications were very important. Simply put, "civilization" was the Christian world, while Muslims were "barbarians." The Crusades of the 11th– 13th centuries, followed by numerous attempts by European monarchs to force the Turks out of Europe, forged a permanent "Turkish" paradigm. In order to realize their imperial ambitions, each new European power had to go through a kind of initiation — participation in a war against the Ottoman Porte.

The Ottoman Empire reached the height of its power by the middle of the sixteenth century, during the reign of Suleiman II, the

---

[1] R. Folz, *L'idée d'empire en Occident du V-e au XIV-e siècle* (Paris, 1953), 178.

Magnificent (1520–1566). By this time, the Ottomans had expanded their borders tremendously. The Ottoman Empire occupied much of Southeastern Europe, the Middle East and North Africa, stretching from the Strait of Gibraltar (and in 1553 the Atlantic coast of North Africa beyond Gibraltar) in the west to the Caspian Sea and Persian Gulf in the east, from the edge of Austria and Slovakia and the hinterland beyond Ukraine in the north to Sudan and Yemen in the south. The northern frontier of the Empire, after the conquest of Hungary, lay close to Vienna, which was attacked several times. In 1571, King Philip II of Spain (1556–1598), the most powerful European monarch of his time, obsessed with the idea of fighting the enemies of Catholicism, waged war against the Ottomans in the Mediterranean Sea. In 1571, his victory at Lepanto, off the Greek coast, earned him the honorary title of a Christian hero. The famous painting by El Greco, *The Dream of Philip II* (1578), which depicts the Turks falling down into the gaping mouth of hell, reflects very well the mystical dreams of a prospective Christian "revenge."

The history of the Russo-Turkish conflict began in 1475 when the Ottomans conquered the Crimean khanate, thus installing the khan as their vassal. Twice, in 1571 and 1591, the khan's army invaded Russian lands, marching as far north as Moscow. The great eastward expansion of Russia in the 16th and 17th centuries, although occurring during the decline of the Ottoman Empire, nevertheless left the shores of the Black Sea in the hands of the Ottoman sultans and their vassals, the khans of the Crimea.

In 1687 and 1689, during the reign of the Russian princess Sophia (1682– 1689), Russian troops, commanded by her favorite, V. V. Golitsyn, marched on the Crimea, but both campaigns failed. Peter I also attempted to shake the power of the Ottoman Porte. He succeeded in seizing the important Turkish fortress of Azov in 1696 and entering the shallows of the Azov Sea. However, his subsequent campaign of 1711 was so unsuccessful (he and all of his forces were surrounded on the Prut River), that he was forced to relinquish Azov.

Meanwhile, the failure of the campaign stirred up Peter's imperial ambitions and initiated the remaking of his political strategy after the model of great Empires. The first true victory over the Turks came in the time of Anna Ioannovna. In 1736, a new war broke out between the Ottomans and the Russian Empire, which was allied at the time with Austria. The Russians recaptured Azov and victoriously entered Moldavia. In August of 1739, Russian troops took over the Turkish fortress of Khotin, a military stronghold in the region. This spectacular Russian success was especially striking, considering that the Austrian Empire simultaneously lost some territories! The seizure of Khotin not only frightened Europe, but also inspired the first Russian military ode, entitled the *Ode to Her Majesty the Empress of Blessed Memory Anna Ioannovna on the Victory Over the Turks and on the Seizure of Khotin in the Year 1739* (Ода блаженныя памяти Государыне Императрице Анне Иоанновне на победу над турками и татарами и на взятие Хотина 1739 года). Mikhail Lomonosov composed the ode while he was a student at Freiburg University in Germany. The poem opened a new page of Russian culture by formulating the poetic language, syntax, style, and rhythm of iambic verse. The verses of the young poet were not published at that time: their first official appearance in print took place only in 1751, in Lomonosov's *Collected Works*. The title itself was added after Anna Ioannovna's death. The ode was known only to a select few, and in 1744, Lomonosov included some fragments of the ode in his theoretical book on versification entitled *Rhetoric*.

The ode combines Lomonosov's poetical ecstasy ("A sudden rapture filled my mind")[2] with his passion for Russia's imperial endeavors. It implies the exhibition of the fiery Russian dream of redrawing geographical boundaries ("<...> Damascus / Aleppo, Cairo will be burnt; / The Russian fleet will circle Crete, / And with your blood Euphrates darken")[3], and predicted the political revenge of Russian "glory" over European "ill envy" ("Let evil

---

[2] *The Literature of Eighteenth-Century Russia. An Anthology of Russian Literary Materials of the Age of Classicism and the Enlightenment from the Reign of Peter the Great (1689– 1725) to the Reign of Alexander I (1801– 1825).* Ed. and trans. by Harold Segel, 1 (New York, 1967), 182.

[3] Ibid, 190.

envy venom pour").[4] Lomonosov also made the first attempt to bring in a very important fraction of a whole imperial paradigm by depicting the joy of Christian peoples liberated by the Russians from the "barbarians":

> Oh, how fair the places
> Which have cast off the cruel yoke become,
> Which have placed in turn upon the Turks
> The same weight which they placed upon them.
> And now those same **barbarian** hands
> Which held them tightly in their grasp
> Already bear the chains of slavery <...>[5]

The Ode on the Seizure of Khotin served as the introduction, both poetical and political, to a great imperial theme in Russian culture. The victory over the Turks was supposed to signify, as Lomonosov espoused, not only Russia's growing power, but also her realized ambition of becoming part of Europe: by fighting the Turks, Russia aligned herself with other European powers, thus associating herself with Western "civilization," as opposed to the "barbarian" Oriental (and Islamic) world.

Lomonosov's ode, written during Anna Ivanovna's reign and published during the rule of Elizaveta Petrovna, became the model for military odes in the time of Catherine II. The ode turned out to be in sharp demand thirty years after its creation and a few years after Lomonosov's death. Moreover, since 1769, the first year of Catherine's war with the Turks, there were no military odes written that did not contain references to Lomonosov's exemplary poem. The ode, however, was not met with universal acceptance: the poem provoked controversy, not only about the representation of the empress, but also about its stylistics. Whether they were modifying Lomonosov's canonical text or entering into an apparent or hidden competition with *The Ode on the Seizure of Khotin*, the poets of Catherine's age struggled for their exclusive rights to create their own image of the empress.

---

[4] Ibid, 191.
[5] M. V. Lomonosov, *Polnoe sobranie sochinenii*, 8, 189–190.

By the end of 1768, Catherine II faced the first strikes of war. The Turks insisted that Russia should cease to dictate the political policy in the region (very important for the Porte), and stop interfering in Polish matters, that is with Poland's internal between King Stanislaw Poniatowski, the former favorite of Catherine II and her ally, and his opposition, the Bar Confederation, supported by the Porte and France as well.

The incident took place in the small town of Balta, which belonged to the Porte. A group of Russian Cossacks entered territory held by the Ottoman Empire while in pursuit of Polish confederates. The Sultan Mustafa III accused these Cossacks of committing massacres at Balta. The Empress denied the accusations and tried to negotiate. Meanwhile, the Ottoman Porte arrested the Russian ambassador A. M. Obrezkov, imprisoned him in the Castle of the Seven Towers, and then refused to set him free. This chain of events was nothing but "the solemn form of a declaration of war, according to the Turkish practice of international law."[6]

All of a sudden, theatrical contests turned into genuine battles, while decorative masques and costumes (the "Slavs" or the "Turks") acquired the most real and menacing meanings. New political events developed very quickly. Catherine declared war and began expedited military preparations. The field of battle dramatically refashioned the field of literature. This transition made it necessary to create a new literary discourse in order to create an appropriate image of the Empress in war.

War and Voltaire:
Imperial Chimeras and Utopias of Enlightenment

From the very beginning of the war the Russian Empress had an ardent ally and ideological supporter. It was Voltaire, who detested the "uncivilized" rule of the Turkish Sultans, and hated both the Pope and the French king Louis XV, an ally of the Turks and Polish confederates. It was Voltaire who actively pushed

---

[6] Albert Sorel, *The Eastern Question in the Eighteenth Century. The Partition of Poland & the Treaty of Kainardji* (New York, 1969), 26.

Catherine to begin this war (even before it started); he invented an entire mythology of war, which he proclaimed throughout his odes devoted to Catherine and her victories. The French philosopher even composed several triumphant odes to celebrate the most glorious episodes of Catherine's military campaigns. He compared the Russian war with medieval crusades ("Voici le vrai temps des croisades") and summoned Catherine (called in his poems "Minerva" or "Pallas") to avenge the "holy places."[7]

In his ode *On the Russian War against the Turks in 1768* (*Sur la guerre des Russes contre les Turcs en 1768*), he had already predicted the great outcome of combat — Russian victories over the Turks in Byzantium, Moldova, Wallachia, and the Crimea:

> La Minerve du Nord vous enflamme et vous guide;
> Combattez, triomphez sous sa puissante égide.
> Gallitzin vous commande, et Byzance en frémit:
> Le Danube est ému, la Tauride est tremblante;
>   Le sérail s'épouvante,
>   L'univers applaudit.[8]

Voltaire was the first to elaborate a conceptual framework for Catherine's strategy of war. He considered the Russian campaign against the Ottomans to be a legitimate action on the part of the "enlightened" "Minerva of the North" to depose a cruel tyrant of the East. The war against the Turks received his utmost sanction as a messianic war in which the Russian troops had to fulfill an old European dream. Voltaire enthusiastically outlined some of the main objectives of Catherine's war: first, to liberate Europe from fanatical barbarians, second, to undermine the strength of the Ottoman Empire (interpreted as a kind of an empire of evil!), and finally, to restore the intellectual cradle of humanity, Ancient Greece, which had perished under a centuries-old religious and cultural yoke. Voltaire's Hellenic cult was especially "mythological": the

---

[7] *Ouvres complèts de Voltaire*, 8 (Paris, 1877), 492.

[8] Ibid., 490. ("Minerva of the North enflames and guides you / Combat, triumph under her powerful aegis. / Galitsin leads you, and Byzantine is trembling; / Danube vibrates, Tauride is shaking; / The harem is in fear, / The universe applauds.")

philosopher believed that the liberated Greeks should re-instate a kingdom of wisdom, culture, and civilization, which would be an alternative to a modern society ensnared by clerical dogmatism and intellectual darkness.

Voltaire vigorously encouraged Catherine to wage war through constant references to her historical "mission" and "mighty wisdom." Thus, he prophesied in his letter written right on the eve of war (on November 15, 1768):

> "S'ils vous font la guerre, Madame, il pourra bien leur arriver ce que Pierre le Grand avait eu autrefois en vue, c'était de faire de Constantinople le capitale de l'Empire russe. Ces barbares méritent d'etre punis <…>. J'espère tout de votre genie et de votre destine. <…> Je pense très sérieusement que si jamais les Turcs doivent etre chassés de l'Europe, ce sera par les Russes."[9]

Catherine, in her turn, was glad to encourage Voltaire to develop his Utopian projects that converged with her own imperial strategy. Voltaire elaborated the concept (which soon became popular in Russian military odes) of Catherine's Russia as a messianic heir in the ancient struggle with the "barbarians." Russia, as he declared in his poetry and letters, had inherited this historical mission, which had been abandoned by France and Austria. The Empress happily accepted Voltaire's symbolic interpretation of her as the ancient goddess Pallas with a spike and shield that protected Europe from an eternal enemy.

In her turn, Catherine willingly relayed news of each new military success to Voltaire. She also spoke about the great mission of her "young" Empire, making particular reference to the obvious lack of will on Europe's part to oppose the Turkish power:

> "In Europe, any desire to act against Turkey is over."[10]

---

[9] *Documents of Catherine the Great. The Correspondence with Voltaire*, 20. ("If you are going to make war, Madame, it could happen what Peter the Great had in mind, it meant to make Constantinople the capital of Russia. The Barbarians deserve to be punished <…> I believe in your genius and destiny <…> I seriously think if the Turks should be chased out of Europe, it could be by Russians.")

[10] *Sbornik russkogo istoricheskogo obsh'estva*, 10 (1872), 351.

She also playfully informed Voltaire that she was learning Greek in order to properly welcome the philosopher in Constantinople, the former capital of Byzantium. [11]

These private letters to Voltaire during the war were a part of Catherine's political strategy: the Empress selected certain facts and opinions, putting aside anything that could jeopardize her image among her French audience.[12] She attempted to ignore and/or hide any points of contention with the Enlightenment philosopher, putting forward instead their ideological parallels. It was especially significant that, in her drafts, Catherine crossed out the most ambitious passages that revealed her "imperial" goals and military vainglory. She eliminated the sections describing her determination to triumph over an erstwhile invincible colossus, and moderated her zealous tone.

The draft of her letter to Voltaire written on January 8, 1770 contained some pompous phrases that were eliminated from the fair copy:

> "You compared my plan to send a navy expedition to the Mediterranean Sea with Hannibal's enterprise. However, the Carthaginians dealt with a powerful colossus, in its full strength, while we face only a weak ghost who falls to pieces as soon as we lay a hand on him."[13]

On the other hand, Voltaire also had his own game. His passionate "militarism" included a good portion of irony. Voltaire's odes and letters contained the everlasting dream of the Enlightenment philosopher to help a monarch establish a just state based on Reason. At the same time, they implied a hidden skepticism on the part of the author of *Candide* toward any kind of rationalistic programming of life.

In his ode *A l'impératrice de Russie Catherine II, à l'occasion de la prise de Choszim par les Russes, en 1769* (*To the Russian Empress Catherine II, on the occasion of the seizure of Khotin by the Russians, in*

---

[11] Ibid.

[12] Alber Sorel, *The Eastern Question*, 52.

[13] *Sbornik russkogo istoricheskogo obsh'estva*, 10, 401.

1769) Voltaire ironically employs the rhetorical devices of solemn hymns by the exemplary king's odist, the Ancient Greek lyric poet Pindar. Thus, he begins his ode by addressing Apollo and the Muses, and he continues by constructing "genealogical" metaphors in which the Russian Tsarina discovers herself to be a "relative" of the Ancient Gods:

> O Minerve du Nord! ô toi, soeur d'Apollon!
> Tu vengeras la Grèce en chassant ces infâmes,
> Ces ennemis des arts, et ces geôliers des femmes.
> Je pars; je vais t'attendre aux champs de Marathon. [14]

Catherine's first military success made Voltaire, as he wrote in his letters, obviously, quite jokingly, "pray to Allah" and "out-prophesy Mahomet."[15] The philosopher apparently got carried away and afterward ironically deflated his poetical adulation for Catherine.

Meanwhile, in comparing Catherine's war to a crusade, Voltaire always (and quite seriously) rejected the notion that his position had any religious basis. In a letter written on May 27, 1769, he ridicules all religious fanatics equally, both Christians and Muslims alike.[16] He emphasizes a great difference between ancient times and Catherine's war, which was aiming, in his opinion, to eradicate fanaticism. Moreover, he includes the Empress in an honorable circle of his atheistic allies. In his poem written in 1770 and entitled *Ode Pindarique. A propos de la guerre présente en Grèce (A Pindaric Ode. On the Russian War in Greece)*, the Goddess Pallas, Voltaire's voice in the ode, makes the statement:

> "C'est moi qui conduis Catherine
> Quand cette étonnante héroine,
> Foulant à ses pieds le turban,
> Réunit Thémis et Bellone,

---

[14] *Oeuvres complète de Voltaire*, 10, 533. ("Oh Minerva of the North, you, a sister of Apollo! / You will avenge Greece by pursuing these infidels, / These enemies of the Arts and jailers of women. / I 'm going away; I shall await you in the fields of Marathon.")

[15] Ibid, 493.

[16] Ibid, 492, 533.

> Et rit avec moi, sur son trône,
> De la Bible, et de l'Alcoran."[17]

Voltaire's image of Catherine as a warrior against the "ignorant" Turks and protector of philosophy and the arts was rather flattering. However, the mention of her "laughter" toward the Bible was very risky, though Voltaire softens the sentence by entrusting it to the ancient (and pagan!) Goddess. In his "Pindaric" ode to the Russian Empress, Voltaire attempts to establish the rules of his game. According to them, Catherine II, having been symbolically accepted to the Enlightenment "republic of letters" as an equal member, had to tolerate all his witty atheistic jokes. For his part, Voltaire pledged to represent her not as a 'Tsarina' and Head of the Russian Church, but as a sophisticated (and devoid of any prejudices) member of an international, non-confessional community of open-minded intellectuals. Catherine II playfully and slyly followed this "rule," but only in her letters to him. It was a part of her image that was used only for the benefit of foreign liberals.

In depicting the Russo-Turkish war, Voltaire persistently returns to Hellenic motifs. He proclaims that, after this war, a resurrected and renovated Greece (liberated by Catherine II) will be the best model of a secular society that has been freed of tyrannical regimes as well as of any form of religious fanaticism. This concept represented a kind of cultural Utopia in which the ancient hero Achilles would be born again, having denounced both the years of the Turkish yoke as well as Byzantium's scholastic rule. Voltaire treated both the Byzantine Empire and the Ottoman Porte as almost equally "tyrannical." According to Voltaire, the former was a kingdom of a scholastic religion that had led Greeks to intellectual degradation and eventually to their slavery under the Turkish yoke. Voltaire wrote in his "Pindaric" ode:

> Et la posterité d'Achille,
> Sous la règle de saint Basile,

---

[17] Ibid, 492. ("It's me who leads Catherine / When this surprising heroine, / Pulling down the turban under her heels, / Unites Themis and Bellona, / And, sitting on her throne, laughs, as I do, / At Bible and Koran.")

Fut l'esclave des Ottomans.[18]

Voltaire apparently ignored the Christian component of the Russian mythology of war and deliberately filled his odes with ancient images and classical myths as a clear alternative to modern — "oppressive" — religions. He never used the paradigm of the "holy war" of Christians against Muslims that would become quite common in Russian military odes.

On the contrary, Russian military odes from the beginning cultivated the ambitious idea of restoring Christianity in Byzantium, which had, many centuries before, given the "light" of Christianity to Russia. Vasilii Petrov declares as much in his ode *On the Seizure of Khotin (На взятие Хотина)*, written in 1769:

> Take miserable Byzantium
> This light from the Russians,
> Who had taken it from you in ancient times. [19]

This cultural Utopia was very characteristic of the entire mythology of war in Russian letters at the time. It constituted a division between Voltaire, who ridiculed the "oppressive" and "schismatic" Christianity of Byzantium's past (before the Turkish occupation), and his Russian counterparts. For later, Byzantium should be returned to the Christian family, and even become a Christian satellite of Russia.

On this point, Russian poets made efforts to "correct" Voltaire and to redirect his anti-tyranny invectives. Thus, Ippolit Bogdanovich, working on his famous translation of Voltaire's ode *A l'Impératrice de Russie, Catherine II* (*To the Russian Empress, Catherine II*, 1771), removes Voltaire's criticism of Byzantium, and instead, inserts his own passage in which he describes the Turks' genocide of the Christians. Bogdanovich writes in this section of the poem entitled *A Translation of some Verses of Voltaire, a Glorious French Writer, 1771*):

---

[18] *Oeuvres complète de Voltaire*, 492. ("And Achilles' progeny, / Under the rule of Basile, / Became slaves of Ottomans.")

[19] V. Petrov, *Sochineniia*, I, 46.

> <...> In order that the unscrupulous pasha's audacious hand
> Would be able to abuse our Christian blood.[20]

Voltaire's poem does not contain any antagonism between the Muslim pasha and his Christian victims. He only protests against the possibility of a poet and a free man becoming playthings in the hands of a tyrant:

> <...> Qu'un bacha dans mon sang trempe à son gré ses mains <...>[21]

Voltaire considered Catherine's successful war with the Turks to be revenge on behalf of the entire civilized world for a kind of historical regression, a miserable retardation in humanity's continual movement from darkness to light. Voltaire's odes to Catherine put her actions in a different perspective by presenting an imperial war as the liberation of oppressed nations and the restoration of law, science, and the arts brought about by the enlightened ruler. This concept played a mobilizing role, helping the Russian Empress to shape the political mythology of her military campaign. At the same time, Voltaire's odes influenced Russian poets to make a turn toward Hellenic culture and images.

The beginning of War: Odes of the Apocalypse

In the summer of 1769, Russians were frightened by the sudden appearance of a huge comet. They immediately connected it with the escalating war and regarded its appearance as a threatening prophecy, a sign of God's anger. Vasilii Petrov depicts the war as a kind of Biblical battle between the forces of good and Hell's troops. In his first military ode *On the War with the Turks* (На войну с турками, 1769), he presents an apocalyptic picture of the impending struggle:

> The Sultan is enraged! Hell's daughters,
> The Furies incited his anger.
> The forest's animals began to howl,

---

[20] I. F. Bogdanovich, *Stikhotvoreniia i poemy*, 213.
[21] *Oeuvres complète de Voltaire*, 10, 435. ("<...> The pasha washes his hands in my blood.")

> The wolf and dog dropped their jaws;
> The cries of night ravens
> Fill our places with horror,
> Foreboding blood and wounds;
> The comet up above the seraglio
> Shakes down, from her fiery tail,
> Misfortunes on our midnight country!
> Oh war, an awful war is in the air,
> Oh Russia, right over your very head <...>.[22]

Petrov, in painting such a cosmological picture, explicitly repeats some of the metaphors from Lomonosov's *Ode on the Seizure of Khotin*. In both odes, the enemy forces are "enraged," "inflamed," "filled" with "anger," "brimstone," and "poison." The physical towns, rivers, and countries become animated, and they act like historical heroes. Petrov also appropriates Lomonosov's "zoological" metaphors as necessary elements of his Baroque style.

By referring to Lomonosov, Petrov not only demonstrates his poetic legacy and his participation in the respectable and politically correct tradition. Through his use of Lomonosov's poetic devices he also, as Lomonosov did, implies that current events can be most accurately described in the Biblical–Apocalyptic context. In the conclusion of his extremely pessimistic ode, Petrov makes an attempt to offer a glimmer of hope for the future. He depicts the Russians as having defeated a terrible animal; this victory is symbolic of Catherine's triumph over all enemies who supported the Turks, most of all France, called in all of Petrov's works by its Latinized name — Sequana. Petrov, as an excellent translator and admirer of Latin poets, knew that, according to Gallo-Roman mythology, Sequana was the goddess of the river Seine. In his ode, Petrov depicts France-Sequana as a serpent dying on the sand:

> Worship Catherine,
> Who has subdued the mighty Beast,
> And turned the battle into peace.

---

[22] V. Petrov, *Sochineniia*, I, 34.

> She must be given honor as her trophy.
> Yes, looking at the mother in laurels,
> Sequana will beat her chest in anger,
> Falling down in unbearable despair,
> Regretting her failed cunning.
> She will shrivel up from envy,
> Barely carrying her body on the river's sands. [23]

Petrov's images refer to passages in the Book of Revelations in which John the Baptist describes the struggle between "a woman clothed with the sun," and "a huge red dragon that had seven heads and ten horns, and on its heads were seven diadem crowns." (Rev.12:1– 3) Petrov's comet that rains misfortunes down upon Russia is also linked with the Biblical dragon: "the dragon's tail swept away a third of the stars in heaven and hurled them to the earth." (Rev. 12:4) The Dragon (or Serpent) in the military odes of that time always stands for Russia's enemies, such as the Turks or France.

Petrov's first military ode explores poetic language, style, and a system of metaphors. Petrov felt a close connection to Lomonosov and even exceeded the latter in terms of the density of his metaphoric devices and Slavonic lexicon, already too artificial for the time (Petrov's language was even more archaic than Lomonosov's!). This ode, written in a time when various writers were competing for the right to be Catherine's exclusive court poet, also exhibits an enormous effort on Petrov's part to find the most adequate style and language with which to worship the Empress during war. The success of the chosen discourse was more than a pure literary achievement: it "signified the *state* success of a poet and his aesthetics."[24]

Petrov's ode gave rise to the creation of another ode about the same comet. Mikhail Kheraskov, the poet and provost of Moscow University, composed an ode entitled *The Comet, which appeared in 1767, at the beginning of the war with the Turks* (Комета, явившаяся в

---

[23] Ibid, 38.

[24] Oleg Proskurin, "Burlesknyi kulachnyi boi I bor'ba za epopeiu: *Elisei, ili Razdrazhennyi Vakkh*, V. Maikova i *Poema na pobedy Rossiiskogo voinstva*, V. Petrova," in *Jews and Slavs*, 14 (2004), 94.

1767 году при начале войны с турками). The poem came out only in 1783, in the magazine *The Interlocutor of the Lovers of Russian Literature.*[25]

Kheraskov also frames his ode in Biblical allusions, but rejects Petrov's pessimistic and apocalyptical views. In his ode, the Russians' struggle with the Ottoman Empire is considered a continuation of the historical clash between Christians and Muslims. The Russians, according to his opinion, inherited the European hope, and had the messianic task of liberating lands taken by the Porte, in particular, Jerusalem. He interprets the appearance of the comet as a dangerous sign only for the Turks: the comet looks, as he writes, like a "menacing sword" above their heads:

> Oh, you! Who fell asleep in luxury,
> Wake up, wake up, and look, Istanbul,
> A sword is hung up above the moon's disk;
> It's bloody and terrifying,
> It threatens to depose your lofty throne
> And destroy you.
> Visible in the sky from far away,
> It's a dangerous sign in the hands of the Russians;
> Their sharp sword is your comet,
> Glinting in your eyes;
> It wants to raze your town to the ground,
> To push Mahomet to Medina.
> The Christian Church has woken up,
> And promises peace to the holy mountains,
> Their black clothing will fall down,
> Jerusalem will arise ,
> Crowned in gold will be
> Love, Faith, and Hope. <...>
> Khotin is already brought to its knees,

---

[25] The title of Kheraskov's poem misled scholars in dating the ode, which suggests that it was written in 1767. However, in 1767 there was neither war with the Turks, nor any comet in the sky. Moreover, the author referred to the seizure of Khotin that took place in September 1769 as a recent event. Most probably, Kheraskov's ode was written just after Petrov's ode, in the autumn of 1769. Very cautiously, Kheraskov had decided not to publish his ode during the time of the apparent domination of Petrov, a young rising star of Catherine's political propaganda machine.

> The East is trembling before the North,
> The holy faith is triumphing; <...>.[26]

The third military ode of the same time period (the end of 1769) belonged to Alexander Sumarokov, who made desperate attempts to overcome both Lomonosov and Petrov and regain the position of poetic leader. His poem of 1769 has a title that indicates not one, but two military victories, and contains a direct statement as to their cause: *Ode to the Empress Catherine the Second, on the Seizure of Khotin and the Conquest of Moldavia* (Ода Государыне Императрице Екатерине Второй на взятие Хотина и покорение Молдавии). Sumarokov's ode offers references to the Bible, a strict and pure "high style" in terms of its lexicon, and a solemn intonation of "high swooping." He filled his ode with implicit polemics addressed to his longtime rival Lomonosov, and through him, to Petrov, who claimed to be Lomonosov's "apprentice."

In 1739, Lomonosov opened his *Ode on the Seizure of Khotin* with a Pindaric preamble, which is saturated with "Pagan" images from Greek mythology. It depicts a joyful and ecstatic Poet who completes an imaginary ascent to the top of the famous Greek mountain Pindus. There he meets the Muses and drinks from the Castalian spring, the source of his poetic inspiration. Lomonosov writes:

> A sudden ecstasy fills my mind;
> It leads to a high mountain summit <...>
> Is Pindus not beneath my feet?[27]

Sumarokov purposely deviates from this traditional "preamble," because it is too "pagan"; instead, he opens his ode with a picture of a spiritual ascent into Heaven. Sumarokov purifies his ode from any pagan mythology, using only Christian symbolism. His poet finds his "inspiration" by visiting Christ and His Angels, not the Muses:

---

[26] M. M. Kheraskov, *Izbrannye proizvedeniia*, 135–136.
[27] M. V. Lomonosov, *Polnoe sobranie sochinenii*, 8, 16, 18.

> To the sky's outermost heights,
> My spirit dared soar.
> Out of the reach of arrows:
> I find myself in Heaven.
> I hear praying angels,
> Who speak to God <...>[28]

Sumarokov deliberately merges the genres of the military ode and the religious hymn. In a very important dispute between the followers of the French "ancients" and the French "moderns," he takes the side of the latter, despite his theoretical sympathy toward the former. The theoreticians of the "ancients" believed it necessary to employ ancient mythology and images in the high genres, even in the depiction of modern events.[29] Rejecting classical heritage, Sumarokov relies on Biblical symbolical capital. Like Petrov, he expresses his utmost concern with the war with the Turks by presenting it in apocalyptical visions:

> Is this not Hell in its new mourning?
> Is not the race of mortals going to drown?
> Is not the world coming to an end?[30]

Apocalyptical motifs helped to maintain a high pathos in odes, but had become outdated by the beginning of the 1770s. The Apocalyptic anticipations surrounding the first months of war in 1769 contradicted the subsequent events of 1770, when the Russian triumphs over the Turks became quite clear. The ideology of war sought a new discourse, and more perceptive poets (like Petrov) had already begun to develop a kind of "Russian" Hellenistic style, which imitated Ancient Greek poetic forms, employing their metaphors and even their rhythms.

Meanwhile, Sumarokov was obstinate, and he continued to compose ode after ode, but success did not come. His archaic poetic principles, his too didactic style and his hymn-like structure

---

[28] A. P. Sumarokov, *Polnoe sobranie vsekh sochinenii v stikhakh i proze*, 2, 106.

[29] V. M. Zhivov, B. A. Uspenskii, "Metamorfozy antichnogo iazychestva v istorii russkoi kul'tury XVII– XVIII veka," in *Iz istorii russkoi kul'tury*, IV (Moscow, 2000), 506– 518.

[30] A. P. Sumarokov, *Polnoe sobranie vsekh sochinenii v stikhakh i proze*, 2, 107.

failed to hit the mark. On September 23, 1770, he sent a new ode to Catherine's secretary, G. V. Kozitskii. The poem was almost completely devoted to war, in spite of its title, *Ode to the Empress Catherine the Second, on the Occasion of Her Coronation, September 22, 1770* (*Ода Государыне Императрице Екатерине Второй, на день Коронования Ея Сентября 22 дня, 1770 года*). Sumarokov assumed the ode would be the best of all his odes, and he asked Kozitskii to present it to the Empress. At the same time, in a rush, he sent a direct letter to the Empress in which he made some theoretical statements about the presentation of her image in war. In his letter, Sumarokov indicates the importance of contemporary aesthetic choices; he suggests accepting his "elevated" pathos in odes, and finally, he distinguishes himself from all modern poets who simply report the facts in their odes.

He writes to the Empress:

> "As a poet, I cannot be silent when the whole universe witnesses the enormous victories of Your Highness and praises the name of Catherine the Great <...>. Perhaps, this is my best ode, and it seems to me, that my ode is quite different from the poems of all our poor poets. <...> Military reports along with a few compliments to your sacred person cannot constitute a live picture that might present to our progeny the whole glory of our century as well as your immortal name. The rule of Augustus needs its Horace. <...> It should be: *The fleet established by Peter the Great, led by God's Providence and yours, for the first time, has crossed the Baltic and Midnight Seas, glimpsed the Western ocean, voyaged along Europe, and reached the Archipelagos where she ravaged the Turkish fleet and moved, with a great noise, all the winds, the seas, and the earth*. And so, the following depiction is poor: *Russian ships arrived, and after some clashes with the Turks, set the enemies' ships on fire, and soon, they all burned down*. The deeds of Catherine the Great require more sensitive explanations."[31]

The letter aimed to convince the Empress to accept and promote Sumarokov's aesthetic views. He justly considered the poet's efforts to be equal to the deeds of a statesman. Not surprisingly, right

---

[31] *Pis'ma russkikh pisatelei XVIII veka* (Leningrad, 1980), 143.

after his aesthetic declarations, the poet found it appropriate to ask Catherine for some financial assistance!

What did he want to prove? Sumarokov protested against using any kind of "narrative" structure in an ode. The ode should remain a poem, not a detailed "report" of facts. As a true high genre, the ode should be built not on plot, but on metaphors or, as he called them, "contrasts" which referred to the Bible.[32] Sumarokov ridiculed the plain, narrative odes of his contemporaries who composed them based on newspapers. On the other hand, he attempted to oppose a pure Christian (Biblical) symbolism to the famous metaphorical "chaos" of Lomonosov's ode, which draws upon both Christian and "pagan" sources.

As a result, Sumarokov's odes consistently depict the war with the Turks against an apocalyptic background and place Catherine's image between the forces of "light" and "darkness," "paradise" and "hell." Sumarokov believed the high genres should not contain any kind of narrative plot, and even criticized Lomonosov for introducing one in his unfinished long poem *Peter the Great (Петр Великий)*. He scorned the narrative as a distinctive feature of the "lower" entertaining genres, like stories or novels.

In 1769, Sumarokov began to write an epic poem entitled the *Dimitriade (Димитрияды)*, devoted to the struggle of Moscow's prince Dimitrii Donskoi against the Golden Horde. He obviously meant to emphasize parallels with modern events. The poem was intended to prove his uncompromised view on the purity of genre as well as the necessity of eradicating Pagan gods and myths from poetry. The opening of his poem gives a picture of personified and animated "passions" (as substitutions for Pagan gods!) that are obstinately based exclusively on a dense Biblical symbolism. He stopped composing the poem, after several unsuccessful attempts to progress beyond the introduction.

---

[32] Sumarokov juxtaposes narrative's strategies of epic poems to contrasts' poetics of the odes (V. M. Zhivov, B. A. Uspenskii, "Metamorfozy antichnogo iazychestva v istorii russkoi kul'tury XVII– XVIII veka," 508).

A Mythological Palimpsest

The Russian war with the Porte turned out to be remarkably in tune with the Baroque perception of the world as a series of historic events that continually repeats itself. Poets and politicians immediately found "similarities," and started to cast Russian triumphs as modern versions of ancient Greek and Roman heroic feats. As a result, the discourse of war had turned into a mythological palimpsest in which modern episodes and their participants are viewed through the prism of ancient history and myths.

The specifics of the geographical setting contributed a great deal to the creation of such a palimpsest. The war happened to take place in legendary locations that made old historical realities and myths quite actual. The names of Crimea, Morea (the southern part of Greece), Greece, Sparta, Archipelago (the part of Aegean Sea between Greece and Asia Minor) sounded like an evocation of the past, the era of epic poetry and myth. Vasilii Petrov rightly perceives connections to Ancient times in his extended *Poem on the Victories of the Russian Army over the Tatars and the Turks, gained under the command of Field-Marshal, Count Rumiantsev, near the town of Zhurzhi (1771)*:

> Here the summit of every smoking hill
> Was known and cherished by the Romans.
> You contain traces of the Trojan troops,
> You witness now the Russian victory![33]

Russian poets interpreted the fight against the Porte through the prism of the Roman invasions and embroidered their military odes with Greek mythology. At the same time, Russian odes of the period quickly adopted the European tradition of the ideological and cultural palimpsest in which the figure of the warrior-king who combats the Muslims acquires a multi-layered system of representation that included Homeric and Virgilian motifs, Biblical

---

[33] [Vasilii Petrov], *Poema na pobedy Rossiiskogp voinstva, pod predvoditel'stvom generala fel'dmarshala Grafa Rumiantseva, oderzhannyia nad Tatarami I Turkami, so vremeni ego voenachal'stva nad pervoiu armieiu do vziatiia goroda Zhurzhi* (Saint Petersburg, 1771), 15.

allusions, as well as the myths about the Argonauts and the Golden Fleece. Later, in his *Historical Laudatory Speech to Catherine II* (1801), Nikolai Karamzin, the sharpest expert in political mythology and its strategies, gave a subtle interpretation of the events of the Turkish war. He writes, recalling the unexpected arrival of the Russian fleet in the Mediterranean Sea:

> "The sacred chronicles of History disturbed the hearts of our sailing Heroes when they got sight of Italy. *It seemed to them* that the great shades of Fabritius, Camillus, and Scipio <...> looked, with curiosity and astonishment, at Catherine's flag, proud and unfamiliar to these seas. *It seemed to them* that Russia, in her splendor, was a new Rome. With such feelings, our Argonauts approached the countries, renowned in chronicles of glory since ancient times <...>"[34]

Karamzin does not describe a real event of war, but the fictionalized feelings of its participants. He italicizes his poetic refrain *"it seemed to them"* and names the Russian soldiers Argonauts with an aim to invoke the ancient myth. Eventually, as a writer and historian, he reconstructs and reveals the main cultural metaphors of the poetry of that time. Karamzin's reading of the epoch's belletristic discourse indicates the most significant paradigms of the military poems.

Russian poetry during the first months of the war began to experience a striking increase in allusions to the Roman Empire. Odes, poems, even military reports and magazine articles abounded in comparisons between the Russian participants of the campaign and Roman patterns of glory and vigor. These metaphors affirmed Russia's claim to be a world power and, on the other hand, through references to the old and well-established imperial symbolism, justified the unconditional rightness of Russia's actions.

Catherine, in her turn, cultivated such metaphors, and even introduced one citation, which enjoyed immense popularity and became the pattern to imitate. When the Field-Marshal Peter Rumiantsev complained to Catherine concerning the numerical supremacy of the Turkish army, the empress reassured him, citing

---

[34] N. M. Karamzin, *Sochineniia*, 8 (Saint Petersburg, 1835), 12.

the Romans' example: "The Romans <...> did not ask how many enemies they had to fight, but where the enemy was." [35] On July 21, 1770, on the shores of the river Kagul, in Moldova, the Russian army successfully defeated the Turks, and 20,000 Turkish troops perished while only 353 Russians died. Recalling Catherine's declaration, Rumiantsev proudly reported to her:

> "Let me liken this feat with the ancient Romans' deeds which your Highness requested to imitate. Is it not so, when the army of your Imperial Majesty does not ask how big the enemy is, but only seeks where he is."[36]

The witty reply by Rumiantsev also became known among contemporaries, and the military epistolary inspired poets to follow suit.

Vasilii Petrov mentions the phrase several times in his *Poem on the Victories of the Russian Army <...> near the town of Zhurzhi* (1771):

> Oh, ancient Rome, the father of invincible warriors,
> The school of the most glorious heroes under the sun <...>
> The empress appreciates your disciples,
> Upon her order her zealot strives to imitate them;
> He gallops toward dangers, spears, fires,
> **He does not observe the number of enemies,**
> **But only seeks where they are.**[37]

The author of the lyric drama *The Russians in the Archipelago* (*Россы в Архипелаге*; 1772), Pavel Potemkin (a distant relative of Grigorii Potemkin), echoes this pattern. The poem portrays Aleksei Orlov, who was recently appointed commander-in-chief of the Russian fleet sent to the Archipelago, as the main protagonist; he lead a very successful attack in which the far superior Turkish navy was completely annihilated at Chesma. The poem reflects the official propaganda, which presented the war as a clash between civilization and barbarity, with the Russian army undertaking a war of liberation. There are two characters, Sophronym and Bukoval, the

---

[35] S. M. Soloviev, *Istoriia Rossii s drevneishikh vremen. 1766– 1772*, 27– 28, 479.
[36] Ibid, 481.
[37] [Vasilii Petrov], *Poema na pobedy Rossiiskogp voinstva*, 15.

leaders of the Greek partisans, who fight under the Russian command to liberate their Christian compatriots from the Muslim yoke. The author implies the motif of the Russian military campaign as a sacred war; he excessively emphasizes the merciful quality of the Russian soul, especially by including the liberation of the captive chief of the Turks, Osman.

Summing up all the most significant ideological motifs of Catherine's military propaganda, Pavel Potemkin, as a result, invokes the Empress's famous Roman comparison. He makes Aleksei Orlov the bearer of Catherine's lucky saying. Thus, Orlov replies to the English general *Elphinstone* who hesitated to attack the Turks because of their numerical supremacy:

> While the Romans did not observe the number
> of their enemies,
> The Russians were not less in courage,
> When they chased the Turkish fleet down to Chesma,
> Everyone recognized the Turks' majority,
> But who was frightened looking at this multitude?
> You recently witnessed an example of Russian courage,
> Why should we discuss the large numbers?
> We are used to triumphing over quantity with bravery.[38]

Moreover, the comparison with Rome was immortalized as a slogan of the epoch when it was engraved on the pedestal of the Morea Column in Tsarskoe Selo. The column commemorates the successful operation in Morea, the southern part of the Greek peninsula. Troops under the command of Fedor Orlov (the youngest of the four Orlov brothers, an admirer of ancient Greece) successfully occupied the territory in February 1770. The Italian architect Antonio Rinaldi (1710–1794) designed the column according to the Roman Doric order, combining a massive Roman base with a Greek style pillar. It corresponded very well not only to the symbolic *translatio* of imperial power, but also, as we will see further, to a rising taste for an amalgam of Greek and Roman culture. The engraved inscription on the base states: "<...> the Russian troops numbered only six

---

[38] Pavel Potemkin, *Rossy v Arkhipelage* (Saint Petersburg, 1772), 20–21.

hundred; they did not ask how many enemies they had to fight, but only where they were."[39]

Rinaldi flooded the empress's country residence with triumphant arches and obelisks: besides the Morea Column, he erected his most famous Kagul Obelisk. The Orlov Gates opened way to the residence. Though the Gates were not directly connected with the war (they glorified Grigorii Orlov's suppression of the Plague Riot in Moscow in 1771), they reproduced the strong and impressive forms of the Arch of Titus, built to celebrate the Roman emperor's demolition of Jerusalem in 70 AD.[40] The event, since the Medieval Ages, had been an emblem of Christian triumph over the Muslims. In this way, the victory over the bubonic plague, which had originated from the Ottoman Porte's dominions, became equal to military triumphs over the Muslim adversary. It is very characteristic that later, in 1789, Catherine ordered the use of the Orlov Gates for another ceremony, already during the second Turkish war. The gates, redecorated with new inscriptions that were more appropriate to the event, assisted in celebrating the triumphant entrance of Grigorii Potemkin into Saint Petersburg after several victorious campaigns against the Turks. [41]

Roman obelisks, columns, and arches invaded Russian territories during the wars with the Turks, thus organizing the symbolic space of the empire. In Europe, their construction began to flourish at the end of the sixteenth century, in the time of Henri the Fourth, which was praised by Voltaire.[42] At the beginning of the 1770s, Catherine initiated the building of a whole park of such monuments. The processions of emperors and troops under the triumphant arches, as always, signified a transition from a real area to a mythological one, thereby supplying the state with additional symbolic capital. In erecting obelisks and columns in her territories,

---

[39] S. Ia. Lastochkin, Iu. F. Rubezhanskii, *Tsarskoe Selo — rezidentsiia rossiiskikh monarkhov* (Saint Petersburg, 1998), 182.

[40] A. Kuchariants, *Antonio Rinaldi* (Saint Petersburg, 1994), 122.

[41] M. I. Pyliaev, *Zabytoe proshloe okrestnostei Peterburga* (Saint Petersburg, 1889), 466–468.

[42] Roy Strong, *A Splendor at Court. Renaissance spectacle and illusion* (London, 1973), 30–31.

the Russian power associated herself with history: all events of the state were to be considered not only in the context of real politics, but also in that of eternal historic triumphs. At the same time, as in a palimpsest, through the Russian events in Moldavia, Morea and the Archipelago, contemporaries sought to read the fading features of the ancient age.

Catherine as Pallas

Meanwhile, Roman metaphors of power did not prevent a parallel emergence of Greek paradigms in Russian political and poetic discourse. The Greek associations in poetry became more and more visible precisely when the Baltic fleet, in summer of 1769, embarked from Kronshtadt on an adventurous journey to reach the Mediterranean Sea, invade the Greek Archipelago, and to attack the Turks in the rear. Aleksei Orlov's daring strategic plan, approved by Catherine, sought to divide the gigantic Turkish army between several frontlines, and to help the Russian ground forces.[43] According to Orlov's plan, after an unexpected arrival on the shores of Greece, the Russian troops were to attack the Turks in different cities, relying on the help of local Greek Christians. The Russian court launched a very intensive pro-Russian propaganda campaign in Greece and Sparta, and sent numerous emissaries who attempted to incite the Greek population to riot against the Turks. Taken as a whole, Orlov and Catherine's ambitious plan intended to repeat the legendary marine struggle near Lepanto of 1571, in which minor Italian and Venetian forces annihilated two hundred Ottoman galleys.

The propaganda (as well as Greek associations in poetry) steadily increased as the troops advanced inside Greece. The turning point in the war discourse was again Petrov's ode addressed to Catherine and written on the occasion of the seizure of the city of Yassy and the conquering of Moldavia (1769). The title contains an inscription that indicates the ode "had been presented to Her

---

[43] E. V. Tarle, *Chesmenskii boi i pervaia russkaia ekspeditsiia v Arkhipelag, 1769– 1774* (Moscow — Leningrad, 1945), 17– 36.

Majesty on October 22. The ode serves as an ideological introduction to the upcoming events in Greece. Petrov, adroit as usual, proclaims the Russian forces to be on a liberating mission to restore the independence (political as well as cultural) of the Greek people. He also draws a contrast between the Russian invasion and the unjust and insidious Roman occupancy of Greece. Speaking to the Greeks, Petrov writes:

> Be calm now heroic race,
> Patiently await changes.
> The longed-for time is coming;
> Your, Greeks, captivity will be over.
> Oh, how grateful you were,
> When the insidious Romans
> Gave you a false freedom!
> Without asking for profit or worship,
> *Catherine* will grant you liberty,
> She is the patron of all who suffer.[44]

Petrov is referring here to the Roman colonization of Greece (by the time of the emperor Augustus's rule, all Greek territories had fallen under Roman control, culminating in Augustus's reorganization of the peninsula as the province of Achaea in 27 BC). The poet implicates those "insidious" Roman rulers, who, while proclaiming the Greeks free for the duration of the Olympic Games, levied taxes on locals and drove many of them out of their lands. At the same time, the poet implies the second target of his sarcasm — the modern heir of Rome, Austria, officially called the Holy Roman Empire. Recently in 1769, Austria, a longtime enemy of the Ottoman Empire, had refused to join Russia in fighting the Turks.

Petrov's image of the empress endows her with some new features. He repeatedly calls her by her Greek name Pallas (or Pallas Athena), not by the Latin version of the goddess' name, Minerva. The change was not accidental: it reflected a search for a new literary code to describe the empress in war. Minerva stood for wisdom, whereas Pallas Athena, equipped with a helmet and shield, implied

---

[44] Vasilii Petrov, *Oda vsepresvetleishei, derzhavneishei, velikoi Gosudaryne Imperatritse Ekaterine Vtoroi, samoderzhitse vserossiskoi na vziat'e Ias i pokorenie vsego moldavskago kniazhestva* (Saint Petersburg, 1769), 11.

associations with battle. Petrov praised Catherine by invoking the name of the Greeks' main patroness and constant protagonist of epic poems. At the same time, he makes use of another — Christian — symbolic system when he mentions the "suffering" Greeks and calls the empress their "Supporter." The Russian word "покров" can be considered in religious terms as a clear reference to the Protective Veil of the Virgin. The poet combines both meanings, and the religious metaphor depicts the Russian invasion not only as a war of liberation, but also as a struggle to restore Orthodoxy in Greece. In the following strophes, Petrov brings in another metaphor by implicitly associating Catherine with a strong warrior who struggles against barbarity in order to usher in civilization; he depicts the Greeks who summon Catherine:

> Oh Pallas, you are severe to barbarians!
> Oh delight of many souls!
> Go quickly to help us,
> Take us under your scepter. [45]

At these early stages of war (and long before the elaboration of the so-called "Greek project"), the Greek theme did not cancel out the most popular Rome paradigms that dominated in imperial symbolism throughout the century. Moreover, the Greek theme gained importance as a rhetorical vehicle for propagandizing Russian colonialism. The Greek entourage of Russian propaganda combined with Russian odes to form a new paradigm of cultural refinement, and therefore, was reminiscent of the Emperor Augustus's age, when Rome imitated Hellenic philosophy, literature, architecture, and even the Greek manner of dress. The Greek theme in Russia at that time often contained colonial connotations. Thus, for example, on June 25, 1779, Grigorii Potemkin, while organizing a special dinner in honor of Catherine II at his dacha in Ozerki (near Saint Petersburg), imitated the Greek symposium. The guests lounged on beds, and a chorus sang some Greek strophes translated by Vasilii Petrov.[46] While maintaining the cultural atmosphere of Ancient

---

[45] Ibid, 10.
[46] *Sochineniia Derzhavina*, 1, 288.

Greece, the place itself also had the look of a "mountain cave in some district of the Caucasus, recently adjoined to Russia and entrusted to Potemkin's governance."[47] Greek and Caucasian accoutrements combined in order to commemorate the recent military triumphs of the Russian empire.

In his experimental *Ode on the victories of the Russian fleet over the Turkish fleet, under the guidance of Count Aleksei Orlov, in the Archipelago, near Chios, 1770*, Petrov develops the concept of the historical betrayal of another cultural descendent of Rome, France. According to his view, in supporting the Turks, France abandons a longtime mission — to fight the Christian enemies:

> Your great grandfathers in old and obscure times
> Following the Roman example went to the South;
>   You secretly fight
> The Russians for Mahomet![48]

As Petrov believed, new political circumstances brought up a paradoxical situation in which the Russians played role of the new Crusaders, a role that had belonged in Medieval Times to European Christians, first of all, to the French. In the Russo-Turkish war, France cooperated with the Porte, sending financial aid and military instructors, as described by the famous memoirist Baron de Tott.[49] The political alliance of the Turks and France did not remain a secret. Mikhail Kheraskov, in his long poem *Fight at Chesma* (1771), had already repeated a well known formula when he wrote about the symbolic union of the national signs of these two countries: "lilies" (France) are intermingled with a "bloody moon" (Turkey).[50]

In 1769, Russia was on extremely difficult terms with three Bourbon Houses, France, Spain, and the Neapolitan kingdom. All

---

[47] Ibid, 287.
[48] V. Petrov, *Oda na pobedy rossiiskogo flota, oderzhannaia nad turetskim, pod predvoditel'stvom grafa Alekseia Grigor'evicha Orlova, v Arkhipelage, pri Khiose* (Saint Petersburg, 1770), 9.
[49] E. V. Tarle, *Chesmenskii boi*, 10– 12; E. I. Druzhinina, *Kuchuk-Kainardjiiskii mir 1774 goda, ego podgotovka i zakliuchenie* (Moscow, 1955), 71– 74.
[50] M. M. Kheraskov, *Izbrannye proizvedeniia*, 145.

three, in addition, were Catholic countries. The Pope expressed a fervent condemnation of Russia, taking the side of the Ottoman supporters among the so-called Polish confederates (the Polish opposition against King Stanisław Poniatowskii), and calling for a crusade against Russia. In a letter to Voltaire from July 14, 1769, Catherine ironically discusses a historical paradox in which a whole distribution of roles becomes reversed: the former crusaders (the Pope and the Catholic countries) go against Russia who is in a fierce conflict with Muslims.[51] While Petrov makes references to the crusaders in his odes, he aims to underline a new paradoxical inversion of a longtime paradigm under new geo-political circumstances.

Petrov not only filled his odes with eloquent imperial metaphors, but also packed his texts with burning political topics; he definitely made all possible efforts to be a mouthpiece for Russian politics.[52] Meanwhile, Petrov's *Ode on the victories* continued the search for the most adequate form in which to describe military themes. He found some new poetic tools for it. First, he transfers to military leaders (not to the empress) a function of the main protagonist; here he imitates Pindar's odes devoted to Olympic heroes. Then, he introduces an exotic strophic structure with a combination of iambic lines of various lengths as a Russian version of the Greek lyric metre (like in poetry of the Greek poetess Sappho).[53] An elegant lyric form transformed the odes into long poems, which better corresponded with his task, giving a narrative account of a military event and, at the same time, implied an examination of its political meaning.

Such an analytical narrative style, with epic elements, allowed him to reinvigorate the established means of glorifying the empress. Petrov's military heroes committed their deeds for the sake of the empress who, in her turn, received an epic role of the protector of the heroes, the honorable role of Pallas Athena.

---

[51] *Documents of Catherine the Great. The Correspondance with Voltaire*, 31.

[52] A. L. Zorin, *Kormia dvuglavogo oral. Literatura i gosudarstvennaia ideologiia v Rossii v poslednei treti XVIII– pervoi treti XIX veka* (Moscow, 2001), 65– 94.

[53] M. L. Gasparov, *Ocherk istorii russkogo stikha* (Moscow, 2000), 105.

Obtaining the Golden Fleece

The Russian military mythology of Catherine's first war with the Turks actively appropriated another imperial paradigm taken from Virgil's *Fourth Eclogue*. There Virgil not only describes the Golden Age, but also prophesies future wars, new Argonauts, and an inevitable navy campaign to destroy a new Troy:

> "Then shall a second Tiphys be, and a second Argo to sail with chosen heroes: new wars too shall arise, and again a mighty Achilles be sent to Troy." [54]

These puzzling lines refer to the Ancient Greek myth about the ship built with the help of the Goddess Pallas Athena and called the "Argo." It also mentions the shipman Tiphys who navigates the ship and possesses supernatural talents. The Argonauts and their leader Jason set off for Colchis (lands on the Black Sea) in search of the Golden Fleece. Among other adventures, the Argonauts raze Troy, long before Achilles. In European history, this ancient myth was recurrently perceived as a symbolic narrative devising a military campaign against an Oriental country, most of all, as a mystical prediction of the Crusades against the Ottoman Porte, the main enemy of Europe throughout the centuries. [55]

An entire system of mythological analogies promoted the concept of the European emperor as a Christian hero, a super warrior who defeated the Muslims, and therefore, belonged to the ancestors of some ancient God or Goddess. In 1430, Duke Philip III of Burgundy even founded the Order of the Golden Fleece. The House of Habsburg used the image of the Golden Fleece as a royal attribute of sovereignty. Despite some controversy over the Pagan symbolism, the emblem became a sign of authority and victorious glory in military conquests. The Argonauts' myth in particular became an important framework for promoting the colonial symbolism and naval victories of European powers.

---

[54] *Virgil's Works: The Aeneid, Eclogues*, 275.
[55] Marie Tanner, *The Last Descendant of Aeneas*, 6.

In Russia, Pindar's well-known odes and translations of Virgil served as sources of Argonaut metaphors. Mikhail Lomonosov, Pindar's translator and a lyric heir to the European ode[56] was the first to show favor to such mythology. He introduced the metaphor in one of his first odes to Catherine, devoted to the celebration of the New Year of 1764. Taking into account the recent establishment of the Committee of the Russian Fleet, Lomonosov urges the naval forces to seize the Golden Fleece:

> Urania looks at the midnight country:
> "Here, from the slopes of ice and snow,
> Russia strives to obtain the Golden Fleece
> And reaches the gates of the dawn <...>"[57]

He appropriates a sublime metaphor of power in order to describe his commercial program of developing the Far East ("the gates of the dawn") and its seas.

A few years later, the war with the Porte, naval expeditions and battles, as well as the Greek environment of the war, all combined to increase the use of the Argonaut myth in Russian lyrics tremendously. Thus, Mikhail Kheraskov writes in his *Ode to the Russian warriors, in February 1769*:

> Not for your Golden Fleece,
> Not for poor Andromeda,
> Oh Russians! The war is imminent,
> And victories are coming;
> Let antiquity sing tales!
> It is not pride that calls you to battle,
> We ought to defend and rescue our neighbors. [58]

Vasilii Maikov, in his *Ode to her highness on the glorious victory over the Turkish fleet in the Laborno bay near the town of Chesma* (1770), compares Aleksei Orlov, the commander of the navy, with Jason who stole the Golden Fleece:

---

[56] Stella P. Revard, *Pindar and the Renaissance Hymn-Ode: 1450–1700* (Tempe, 2001).
[57] M. V. Lomonosov, *Polnoe sobranie sochinenii*, 8, 797–798.
[58] M. M. Kheraskov, *Izbrannye proizvedeniia*, 68.

> Are they same glorious heroes
> Who came to destroy Troy?
> Is it brave Jason
> Who stole the Golden Fleece? <…>
> Their glory is over, like a dream![59]

However, the Russian poets invert this paradigm: they provide Jason and the Argonauts with negative connotations. Russian warriors do not steal anything; to the contrary, they go to fight in order to restore justice and order. An enlightened perception enables Petrov to construct an image of the Russian fighters as the ***new Argonauts***, through a comparison to the mythical ones. He writes in his *Ode on the victories of the Russian fleet <…> near Khios, 1770*:

> We ought to bring our law to the barbarians,
> Fighting with an elite army, like daring Jason.
> He went abroad to steal the Golden Fleece,
> You are coming to shake up the brandisher of the law,
> To save the Fatherland,
> And to defend Greece.[60]

Petrov does not merely decorate his ode with the Golden Fleece metaphor, he inverses it, while appealing to history. According to his interpretation, the Turks violated the Christian "law" of Byzantium: they denied the Greeks their Christianity. The Russian army, as the new Argonauts, must restore law and history. This ode reflects a major change in interpreting an ancient imperial symbolism. The Russian fighters prove to be the bearers of an enlightened imperialism, and their victories surpass old European deeds by virtue of their ideological fairness. The concept was meant to stress the prophetic, missionary task of Catherine's expansionism. It also presented the war as the just conclusion of the longstanding European struggle against the Ottomans in which Russia took in her hands the lance that had fallen from the old empires' grasp.

---

[59] Ibid, 210.
[60] V. Petrov, *Oda na pobedy rossiiskogo flota*, 10.

Chapter Six

The Birth of Felitsa

Since the mid-1770s, the Russian government began to implement a brand new cultural strategy which aimed to consolidate the nation, and, most of all, its gentry. This strategy was designed to ensure social peace after the devastating Pugachev rebellion in 1773–1775, as well as to soften the image of the sovereign who had cruelly put down the peasant revolt. Pugachev, a fugitive Don Cossack, acting under the guise of a miraculously rescued Peter III (Catherine's husband), managed to gain popularity not only among the serfs, but also among provincial law officers. By the end of 1775, Catherine and her court had issued an edict that was supposed to grant amnesty to all the accused officers and even consign to "eternal oblivion"[1] all charges against them. The manifesto put an end to a terrible period of unrest during which the Russian government faced the serious threat of civil war.

In 1774 the war with the Ottoman Porte was over; the victory strengthened Russia's status in the South and lead to the peaceful annexation of the Crimea in 1783. A period of peace started on July 10, 1774 (when Russia signed a peace treaty with Turkey) and continued for 13 years. This era became the apogee of Catherine's glory and success. The second period of Catherine's reign reached its peak in 1782–1783, when the monument to Peter I was erected and Catherine celebrated the twentieth anniversary of her ascension to the throne. The new era required a different mythology to represent the empress, and the culture immediately began to develop

---

[1] A. S. Pushkin, *Sobranie sochinenii v 10 tomakh*, 7 (Moscow, 1962), 103.

a new symbolism of power. Given the new situation, a mythology of splendor, prosperity, and happiness for the entire nation under Catherine proved to be the most auspicious for a successful reign.

On July 16, 1775, the Russian court was busy organizing elaborate festivities in Moscow on the occasion of Russia's victory over the Turks. While living in the favorite palace of Peter's father, tsar Aleksei Mikhailovich, located in the Moscow suburb of Kolomenskoe, Catherine II worked on drafting new laws and, at the same time, extensively discussed the plans for the upcoming celebration with her foreign correspondents. In a letter to Grimm, she gave a detailed account of her proposal:

> "The plans put forth for the celebration were the same as usual: the temples of Janus, Bacchus, and various other devils; all those stupid, unbearable allegories, and of an immense size at that; in short, an extraordinary effort to produce something senseless. I had become angry with all these schemes, and one fine morning, I summoned Bazhenov, my architect. I said to him: "My dear Bazhenov, there is a meadow located three miles from Moscow. Imagine that the meadow is the Black Sea; there are two roads from here to the city: one will be Tanais (the ancient name of the river Don. — V. P.), and the other will be Borysphen (the Dnepr river. — V. P.) You will build a cantina on the estuary of the first one and call it Azov, and you will erect a theater on the estuary of the second, called Kinburn. You will create the Crimean peninsula out of sand. There will be ballrooms set up in Kerch and Enikale (two towns that the Turks had recently given up. — V. P.) To the left of Tanais, there will be a buffet with wine and refreshments for people. In front of the Crimea, we will have an illumination that expresses the joy of both countries on the occasion of the peace treaty. There will be fireworks on the other side of the Danube. You will also distribute boats and vessels all around the area designated for the Black Sea. All along the rivers (that are roads at the same time), you will place pictures, windmills, trees, and illuminated homes. Thus, I will have a celebration without any frills, done in a simple way. <...> At least, it will not be worse than the absurd pagan cathedrals that made me sick."[2]

---

[2] *Russkii Arkhiv*, 3 (1878), 16–17.

Catherine disapproved of the old Baroque ceremonies and instead planned a new kind which she considered "simple." In actuality, the design was not so simple; it featured a symbolic geography in which the slightly transformed landscape of a Moscow suburb corresponded to the real battleground. A new space relating to the "reality" of the recent war became the court playground where the empress, her courtiers and the people found themselves the players in a splendid performance. If the allegorical places (i.e., the pagan gods' temples) clearly revealed the artificial essence of the ceremony, Catherine's endeavor, though it imitated genuine places, shifted the event to a higher level of symbolism. This duality pervaded the festivities: the artificial homes, rivers, and trees made a peculiar combination with the real theater, ballrooms, and buffet. The natural became unnatural, while the artificial was supposed to look much more authentic. Catherine's design expressed her complete control not over the war (which she had won), but over the image of the war. In rejecting the traditional scenario, she attempted to be in command not only of the political situation (a real war), but also of the cultural paradigm of its representation.

It was also very characteristic that she wanted to portray the "joy" of the people. The image of a happy nation enjoying peace and prosperity was of great political importance at that time. Vasilii Maikov, in his work *Description of the ceremonial buildings in Khodynka*, makes the metaphors of happiness and prosperity even more explicit:

> "Azov, where the dining hall was, exhibited abundance as a result of the peace <...> Kerch and Enikale, where the halls and galleries for masquerades were, depicted the delight of different peoples at having become subjects of Russia."[3]

The poems of the time take as their main motifs *happiness, celebration,* and *excitement.* In his *Ode on the Arrival of Her Majesty in Moscow in January of 1775 (Ода на прибытие Ея Величества в Москву. В Генваре 1775),* Mikhail Kheraskov exhibits the common feeling of having transitioned from gloomy anxiety to pure delight:

---

[3] Vasilii Maikov, *Izbrannye proizvedeniia,* 307–308.

> Moscow! Decorate your head with flowers,
> Take a green branch in your arms,
> Appear in the best of your beauty!
> Cover roads with flowers,
> Open your soul and palaces,
> Rejoice, celebrate, enjoy!⁴

The new era was understood to be a renaissance of science, art, and literature. Ippolit Bogdanovich, following the new political agenda, started a political and literary magazine called *The Collection of News* in September of 1775. In his first issue, he declares:

> "We can say that we are now living in a time of exceptional joy and tranquility which has been restored throughout the land by the unflagging concern of our glorious Empress: in which the foreign war is over, in which domestic rebellions and uprisings have been destroyed, in which the exhausted people rest in the bosom of tranquility and benevolence, when abundance, science, and the arts are once again on the rise; therefore the Muses have discovered an unlimited field, having celebrated the triumphant empress, to glorify the peace, silence, and felicity of her subjects."⁵

Bogdanovich's *manifesto* opened the doors to fresh cultural paradigms. The old Baroque tradition of comparing Catherine to such figures as Minerva, the Amazon Queen, Augustus, Virgil's Astraea, and Pallas, lost its appeal. The old-fashioned sanctification of the monarch as the earthly embodiment of a deity gradually evaporated. The empress herself expressed her dissatisfaction with the Baroque system of allegoric identification. She began softening her own imperial image: she made the official court ceremonies less official and avoided pompous receptions. Eventually, she transformed court life into a salon led by an educated lady of taste, not by the empress. Vasilii Kliuchevskii pointed out that, overall, the court under Catherine became more civilized and polite. ⁶ Catherine behaved with her courtiers and servants as though

---

⁴ M. Keraskov, *Tvoreniia*, Vol. 7 (1799), 152–153.
⁵ *Sobranie novostei*, 9 (1775), 4.
⁶ V. O. Kliuchevskii, *Sochineniia*, 5 (1989), 26.

she was with friends.⁷ She conducted herself as a private person at court ceremonies: she played cards or chess, listened to music, and had vivid and quite informal talks with those around her. Her contemporary Lev Engelgardt writes in his *Memoirs*:

> "Once a week, there were gatherings in the Hermitage, sometimes accompanied by theatrical performances; they invited only the most famous; all formalities were forbidden there; the empress, having forgotten, so to speak, her royal position, treated everyone cordially; there were rules established against etiquette; those who forgot them were required, as a kind of punishment, to read several verses from the *Tilemakhida*, an old poem by Trediakovskii."⁸

A playful punishment — to read Trediakovskii's translation of Fénelon's *The Adventures of Telemachus*, rendered into Russian in old-fashioned hexameters — testified to an obvious shift in cultural tastes. The poem's epic grandeur as well as its complicated and heavy style made it an easy target for enlightened ridicule. The empress made all possible efforts to present herself not only as a human being, but as a witty one as well. The second phase of Catherine's rule exhibited a clear search for a *new style*.

Derzhavin was very perceptive to this new trend and actively developed innovative ways of representing royal power in literary forms. In 1777, he composed an ode written in a newfangled manner and devoted to the birth of Catherine's beloved grandson Alexander (the future emperor Alexander I). His ode, entitled *On the birth in the North of a Royal Scion*, gives a playful account of the gifts bestowed upon the newborn by the gods of fate, the Genii. One Genius brings "beauty of the body," another one, "beauty of the soul."⁹ Then, the baby is given the gifts of riches, abundance, divine insight, and reason. Finally, the last Genius presents him with an original gift:

---

[7] Richard S. Wortman wrote: "At court functions, she appeared as an effacing and friendly companion of her servitors and favorites." (Richard S. Wortman, *Scenarios of Power*, 132.)

[8] L. N. Engel'gardt, *Zapiski* (Moscow, 1997), 45.

[9] *Sochineniia Derzhavina*, 1, 51. The translation is taken from the book G. R. Derzhavin, *Poetic Works. A Bilingual Album*. Ed. By A. Levitsky (Providence, 2001), 144.

> But the last, who wished to waken
> Virtue in the infant, said:
> May you govern well your passions,
> Hold the throne, yet be — a man![10]

Dwelling upon the concept of the imperial essence, Derzhavin, for the first time in the Russian odic tradition, considered human characteristics to be even more valuable than divine ones. He did not know what Catherine herself, right at the same time, wished for her grandson, as she stated in her letter to Grimm: "It is pity that Fairies went out of fashion: they endowed a child with everything you could want. I would generously reward them and whisper my wish: "A nature, give him a nature, my dear ladies.""[11] Undoubtedly Derzhavin was unfamiliar with the empress's personal correspondence at that time, but somehow he managed to echo this new cultural turn toward the softening and the humanization of the sovereign's image. Derzhavin suggested that to be a king meant to be a great man, to have character and feelings.

The quest for a cultural change concerned not only courtly ceremonies and literary works. The visual arts quickly appropriated this new tendency as well. Thus, the most famous portrait of Catherine, painted by Dmitrii Levitskii in 1783 (designed by Derzhavin's close friend, the poet, artist, and architect Nikolai L'vov)[12] shows the empress wearing a small, so-called "civil" crown; there is an altar where she burns poppies, a symbol of peace. Her dress is decorated with the ribbon and the order of Saint Vladimir. Catherine established the order in September of 1782, as a civic parallel to the military order of Saint George. The order was designed to recognize personal and civic achievements regardless of dynastic or courtly rank differentiations, in contradistinction to the two orders introduced by Peter I to honor the royal family and highest man and woman at court: the order of Saint Andrew the First Called and the order of Saint Catherine.[13] In exhibiting the

---

[10] Ibid.

[11] *Russkii Arkhiv*, 3 (1878), 39.

[12] *Sochineniia Derzhavina*, 3, 486.

[13] See the discussion on the orders in Chapter 1.

order of Saint Vladimir, the artist and designer (as well as Catherine herself) sought to portray a much more civic and private image of the empress as well as a peaceful Russian government that was preoccupied not with war, but with law (represented by several books placed at her feet) and trade (the staff of the god Mercury, the protector of trade, is painted on the Russian flag).

It was also very important that Levitskii wrote a detailed commentary in which he explained and stressed his painting's political symbolism. His description appeared in the literary magazine the *Interlocutor of the Admirers of Russian Letters (Собеседник любителей Российского слова)* edited by Ekaterina Dashkova with Catherine's active participation.[14] Derzhavin relied a great deal upon Levitskii's model for the description of Catherine in his poem *A Vision of Murza (Видение Мурзы)*:

> A crested crown adorned her tresses,
> Upon her breast — a sash of gold;
> Of jetty tissue, flame-black byssus
> All rainbow-hued, her mantle's fold
> Cascading, fell from her left shoulder
> Along her left flank thence to lie,
> Her arm outstretched above the altar,
> She, onto sacrificial fire
> The sweetly fragrant poppies pouring,
> Made worship unto the Most High <…>[15]

After her victory over the Pugachev rebellion, Catherine positioned herself as the empress of the gentry, demonstrating her protection, support and friendship towards the gentry as a class. In 1775, she began a series of significant political and social reforms that aimed to organize the gentry into an independent, enlightened, and, at the same time, loyal and reliable force. In general, all of Catherine's famous reforms of the second part of the 1770s to the 1780s carried out the political task of unifying the different groups of the Russian gentry: the provincial and the courtly, aristocratic

---

[14] *Sobesednik liubitelei rossiiskogo slova*, 6 (1783), 18–19.
[15] Sochinenia Derzhavina, I, 108. The translation is taken from the book G. R. Derzhavin, *Poetic Works*, 40.

nobles, as well as the officers in the military and civil service who were promoted to the ranks and entitled to personal or hereditary nobility, according to the Table of Ranks, established in 1722 by Peter the Great.

In 1775, the Manifesto on Free Enterprise was issued, followed by a major administrative reform that concerned the status of the provinces. In 1782, the Police Code appeared, followed by the Charter to the Gentry in 1785. These reforms were enacted to strengthen and consolidate the gentry as a class and to establish a social contract by a system of rules. The authorities invited the gentry to form a partnership. Derzhavin, in his *Felitsa (Фелица)*, put the contents of these edicts in verse.

Catherine cultivated the concept of the patronal monarchy based on a direct relationship between the throne and the gentry without political arbitration or intervening social institutions. The notion of a parliament as such an institution was completely buried in 1782 when the empress forced Nikita Panin, the main proponent of the aristocratic legislative body, to retire.

In Felitsa, Derzhavin attempts to put Catherine's political strategy into verse. As a result, he combines the new concept of a patronal monarchy with the old vision of a king's sacred power. He does not reject the latter, but he strives to make it more "modern." Paradoxically, he comes to the conclusion that a ruler's divine nature is embodied in a system of state laws. Derzhavin writes:

> 'Tis you alone who wounds no feelings,
> Nor gives offence to anyone;
> Toward foolishness you can be tolerant
> But suffer evil not a whit.
> Misdeeds you treat with condescension;
> As wolves do sheep, you choke no people,
> But know wherein their merit lies.
> To rulers' wills are people subjects,
> But to their righteous God more greatly,
> Who lives within their very laws.[16]

---

[16] *Sochineniia Derzhavina*, 1, 87. The translation is taken from the book G. R. Derzhavin, *Poetic Works*, 32.

Earlier, in his ode *On the Departure of Her Highness to Byelorussia (На отсутствие Ея Величества в Белоруссию)*, written in 1780, Derzhavin already made the first sketches of this concept. Addressing the empress who had traveled to the newly acquired lands, Derzhavin calls out:

> Come back — and make your laws
> Sacred with you <...>[17]

Later, in a draft of his poem *A Vision of Mirza,* Derzhavin conveys the same concept even more openly:

> Ones did not recognize at all
> The God made dwelling in your laws.[18]

In Derzhavin's poetry, the sanctity of the laws and edicts established by Catherine in the 1770s–1780s, coexists with the old-fashioned perception of the king as a model of behavior. The poet implements the notion that the king's life (like the life of Christ) serves as a pattern to be emulated. In his *Felitsa*, Derzhavin appeals to Catherine (though not without a hidden irony!) in order to obtain moral instructions on how to be happy:

> Felitsa, help me with instructions
> On living uprightly but well,
> On taming passions' agitation
> And being happy on the earth![19]

However, the poet also alludes to modern notions in his text: he seeks models of happiness, not of morality. The search for personal happiness as well as a meditation on the different ways of acquiring a happy life pervades the whole poem.

Meanwhile, a shift toward the ideology of social harmony, that is, a peaceful partnership between the sovereign and her noble subjects, posed new cultural challenges. The allegories of

---

[17] *Sochineniia Derzhavina,* 1, 62.

[18] Ibid, 117.

[19] Ibid, 83–84. The translation is taken from the book G. R. Derzhavin, *Poetic Works,* 28.

the classical ode gradually lost their attractiveness as vehicles for representing power. Derzhavin as well as his friends and literary allies Vasilii Kapnist, Ivan Khemnitser, and Nikolai L'vov disdained the old, cumbersome machinery of solemn odes and epic poems. They put forward instead small genres and the so-called "light poetry." They proclaimed the clarity of style and language, thereby dramatically diminishing the usage of archaisms. Dwelling upon the neo-classical hierarchy which determined the appropriate style and language for a given subject, they began deconstructing the system, choosing instead to describe the private life of kings and modest peasants with the simple means of a neutral language. The old-fashioned style of praising the empress, practiced by poets such as Vasilii Petrov and Vasilii Ruban, looked quite outmoded, and they soon became the constant objects of ridicule.[20] The new post-war age of peace, happiness, and prosperity brought new configurations of culture, and the empress found herself their architect.

Patronizing the Russian Muses

At the beginning of the 1780s, the Russian authorities undertook one of the most visible invasions into the literary field in order to consolidate the most appropriate tendencies. Catherine strove to institutionalize culture as well as to incorporate it into the civil service and, therefore, to control it. Quite incidentally, Princess Dashkova, who returned in 1782 from her life abroad in quasi-exile, was invited to reprise her role as Catherine's cultural emissary. Twenty years prior, both had, side by side, taking command of the army in order to take political control of Russia. Now, the empress mobilized Dashkova, with her enormous energy, to initiate cultural institutions and, at the same time, to maintain the necessary control over them.

On October 30, 1783, the empress issued an order which established the Russian Academy, with Dashkova as president. Even earlier, at the beginning of 1783, the Saint Petersburg

---

[20] Ilia Serman, "Derzhavin v krugu druzei-poetov," in *Gavrila Derzhavin. Simposium devoted to his 250th Anniversary* (Norwich, 1995), 321.

Academy of Science, founded by Peter I in 1724, had been entrusted to Dashkova's leadership. While the latter dealt with science, the former was devoted to the humanities. As a result, they published the first *Complete Works by Mikhail Vasilievich Lomonosov* in six parts (1784–1787) and began intensive work on the *Academic Dictionary of the Russian Language*.

The Russian Academy was based on the assumption that language and literature — *the letters* — could unify, consolidate, form and eventually, represent the nation as well as its political or economic forces. Dashkova's appointment was not temporary and politically neutral. It acknowledged the central role of the empress in shaping and patronizing culture: the empress simply delegated her power to her cultural emissary. The newly founded magazine the *Interlocutor* was meant to be a laboratory and, at the same time, an exhibition of a new cultural trend.

In terms of her cultural strategy, Catherine relied upon the model of the French Academy, which was founded in 1635 by Cardinal Richelieu, the chief minister of France. Attempting to replace the decreasing role of the king's sacred image with a more rational system of incorporating *gents de letters* into the state's service, the French authorities organized cultural institutions in order to formulate new ways of ensuring the king's power. While the king claimed to be equal to the state or nation, his cultural ambassadors tried to unite all of them by regulating the French language.

The Académie française was devoted to letters and was, first and foremost, responsible for the codification of French grammar and spelling as well as the development of French literature. The so-called "small Academy" of language and literature — in contradistinction to the Academy of science — played a central role in organizing and patronizing culture. It was also significant that initially, the French Academy grew out of literary circles and salons. Later, in the time of Louis XIV, royal minister Jean-Batiste Colbert successfully carried out the reorganization of academic and cultural life.[21]

---

[21] Jean-Marie Apostolidès, *Le roi-machine. Spectacle et politique au temps de Louis XIV* (Paris, 1981), 29.

Catherine's imitation of the French Academy was clear to her contemporaries. The French diplomat Chevalier de Corberon noticed that "a new Russian Academy was established after the model of the French Academy."[22] The poetess Maria Sushkova, in her epistle written under the mask of a Chinese man, published in the *Interlocutor* and addressed to the famous Murza-Derzhavin, declares:

> Befriending the Muses and producing exhilaration,
> France ascended to the sky in recent times
> Not by the power of the sword, but through her enlightenment;
> She provides models in taste and science,
> The language, renowned with excellent authors,
> Developed into a universal tongue in all of Europe.
> Therefore, the age of Louis, praised by the Muses,
> Afterward is shining in immortal glory.
>
> This is, Russian Muses, your great destiny!
> You should seek to rise up similar honors!
> How can you be silent? Catherine herself
> Gives you protection and revives your voices.
> Oh what a beautiful field is opened for you!
> You ought not to mix any fables into your songs.
> You should only sing wisdom on the throne,
> Describing simply the Russian Golden Age as well.[23]

The poem advocates several positions at once. First, it indicates the paradigm to imitate (France) and pays tribute to the efforts of the French Academy in strengthening the country by supporting her excellent writers. Second, it underscores the advantages of enlightenment over force. It also outlines the themes to be elaborated upon (Catherine II and the Golden Age in Russia under her rule.) Finally, it stresses that the empress herself supports the poets; therefore, they should not refrain from praising her — in a new, "simple" way. In addition, the poem written to Murza from a humble Chinese man apparently pretended to be a programmatic

---

[22] *Un diplomate français à la court de Catherine II. 1775–1780. Journal intime du chevalier de Corberon*, I (Paris, 1901), 119.

[23] *Sobesednik*, 9 (1783), 21.

declaration, a claim to express a new cultural situation and a new style as well.

Despite an obvious orientation toward France, the Russian situation proved to be different. Salon culture did not exist in Russia in the eighteenth century, and the court remained an almost unique initiator and architect of cultural renovation. As a result of Richelieu's and Colbert's reforms, France developed a very productive cultural paradigm. While the French Academy cultivated the state-oriented, serious art which corresponded to the masculine community, the salons were the kingdom of women who promoted a playful style of conversation, gallant ridicule, and the central role of a witty woman.[24]

In Russia, Catherine did not want to promote salons outside her palace walls. Salons stand for a measure of equality among members. The Russian empress wanted to be the center of a salon-like culture developed and propagated by her courtiers and sponsored writers. *Despite the fact that she accepted some elements of salon culture (witty conversation, light style, new genres), she refused to establish equality. Catherine promoted an amusing style and a new trend in culture — in an authoritarian way.* She had to be entertained, not the other way around.

The Birth of Felitsa

In the 1780s, Derzhavin composed a set of odes which were united by their political rhetoric, their dedication to the empress Catherine-Felitsa, and the concept of the so-called "amusing style": *Felitsa* (1782), *Thanksgiving to Felitsa* (Благодарность Фелице; 1783), *To Reshemysl* (1783) (the first publication of the ode contained the subtitle: "written in imitation of the ode to Felitsa"), *A Vision of Murza* (1784; 1791), *To Fortune* (1789), and *A Portrait of Felitsa* (1789).

The first ode, *Felitsa*, composed by the end of 1782, established paradigms that represented the second period of Catherine's

---

[24] Dena Goodman, *The Republic of Letters. A Cultural History of the French Enlightenment* (Ithaca & London, 1994, 130); Benedetta Craveri, *The Age of Conversation* (New York, 2005), 27–44.

administration as the apogee of the Russian kingdom. This playful ode was devoted to Catherine, who is disguised in the text as Felitsa. The Latin word *felicitas* means happiness and became a key word of the moment. The triumphant empress wanted to be placed among civilized, happy, and unified society. The new epoch brought in a new ideological program, along with prosperity, abundance, grandeur, and, especially, the happiness of the nation under Catherine, which became the most important focus of her rule.

The name of the protagonist of Derzhavin's poem refers to the heroine of Catherine's own literary work, the *Tale of Prince Chlorus (Сказка о царевиче Хлоре)*, written in 1781 and devoted to her beloved grandson Alexander. Wrapped in the fashionable garb of the oriental tale, quite popular in French and German literature, the story depicts a young boy (Prince Chlorus) who is abducted by the Khan and forced to search for "a Rose without thorns." He goes on several adventures, meets the Kyrgyz-Kaisak Tsarina Felitsa and her son Rassudok (Reason), and eventually scales a mountain that has the rose in question. The tale provides an allegoric lesson about a young boy whose wrong passions lead him away from the road of virtue and reason (the meaning of the abduction of a young boy). Eventually, the wise council of Felitsa and her son restores him to his home — an allegoric embodiment of good moral character.

By exploiting the popular genre of the oriental tale, which was introduced by Joseph Addison and refined by Voltaire,[25] Catherine attempts to foster this European tradition in Russian culture. Quite significantly, she chooses, as an oriental *couleur local*, the Kyrgyz-Kaisak setting to emphasize the extensive dimensions of her empire, which stretched out from Europe to Asia, from the Northern seas to the Southern steppes. The term "Kyrgyz-Kaisaks" refers here to the nomadic Kazakh population that occupied the steppes between the Urals and the Volga River. At that time, Russian readers had only foggy ideas about the ethnic, linguistic

---

[25] Marta Pike Conant, *The Oriental Tale in England in the Eighteenth Century* (New York, 1908); Katerine Astrury, *The Moral Tale in France and Germany 1750–1789* (Oxford, 2002.) On Addison and Derzhavin see Pierre R. Hart, *G. R. Derzhavin: A Poet's Progress* (Columbus, 1978), 52–53.

and religious roots of this people. The tale carries out a dual task: it provides moral instructions wrapped in a delightful and fashionable cover, and, at the same time, implies a colonial subtext. The peaceful and playful setting did not contain any hints to the recent and troublesome circumstances involving the participation of Kyrgyz-Kaisaks in the Pugachev rebellion. Instead, the tale — in an imaginative way — undertook a literary acquisition of this remote territory.

An appeal to the far-off corners of the Empire, to its extreme poles, usually served as a vehicle to convey the image of a triumphant sovereign. Thus, the full title of Derzhavin's poem is *Ode to a Wise Kyrgyz-Kaisak Tsarina Felitsa, Written by the Tatar Murza Who Had Settled in Moscow Long Ago, and Lives in Saint Petersburg on Business*. *Felitsa*, as do the other odes in this cycle, exposes an unfolding story of a special relationship between the Empress, personified as the Kyrgyz-Kaisak Tsarina, and Derzhavin, represented by the Tatar Murza.

Derzhavin borrowed his literary mask from Addison's prose tale *A Vision of Murza*, published in 1711 in the *Spectator*. The fact that Derzhavin's poem has the same title proves his acquaintance with the British tale, which had been translated into Russian by Grigorii Kozitskii in 1757. The tale enjoyed enormous popularity, and Catherine also was most likely familiar with the text, since she knew its translator very well. Kozitskii was Catherine's state secretary (a position he had held since 1768) and even earlier worked as an assistant on the empress's literary works and translations. Meanwhile, appealing to this popular trend was not only a tribute to the genre form. Stressing the "outskirts" associations of both names symbolized the imperial context of the dialogue between the poet and the empress.

Since that time, Derzhavin liked to emphasize his Tatar origins. He called his verses "the Tatar songs," and later, an honorary ancestry was provided for "Tatar Murza" in his poem *My Queen! (Монархиня!)*. This poem was a lyric dedication to Catherine that began a manuscript collection of Derzhavin's works and was presented to the empress on November 6, 1795. In his introductory verses, Derzhavin makes a reference to his ancestor

Bagrim, a descendent of the Golden Horde enlisted in the troops of the Russian Prince Vasilii the Dark. Derzhavin writes:

> When long forgotten is Bagrim and his last scion <...>[26]

The author's glorious pedigree elevated the status of the dialogue with a tsar, and gave the Tatar Murza the exclusive status of being a representative of an old noble family accustomed to being in the service of the Russian court. Among the Russian gentry, Tatar origins indicated a prestigious lineage, dating back at least three centuries. Thus, in praising Felitsa under the mask of the Tatar Murza, Derzhavin relies upon a section of the Russian noblemen as though they were the whole class.

Derzhavin's intertextual links with Catherine's tale were not limited to a mere oriental facade. In his extended commentary on *Felitsa*, Derzhavin gives an explanation for his newly elaborated method:

> "The model for such an ode <...> was the tale about Chlorus composed by the Empress. As Madam liked amusing jokes, I wrote my poem in a manner she loved, addressing her circle, with lots of mockery and pranks, though avoiding any spitefulness."[27]

In producing the playful ode *Felitsa*, Derzhavin, once again, declared that the empress began the method. Indeed, Catherine's *Tale of Prince Chlorus* introduced an allegoric narrative which was filled with allusions to her closest courtiers. Readers easily recognized Prince Potemkin in Lentiaga-Murza (the Lazy Murza) and Prince A. A. Viazemskii in Bruzga (the Grumbler). The same readers had no trouble identifying the wise tsarina Felitsa, the mother of the young Rassudok (Reason), as the empress. The tale's moral message coexisted with some gallant ridicule. In this way, the imperial power indicated its desire for laughter. Derzhavin perceived this signal, and by the end of 1782, he had composed his *Felitsa*.

---

[26] *Sochineniia Derzhavina*, I, 492. The translation is taken from the book G. R. Derzhavin, *Poetic Works*, 15.

[27] Ibid, 3, 482.

The Birth of a Literary Myth

Felitsa's publication quickly acquired the features of a literary myth. First, Derzhavin made his literary friends (Kapnist, L'vov, and Khemnitser) acquainted with his new work. Despite their enthusiastic approval of the ode, the poets dissuaded Derzhavin from publishing it: they believed that the unusual ode contained too many pointedly satiric hints toward the powerful boyars. The poem remained concealed in Derzhavin's bureau for a year. Then, the situation was altered dramatically.

Derzhavin observed a change of literary taste among Catherine's courtiers. According to his memoirs, some influential people in Catherine's court (I. I. Shuvalov, A. P. Shuvalov, A. A. Bezborodko, and P. V. Zavadovskii) expressed their concern about the absence of a "light and entertaining poetry" in Russia.[28] In response to this statement, Derzhavin's acquaintance Osip Kozodavlev, a future executive editor of the *Interlocutor*, mustered the courage to recite the ode as evidence of the existence of a new poetry in Russia. The privileged audience highly appreciated the ode. Meanwhile, Derzhavin stressed the hesitation among experienced courtiers about the propriety of publishing such an ode. Ivan Shuvalov, a former favorite of Elizaveta Petrovna, especially opposed making the ode public. The old-fashioned mastermind of court intrigues was more concerned about Potemkin's reaction than ever. He apparently did not grasp that a new fashion had arrived at the Russian court.[29]

By contrast, Kozodavlev immediately valued the poem's innovative quality, as he makes clear in his article entitled *Historical, Philosophical, and Critical Considerations on the Rise and Fall of the Interlocutor* (1784). He was very close to Dashkova, and he shared his excitement with his high-ranking patron. The ode *Felitsa* gave Dashkova the idea to organize a new magazine, and so the *Interlocutor* was born. Finally, the first issue came out with the ode in May of 1783. Soon after that, according to this account, Dashkova was summoned to the empress early in the morning. Frightened,

---

[28] Ibid, 483.
[29] Ibid.

Dashkova rushed to the palace and, to her great surprise, found Catherine in tears, with the magazine in her hands. Catherine calmed Dashkova down and cordially inquired about the author "who knew her so well and could portray her so delightfully, that she began to cry like a fool."[30]

Afterward, a playful scenario began to develop. A few days later while dining at the house of his supervisor Prince A. A. Viazemskii, Derzhavin received a letter with a golden snuff-box and 500 gold rubles inside. The letter was signed: *Orenburg, from Kyrgyz Tsarina to Murza*. This impressive gesture of royal confidence made Derzhavin the leader of modern poetry overnight. Derzhavin had been awarded the status of a poet with whom the empress enjoyed making jokes (as Vladislav Khodasevich rightly pointed out).[31]

Catherine was happy to identify herself with Derzhavin's image of a kind, witty, truly liberal-minded tsarina who allowed her subjects to disapprove of her. Amazingly, soon after that episode, in order to conform to the accepted role of Felitsa, Catherine sent a secret decree to the Tambov province ordering that the sentences of all criminals who had been accused of crimes against the empress be commuted. The new dress and its tailor were warmly embraced.[32]

The imperial authority stopped modeling itself on the old patterns of the Roman emperors and heroes, as well as on Greek and Roman mythology. Instead, Catherine expressed her preference for modern salon culture and gallant literary models. She no longer wanted to be compared to Minerva, Titus, or even Augustus. She strove to foster an enlightened and unofficial "republic of letters." She claimed to be the bearer of a culture of laughter, to be part of a civilized system of ridicule. After reading Derzhavin's ode, she underlined verses related to certain boyars and sent them copies of *Felitsa*, with her personal remarks. She established a sort of test: the ability to understand mockery that is directed at oneself and not take offense served as admission to the enlightened community. Catherine even played with Derzhavin's poem, picking up some

---

[30] Ibid, 484.

[31] V. F. Khodasevich, *Derzhavin* (Paris, 1931), 122.

[32] Ia. Grot, *Zhizn' Derzhavina* (Saint Petersburg, 1880), 198.

useful formulas for her own literary endeavors. Thus, in drawing a portrait of a free minded empress who is tolerant of critics, Derzhavin writes with a subtle humor:

> And you do prohibit no one
> To speak of you both in truth and fable.[33]

Starting in June of 1783, just a month after Felitsa came out, Catherine started to publish her own satirical mélanges under the title *Truths and Fables ("Были и небылицы")*, making a clear reference to Derzhavin's verse. There, she ironically chatted with readers about herself and her courtiers, recounted stories that were without plot under the multiple masks of different narrators, and enjoyed her own wit. The work was quite innovative and had tremendous success. In her letters to Baron Melchior Grimm, Catherine proudly called her work the amusing rubbish which makes readers happy.[34] She openly proclaimed that witticisms and a tolerant attitude toward laughter constituted the main qualities of a man of the Enlightenment. This gallant laughter was supposed to demonstrate not only a cultural shift toward light poetry and small entertaining genres, but also the great success of her rule.

The Philosophy of Pleasure

The word *happiness* was understood as a political term. It was associated with the name Felitsa (Catherine) and became the main slogan of the second epoch of her rule. The Russian nobles should be thankful, according to Derzhavin, for the happiness being sent from "high spheres" as a kind of political edict. The "happy age" of a triumphant Catherine began with Derzhavin's *Felitsa* in 1782–1783 and ended in 1791 with Derzhavin's *Description of a celebration organized on the occasion of the capture of Ismail in the house of the General-Fieldmarshal Prince Potemkin-Tavricheskii in the presence of Catherine II.*

---

[33] *Sochineniia Derzhavina*, I, 87.

[34] "Pis'ma Imperatritsy Ekateriny II k Grimmu," 281.

Derzhavin became renowned for his ideologically correct and politically motivated descriptions of the paradise under Catherine's rule in the 1780s. He exceeded himself in creating a mesmerizing panorama of the everyday life of the Russian gentry, in which he depicted them enjoying an eternal holiday and an endless chain of carnal pleasures. This gastronomic and erotic bliss was meant to symbolize the triumph, abundance, and splendor of Catherine's time. The word "holiday" also became a key-word of the epoch. In his *Felitsa*, Derzhavin writes about these banquets with a solemn gravity:

> Or I am at a sumptuous banquet,
> Which has been tended in my name,
> Where gold and silver deck the table,
> Where courses by thousands come;
> The famed Westphalian ham is served there,
> And fish of Astrakhan in slices;
> Pilaff and pirogi in mounds,
> I wash down waffles with champagne
> And leave my worldly cares behind me
> Midst sweetmeats, wines, and nice aromas.[35]

Meanwhile this inventory of dishes not only played an aesthetic role (the use of such material was a provocative innovation in terms of the odic tradition), but it also contained political connotations. The "thousands of courses" from around the world, and especially from the exotic provinces of Russia, signified achievements in economy and commerce as well as in colonial policy.

Meanwhile, there was a metaphysical foundation underneath Derzhavin's poetic cult of abundance and his well-known ability to imbue his verses with detailed descriptions of life, the luxuries of food and wine, and even the joys of Eros. The exceptional attention he paid to the material world was not a mere tribute to the so-called "realistic" tendency of his style. Rather, it demonstrated his respect for plenitude and the large variety of substances and beings in the universe. In accordance with the post-Leibnitzian vision of the

---

[35] *Sochinrniia Derzhavina*, I, 84–85. The translation is taken from G. R. Derzhavin, *Poetic Works*, 19.

world, every element has its place and reason to exist within a *great chain of being*. Every grain of sand has its place in a strict hierarchy that makes up the chain. Each level is considered to be constant, coherent, and limited only by the death of a particular "grain of sand."[36]

The theory of the Great Chain of Being was as popular in the eighteenth century as the theory of evolution was in the nineteenth. After Leibniz, there were Milton and Fénelon, Addison and Pope, Diderot and Goldsmith, Locke and Buffon who contributed to the theory's discourse. The concept had a strong impact on poetry, inspiring the two major sources of Derzhavin's verse: the Prussian emperor and philosopher Frederick II the Great and the British poet Edward Jung. Derzhavin's early poetic experiments of the 1770s, such as *Odes, Translated and Composed near Mount Chitalgai in 1774 (Оды, переведенные и сочиненные при горе Читалгае в 1774)*, dealt with German translations of Frederick's French poems *Poésies diverses*.[37] Later, Derzhavin was deeply influenced by Jung's *Night Thoughts* (three Russian translations of the book had come out by the beginning of the 1780s).[38]

Derzhavin apparently introduced the theory's paradigms into his poems. There he found theological grounds for his famous poem *God (Бог)*, which was published in the *Interlocutor* (1784) The assumption that man occupies a transitional position between the higher spiritual world and the lower physical world in a great chain of being reflected the European quest to combine religion, science, and politics. In his poem *God*, Derzhavin declares:

---

[36] Arthur O. Lovejoy, *The Great Chain of Being. A Study of the History of an Idea* (Cambridge, 1948), 184.

[37] Anna Lisa Crone, *The Daring of Derzhavin.The Moral and Aesthetic Independence of the Poet in Russia* (Bloomington, 2001), 117–126.

[38] The first works on Jung's influence on Derzhavin appeared already in the nineteenth century. Ia. K. Grot made a detailed comparison of the first *Night* and Derzhavin's poem *The God* (*Sochineniia Derzhavina*, I, 142–143.) On Jung's influence on Derzhavin see Iu. D. Levin, "Angliiskaia poeziia i literatura russkogo sentimentalizma", in *Ot klassitsizma k romantizmu* (Leningrad, 1970), 210–223; Jane Harris, "Derzhavin i Iung: K voprosu o vliianii perevodov na literaturnyi protsess," in *Gavrila Derzhavin. Simposium devoted to his 250th Anniversary*, 202–223.

> A fraction of the universe's whole,
> I put, it seems, in a worthy spot
> Midway between where you finished
> The creation of corporeal beasts,
> And started that of the heavenly spirits:
> Through me, you linked together the chain of being. [39]

Derzhavin's famous juxtaposition "I am a God — I am a worm" (instead of a "worm" here it could also be a "grain of sand," or "fraction") reflects the most popular dyad for defining the vertical poles of the great chain of being.[40] According to the theory, plenitude and a strict structure prevent any transformations: there is no possibility for beings created by God to change levels for any reason. As every being created by God is reasonable and perfect, therefore man, with his sins and his routine and idle everyday life, should also be understood as "reasonable." As Edward Jung writes in his *Night First*:

> How poor, how rich, how abject, how august,
> How complicate, how wonderful, is man![41]

The only consolation for a man, according to this concept, is to live his life and enjoy his existence without reproach. The optimism of these speculations consists in the pathos of joy, happiness, and pleasure that were destined for men by the nature of their "level." Participating in this discourse, Derzhavin describes varied and boundless feasts of pleasure in his *Felitsa*. He even makes the blissful statement: "You see, Felitsa, my debauchery!"[42] All debauchery should be forgiven since man is destined for such behavior and sin. Confined to a strict level in the ladder of beings, man cannot not be

---

[39] *Sochineniia Derzhavina*, I, 132. Compare with Jung's *Night I. Life, Death, and Immortality*: "Distinguished link in being's endless chain! / Midway from nothing to the Deity!" See Edward Young *Night Thoughts* (Boston, 1841), 27.

[40] Arthur O. Lovejoy, *The Great Chain of Being. A Study of the History of an Idea*, 249–250. On the influence of the concept see Thomas Barran, *Russia Reads Rousseau, 1762–1825* (Evanston, 2002), 173–180.

[41] Edward Jung, *Night Thoughts*, 7.

[42] *Sochinrniia Derzhavina*, I, 84–85. The translation is taken from G. R. Derzhavin, *Poetic Works*, 31.

seriously penalized for his transgressions. Mankind is practically unable to change or has only limited possibilities for change within a horizontal layer of the entire ladder. The most appropriate attitude would be excitement before the Almighty Creator and a feeling of man's ambiguous nature as a transition between animals (worms) and higher beings (kings, angels, God).

The concept had political implications in praising the *status quo* and proclaiming the ruinous nature of social revolutions, civil wars, and the idea of egalitarianism. The theory combined conservatism with philosophical optimism and was harshly ridiculed by Voltaire in his *Candide, or Optimism*. Leibnitzian optimism had influenced German ethics and then formed a pietistic culture that was concerned with the right understanding of happiness and the appropriate ways of reaching it. Catherine's *Tale of Prince Chlorus* exhibits some practical applications of the pietistic moral: "The one who has the strength to overcome all difficulties in his way honestly will be happy."[43] Not by accident, the lyric hero of Derzhavin's ode asks Felitsa to give him instructions on how to be happy on this earth:

> Felitsa, help me with instructions
> On living uprightly but well,
> On taming passions' agitation
> And being happy on this earth.[44]

It was not mere flattery to ask Felitsa-Catherine's advice. It also was not a simple jest with a direct reference to Catherine's *Tale*. Derzhavin had positioned his tsarina above himself and his personae, with a vision of her occupying a structurally higher "level" in a great chain of being, near the angels or God. Rather, he found metaphysical grounds for his poetic veneration.

---

[43] *Sochineniia imperatritsy Ekateriny Vtoroi*, III, 102.
[44] *Sochineniia Derzhavina*, I, 83–84. The translation is taken from G. R. Derzhavin, *Poetic Works*, 28.

Speaking Truth to Sovereigns

According to popular literary mythology, Derzhavin, until his last days, liked to wear the honorable uniform of a poet who dared to reveal an uncompromised truth to the Russian Empress Catherine II. He regarded the poem as a programmatic statement on his public function and usually placed this poem at the end of his works.[45] This "truth," however, was packaged in the palatable form of a "funny Russian style," and he exposed it "with a smile," because he had the privilege of being in the empress's inner circle. Thus, in his poem *Monument* (*Памятник*; 1796), while summarizing the poetic achievements he accomplished during Catherine's reign, Derzhavin makes an almost terminologically clear statement:

> As first to dare proclaim the virtues of Felitsa
> *In Russian in a light and entertaining style*;
> To speak sincerely of the Deity, but simply,
> And with a smile to tell the truth to sovereigns.[46]

Lev Pumpianskii, while commenting on these verses, justly underscores the two important questions here: what and how.[47] Meanwhile, Derzhavin, in his own *Explanations*, rather clearly explains the meaning of this quatrain. He writes: "The author was the first among Russian writers to compose his lyrics in a simple, funny style, and jokingly, praise the Empress; thanks to that he became well known."[48] Behind this modest statement lies a very significant ideological and literary declaration.

The "what," that is, the substance of his odes, was always focused on Catherine. Derzhavin replaces Russian poetry's traditional opposition of *the poet vs. the tsar* with a pair of

---

[45] Pierre R. Hart, *G. R. Derzhavin, A Poet's Progress*, 87.
[46] Translation is taken from the book: Pierre R. Hart, *G. R. Derzhavin*, 87. The deepest examination of the poem *Pamiatnik* see in Yoakhim Klein, *Puti kul'turnogo importa. Trudy po russkoi literature XVIII veka* (Moscow, 2005), 498–520.
[47] L. V. Pumpianskii, "K istorii russkogo klassitsizma, in *L. V. Pumpianskii, Klassicheskaia traditsiia* (Moscow, 2000), 83.
[48] *Sochineniia Derzhavina*, III, 538.

conventional literary masks "the Tatar Murza" and "the Kyrgyz-Kaisak Tsarina." He continues to develop this plot in the subsequent poems of the "*Felitsa* cycle," combining fantasy and reality, fiction and imagination, in a newly created narrative. Murza emphasizes his close relationship with Felitsa, who visits his house and secretly sends him gifts. In his turn, he sings "Tatar songs" to her, and, at the same time, overcomes the intrigues and calumnies of his enemies (*A Vision of Murza*).

Derzhavin considered his approach non-hypocritical and his style simple. In his poem *Thanksgiving to Felitsa*, written in response to Catherine's generous gifts, Derzhavin affirms:

> Since you like a simplicity
> In my non- hypocritical style,
> Listen <...>[49]

The poet renders his dithyrambs to the Empress as the honest expression of a truth (not flattery!) that he dares to reveal, even though he might provoke the vicious intrigues of envious courtiers. Moreover, Derzhavin is so bold as to claim that only he, in his poems, sees a strategy that provides wealth and happiness for the people in the logic of Catherine's political actions. Derzhavin even addresses this almost secret knowledge — *of Catherine's greatness* — not to his jealous contemporaries, but to his more appreciative successors. In his ode *Vision of Murza*, which remained unpublished until 1791 but was well known in literary circles, the poet declares:

> O thou, so virtuous and royal!
> I sang not flattery nor dreams,
> But that to which the world was witness:
> Thy virtue's deeds are fair to see.
> I sang them, and shall sing them always,
> And, jesting, raise on high the **Truth**.
> With Tatar strains, like hidden candles,
> I shall present to future days <...>[50]

---

[49] Ibid, I, 105.
[50] Ibid, 111. The translation is taken from G. R. Derzhavin, *Poetic Works*, 43.

This new approach, as established by Derzhavin, determined the "truth" as the deeds of the empress's virtue, as her greatness, generosity, and kindness. Therefore, Derzhavin introduced a very clever and subtle game. *He told the truth, but his truth was not bitter, but rather sweet.*

Such a new method of representing and praising the sovereign was highly cherished in the *Interlocutor*'s literary circles. Soon after *Felitsa* appeared, one of the magazine's contributors, Maria Sushkova, published her poetic epistle *A Letter from a Chinese man to the Tatar Murza who is Living in Saint Petersburg on Business*. The poem was published in the magazine anonymously under the initials "M. S." The author openly used Derzhavin's playful manner, imitating both his and Catherine's oriental masks (in her introduction, Sushkova informs readers that she had found a piece of paper containing this *Letter* during her travels in China.) Sushkova writes:

> At the edge of the earth we know
> What happens in the other corners.
> In Beijing, O Murza, we read your poems.
> Admiring ***truth***, we say in agreement:
> We see Confucius on the Northern throne.
> For twenty years glory has resounded everywhere:
> A lofty spirit, wisdom, gentle character,
> Commonwealth laws and deeds
> With which you have raised yourself so high,
> The Tsarina of the Northern lands, an exemplary Sovereign,
> Felitsa, lately praised by you, Murza.[51]

Contributors to the *Interlocutor* began at once to cultivate the genre of an epistolary ode that made references to Derzhavin's *Felitsa*. An anonymous author writes in a poem entitled *To My Friend NN*:

> Murza, in his verses to Felitsa,
> Displays only the ***truth***.
> With no flattery to the Tsarina
> He spoke about her deeds.

---

[51] *Sobesednik*, 5 (1783), 6.

> Sounds of truth resonated,
> Tears began to shed
> From many happy eyes <...>
> I would wish, like Murza,
> To describe Felitsa's virtues,
> Like him, in unbounded verse,
> To expose all my feelings <...>[52]

When Derzhavin summarized his lyric achievements in his famous poem *Monument* ("And with a smile to tell the truth to sovereigns") he relied upon the tradition and style which he himself attempted to create. The "daring" of Derzhavin tended to be represented as the unbelievable courage of an individual who spoke the bitter truth to the tsars. The first part of the formula — speaking the truth to sovereigns — does not signify a bitter truth that a courageous liberal mind dares to say to a monarch's face (such was the interpretation unanimously expounded in Soviet literary criticism). Rather, it was a clever rhetorical tool in which the "truth" meant the highest approval of Catherine's politics. Thus, in a letter to Dashkova written in May of 1783, just after the triumph of *Felitsa*, Derzhavin asked his correspondent to send him "some of Felitsa's letters in order to obtain new truths, new manifestations of her soul."[53]

The Liberal Agenda of Catherine-Felitsa

To make Catherine's achievements more apparent, Derzhavin began portraying Catherine II against an historic background that was very peculiar in comparison with the times of the Empress Anna Ivanovna. In *Felitsa*, he clearly juxtaposes Catherine's illuminated era to the time of Anna Ivanovna by emphasizing the latter's unenlightened autocratic approach, the restoration of the Secret Chancellery, her oppressive methods of ruling, her disrespect for the Russian nobles, and the barbaric culture of the court jesters. According to Derzhavin, in Catherine's time, by contrast, the

---

[52] Ibid, 6, 40.
[53] G. R. Derzhavin, *Sochineniia* (Leningrad, 1987), 406.

Russian gentry enjoys tranquility and freedom from the tsar's abusive power:

> There one may whisper conversation,
> And without fear of being punished,
> At dinners not toast sovereigns.
> There one need have no fear of blotting
>
> Felitsa's name in any line,
> Or carelessly permit her portrait
> To drop somewhere upon the ground.
> There jesters' weddings are not feted,
> Nor are there people steamed in ice baths,
> Or noble's whiskers tweaked for fun.
> Like brood-hens princes do not cackle,
> Nor favorites laugh loudly at them,
> And smear their faces black with soot. [54]

In his *Explanations*, Derzhavin gives a detailed commentary on these verses in which he connects the rude and unenlightened kingdom of Anna Ivanovna with the peak of the humiliation of the old nobility (which had started under Peter I). The envoy of France, the Marquis J. J. de La Chetardie, reports on the comic wedding of the elderly Prince M. Golitsyn to Anna's "fool," a Kalmyk woman named A. Buzheninova: "By these means, from time to time, she (Anna Ivanovna. — V. P.) reminded the boyars of her country that neither their origin, nor any granted status, ranks, or awards could protect them from the whims of their sovereign."[55] This notorious event, mentioned in *Felitsa*, became the canonical example of the cruelty of Anna's rule that became an open topic of discussion since Derzhavin's ode. Catherine's portrayal of Anna Ivanovna, endowed with accusatory and revealing hints, was very characteristic of this discussion. In the mid-1780s, she composed an extravagant tale in French entitled *The Palace of Chesma*. Framed as a discussion between portraits and medallions depicting the most famous sovereigns, this political tale presents the cruel and sadistic Anna, the drunk and

---

[54] Sochineniia Derzhavina, I, 88. The translation is taken from G. R. Derzhavin, *Poetic Works*, 33.

[55] "Doneseniia frantsuzskikh poslannikov pri russkom dvore", in *Sbornik Imperatorskogo russkogo istoricheskogo obsh'estva* 86 (1893), 227.

undedicated Catherine I, and the spoiled, lazy, and light-minded Elizaveta Petrovna.[56]

In comparison to his contemporaries, Derzhavin appeared rather indifferent to the historical past and, by contrast, was very strongly and even metaphysically attached to the present. Why did he undertake such an extended excursus to the barbaric times of Peter's niece? He consciously painted unpleasant pictures of that epoch, which was comparatively worse for the Russian nobility, in order to create an idyllic panorama of the "gentry's freedom" in Catherine's Golden Age. The distance between the 1730s and the 1780s seemed especially impressive, and it allowed Derzhavin to make innocent jokes and sling gentle arrows toward the boyars.

Anna's time turned out to be a kind of an anti-locus, or an anti-world. Anaphoric lines with a recurring word "there" («там») were addressed to Catherine's joyful reign which *did not* practice such disgusting customs and rituals. In his ode, the poet inverts the structure of Alexander Sumarokov's didactic choruses built on the opposition *"here — there."* Sumarokov's "there" has always been associated with an idyllic place "overseas," as opposed to the real Russia. Sumarokov's "there," or "overseas," social and political crimes *did not* exist. In his *Another Chorus to a Topsy-turvy World* (1762–1763), Sumarokov writes:

> <...>Money there is not buried in the ground,
> Nor are skins flayed from the backs of peasants.
> Villages they never stake at cards;
> Overseas they do not trade people.[57]

In Sumarokov's poems, "there" (or "overseas"), the nationals do not steal, take bribes, or judge unfairly: negative constructions belong to an ideal place, not to reality. Derzhavin inverts Sumarokov's verses. In his text, "'there" turns out to be equal to Catherine's rule. The idyllic world overseas has come to the Russian lands. ***Derzhavin implies Sumarokov's poetics in an inverted structure.***

---

[56] *Zapiski imperatritsy Ekateriny Vtoroi*, 600–604.
[57] A. P. Sumarokov, *Izbrannye proizvedeniia*, 280.

Thus, Derzhavin writes:

> 'Tis you alone who wounds no feelings,
> Nor gives offence to anyone. [58]

Derzhavin openly plays with Sumarokov's poetics in order to draw a picture of the Golden Age "here," that is, in Russia under Catherine's rule. The negative construction, with playful reference to Sumarokov's didactic poems, became one of the favorite tools of Derzhavin's complimentary strategy. A few years later, in his ode *To Fortune* (1789), Derzhavin repeats the same poetics of negative constructions, and adds Catherine's successes in international affairs to the list of her domestic achievements:

> In these days, when Wisdom is the only one
> Among thrones who does not knead macaroni
> Nor goes to the blacksmith to forge <...> [59]

Sumarokov linked the world abroad with order, reason, prosperity, and justice. Instead, Derzhavin reverses the whole picture. Overseas, absurdity rules and kings are engaged in inappropriate activities, while Catherine (Wisdom) remains the only stronghold of reason in a mad world.

Derzhavin continued to dwell upon Catherine's "liberal agenda" in his ode *To Reshemysl* (1783), devoted to Grigorii Potemkin and written in response to Dashkova's request to create a new ode in *Felitsa's* style. He inserts a brief but impressive historical picture into his playful yet utterly flattering images of both Catherine and Potemkin. His description again targets Anna's rule, when her favorite Biron possessed an almost unlimited power to punish his enemies (like the Dolgorukovs or Artemii Volynskii).

The contrast between Anna's barbaric kingdom and Catherine's enlightened monarchy was very comprehensive: the elimination of cruelty and uncivilized methods of ruling transformed the classical pattern of Montesquieu's despotic system into a monarchic one.

---

[58] *Sochineniia Derzhavina*, I, 87. The translation is taken from G. R. Derzhavin, *Poetic Works*, 32.

[59] Ibid, 173.

Derzhavin believed this to be an enormous change that brought freedom to his class.

The poet makes an additional contrast: in his ode *To Reshemysl*, he depicts Elizaveta Petrovna as a "tsarina" who "was shining with her glory and beauty from under a sable blanket."[60] He juxtaposes the handsome, but idle and spoiled Elizaveta to "another tsarina" (Catherine) who "worked hard for the sake of her land."[61] It was also very significant that while describing Elizaveta, Derzhavin alludes to several of Catherine's phrases from her story *The Tale of Prince Fevei* (Сказка о царевиче Февее; 1783). Without mentioning the name of her predecessor, Catherine ridicules Elizaveta's indolent habits. Once again, Derzhavin echoes Catherine's expressions (the sable blanket), and places the "treasure" of the empress's wit into his own lyric narrative.

Talk with a smile, or the creation of the "amusing style"

The second part of the formula — **to speak the truth with a smile** — concerns Derzhavin's playful way of conveying the "truth." The expression "with a smile" means to praise Catherine's deeds in a new way — amusingly, jokingly, or wittily. Instead of the old tradition of the pompous, serious, direct and archaic worship of the sovereign (as in Petrov's or Ruban's odes), Derzhavin uses a gallant, "indirect" and subtle style to represent the empress's image in poetry. In his late *Discourse on Lyric Poetry, or on the Ode*, Derzhavin retrospectively discusses the principles of the so-called "entertaining odes," providing a fragment from *Felitsa* by way of illustration:

"Only in such odes can the poet speak about everything. He can, at the same time, praise his subject and glorify God, or he can describe truth and preach good morals, etc. A variety of things makes odes richer and more distinguished in style, and it exhibits the author's wit, like lightning striking the heavens from one side

---

[60] Ibid, 118.
[61] Ibid.

to the other <...> In such "varied" odes, one can easily imply praise via allegories or hints that appear not explicitly, but from a distance, like a delicate fragrance or gentle melody coming from afar. These odes give pleasure only to people with taste and entertain sensible and gentle hearts in a more effective way than any direct, noisy, and robust song of praise."[62]

In such a retrospective overview of his poetry, Derzhavin reveals the strategy of a new type of ode and names *Felitsa* as its exemplar. Derzhavin suggests that his odes were oriented towards people with taste, to those who could interpret the subtle hints and metaphors which concealed his hidden flattery, and who could enjoy an author's wit. The poet emphasizes his skill of singing praise to Felitsa-Catherine "indirectly" in a funny or amusing style.

Contemporaries decidedly cherished Derzhavin's innovation. Almost every issue of the *Interlocutor* contained references to Derzhavin's *Felitsa*. The poet Ermil Kostrov, who had already composed eight laudatory odes to Catherine, nominated, in lyric form, Derzhavin for the position of first poet. In his poem entitled *A Letter to the author of an ode praising Felitsa, the Kyrgyz-Kaisak Tsarina* (*Письмо к творцу оды, сочиненной в похвалу Фелицы, царевне киргиз-кайсацкой*), Kostrov sincerely declares:

> You, as we see, came over all the roads
> On the summit of Pindus,
> And in a grassy valley of pure Muses.
> To glorify the tsarina so much,
> To comfort, entertain, and ***amuse*** her,
> You found a new and untrodden way.[63]

Kostrov expresses the opinion of elite readers who enjoy a "new and untrodden way" of praising and, at the same time, of amusing and entertaining the empress. Kostrov as well as the rest of *Felitsa's* privileged audience still could not refrain from re-reading the poem "in order to enjoy again the ***amusing*** playthings."[64]

---

[62] G. R. Derzhavin, *Poetic Works*, 569.
[63] *Sobesednik*, 10 (1783), 26.
[64] Ibid.

The poet Kozodavlev, Dashkova's co-editor at the *Interlocutor*, while expressing the highest opinion of his patrons, asked Derzhavin to repeat his successful lyric experiment by constructing a new image of Catherine in poetry. Undoubtedly, he articulated the request of his royal protectors who wanted Derzhavin to continue to develop a new canon. Soon after Derzhavin's *Felitsa* came out, Kozodavlev composed a poem under the title *A Letter to Tatar Murza Who Composed the Ode to the Wise Felitsa* (Письмо к татарскому Мурзе, сочинившему Оду к премудрой Фелице) in which he writes:

> To *amuse* good souls, let your verses depict
> The deeds of the glorious and wise tsarina,
> Who is known to us by the name of Felitsa.[65]

The word "zabavnyi" in Russian and "amusant" in French grew to be one of the most fashionable *bon mot* in high society parlance. Both Kostrov and Kozodavlev were immediately caught up with a trendy term which had already penetrated the palace walls. In a letter to Grimm dated August 16, 1783, Catherine proudly describes the *Interlocutor* and her own *Truths and Fables* (calling them "NB" and "commentaries") using the word "amusing" and even underlining it:

> "<…> I have to tell you about a magazine which began to come out four months ago in Saint Petersburg; there are the hilarious *NB* and commentaries there; in general, the magazine is a ***collection of most amusing things***. <…> It has enjoyed enormous success."[66]

The word "amusing" became synonymous with the new literary fashion. In 1786, Ippolit Bogdanovich boldly employed the term while discussing Catherine's recently staged comedies. Describing the principles of the new strategy which had initially emerged as a mechanism for refreshing the literary image of the Empress, he found its best embodiment in the works of Catherine

---

[65] Ibid, 8, 8.
[66] "Pis'ma Imperatritsy Ekateriny II k Grimmu", 281.

herself. In his *Verses to the Author of the New Russian Comedies (Стихи к сочинителю новых русских комедий)*, Bogdanovich declares:

> Loving your people,
> You show them the ways of peace, happiness, and glory,
> Softening cruel and rude laws,
> You blend joy with profit in your **amusing things**,
> You correct morals with your **amusements**,
> Avoiding any insults in your goals,
> Are not such deeds worthy of your attention?[67]

In his long poem *Dobromysl* a few years later, Bogdanovich repeats the word and — again — describes Catherine as embracing the new literary strategy.

Replying to the Empress's unofficial request that he collaborate with the members of the new literary elite (Derzhavin, most of all), he writes:

> Finally, you want the author of *Dushen'ka*,
> A simple teller of the old stories,
> To follow in a long line of **amusing writers** <...>[68]

The expressions "amusing toys," "amusing style," "amusing things," and "amusing writers" indicated belonging to the most fashionable and politically advantageous new style, which Derzhavin deemed "a light and entertaining style" in his *Monument*. The poet always liked to stress the humorous or entertaining quality of his odes as well as his informal standing at court — his ability to speak to the empress with a smile. In his preliminary outline of the *Vision of Murza*, Derzhavin makes an explicit assertion as he jokingly distributes the roles of both parties (his and Catherine's) as well as classifies his "songs" to the empress as "humorous." He writes: "You are destined, my Godlike tsarina, to rule and surprise the Universe, while my fate is to praise you and your deeds in my humorous Tatar songs."

Meanwhile, what was Derzhavin's "amusing style" in the context of Russian literary history? First of all, it was a stylistic

---

[67] I. F. Bogdanovich, *Sochineniia*, 2 (Moscow, 1810), 188.
[68] I. F. Bogdanovich, *Sochineniia*, 1 (Saint Petersburg, 1848), 227.

revolution with regards to the well-known theory of the three styles that were bound to specific genres: high style was supposed to be employed in epics and odes; middle style, in didactic poems, satires, and tragedy; low style, in fables, epistles, epigrams and comedy. Derzhavin dared to compose his odes using the illegitimate "middle style" (instead of the high one), a method that allowed him to synthesize different levels of speech and even play with such "macaroni" blends, as Boris Uspenskii called them.[69] In addition to obliterating the boundaries between style and genre, Derzhavin eliminated another neo-classical rule. In his ode, he did not maintain the stylistic and linguistic correlations between "high" and "low" objects of depiction. ***Stylistically, Derzhavin established a visible and accentuated linguistic equality between the image of the empress on the throne and that of a sleepy chum who smokes tobacco in the morning.*** Neither object had any privileges, and their images were equally "macaronic." By lowering stylistic devices by one level within the high genre, Derzhavin produced a colossal shift not only in form, but also in meaning. He deconstructed the cosmology of the ode which usually had "cosmic" settings that were separate from the everyday realm. Instead, he portrayed his tsar seated at a desk, sipping lemonade, and taking a simple dinner (not in the sky amid angels and clouds!).

On the other hand, Derzhavin stopped interpreting "low" things as "low" and therefore unsuitable for the "high" genre. By shifting "low" things to a neutral level, the poet deemed them worthy of being depicted in close proximity to the tsar. Such double destruction (the lowering of high objects and the elevation of low ones) did not desecrate the empress. On the contrary, the whole arsenal of odic sanctification acquired new power. As Vladislav Khodasevich noted, in *Felitsa*, Catherine recognized herself not as "Godlike" (she already could not enjoy such an abstract idealization), but as a human being.[70] Derzhavin endowed the Empress with the ideal enlightened persona that she herself cultivated in the *Interlocutor*.

---

[69] B. A. Uspenskii, "Iazyk Derzhavina", in *Lotmanovskii sbornik*, 1 (Moscow, 1994), 345.

[70] V. F. Khodasevich, *Derzhavin*, 122.

She skillfully interpreted the poet's message and immediately put on her new image, as though it were a new dress. *Felitsa*'s author provided Catherine with a new mirror, and she in turn recognized its reflection as her genuine image.

Chapter Seven

POLITICS AND CARNIVAL IN DERZHAVIN'S ODE TO FORTUNE

*I*n the 1780s, Derzhavin composed a set of odes which were united by their political rhetoric, dedication to the Empress Catherine-Felitsa, and the concept of the so-called "amusing style" ("забавный слог"). The odes of this cycle expose the unfolding story of the special relationship between the Empress, personified as the Kirgiz-Kaisak Tsarina, and Derzhavin as Tatar Murza. The odes contain references to Catherine's works, sayings, bon mots, and quite intimate judgments of political and personal events. Thus, good information about rather intimate details of court life as well as Catherine's life and opinions was essential for Derzhavin's odes. In addition, these odes are saturated with self-citations and references to Derzhavin's own life as well as with allusions and hints that target Catherine's close courtiers. In fact, the odes of this cycle contain a very complicated intertextual structure which has been provided with multiple keys to decode their meaning.

Of all the odes, Derzhavin's poem *To Fortune* (*На Счастие*), which involves a dubious game with two main addressees — Felitsa and Fortune — would seem to be the most "amusing," even buffoonish. In his ode, the poet ridicules recent European political events and diplomatic affairs by placing them in a context of enduring lyric play. Derzhavin's tricky system of allusions and grotesque political metaphors has remained puzzling until the present day, and the intrinsic perplexity of the ode makes it necessary to examine the ode's poetics in detail and to decode its political contexts.

Amusing style or the Russian version of "persiflage"

The ode *To Fortune*, written in 1789, was the only one in the series of odes that remained unpublished during Catherine's lifetime. However, as Andrei Bolotov's memoirs state, the ode circulated in manuscript form, and was rather well-known.[1] Lev Pumpianskii considers this ode the most ironic of the series, even buffoonish, presenting the world as nonsense and carnival (depicting, like Shakespeare's plays do, a mad world with mad kings).[2] Derzhavin, though mockingly, asks readers to excuse the frivolous style of his poem due to special circumstances: in his *Explanations*, the poet indicates that he wrote the poem during Shrovetide, while he was quite tipsy.[3]

The ode's publication in Derzhavin's *Works* (1798) took place after Catherine's death (during Pavel I's reign), and included a few remarkable details. The poet put an incorrect date on his own poem (he dated it one year later than the actual time of its creation), and endowed the title with a peculiar statement: *To Fortune. Written during Shrovetide, 1790.*[4] Scholars never had any doubts that the poem *To Fortune* had been composed in 1789, and not in 1790. The poem reflects political events as well as Derzhavin's personal circumstances during the beginning of 1789, when the poet found himself in Moscow in the middle of a scandal which culminated in a Senate trial. The poet consciously confused his readers since he apparently did not like to recall the most difficult and stressful period of his life, and did not want to link his ode *To Fortune* to the most painful crisis of his career.

In 1788, Derzhavin was fired from his assignment as the governor of Tambov, and since January 1789 he lived in Moscow, in

---

[1] Ia. Grot, *Zhizn' Derzhavina* (Saint Petersburg, 1880), 577. At that time, Derzhavin called almost all his poems odes; see Mark Altshuller, *Beseda liubitelei russkogo slova. U istokov russkogo slavianofil'stva* (Moscow, 2007), 70–71.

[2] L. V. Pumpianskii. *Klassicheskaia traditsiia. Sobranie trudov po istorii russkoi literatury* (Moscow, 2000), 96.

[3] *Sochineniia Derzhavina s ob'iasnitel'nymi primechaniiami Ia. Grota*, I (Saint Petersburg, 1868), 177.

[4] G. R. Derzhavin, *Sochineniia* (Saint Petersburg, 2002), 575–576.

anxious anticipation for the Senate's verdict on his trial. Accused of some severe administrative violations by his superior, I. V. Gudovich, Tambov's general governor, he had grounds to believe that the intrigues of some high ranking enemies, such as A. A. Viazemskii (the General Prosecutor, Derzhavin's former superior) and P. V. Zavadovskii (a Senator and member of Catherine's cabinet), were involved. These influential politicians, at the same time, turned out to be adversaries of Grigorii Potemkin, Derzhavin's supporter.

Meanwhile, at the beginning of January 1789, Derzhavin arrived in Moscow, with an order in hand requiring him to stay in Moscow until the end of his trial. The Moscow Senate, headed by Prince Petr Volkonskii and influenced by the poet's enemies, deliberately postponed the hearings. Derzhavin passionately waited for a verdict for almost six months, until June 1789 when all the charges were dismissed.

The ode was written in the first months of 1789, and most likely, in February, during the week of the Russian carnival. It was quite distinctive that the ode, making a comical overview of international affairs, does not even mention the French revolution, the main event of 1789. Iakov Grot, while preparing the edition of Derzhavin's *Works*, immediately rejected the poem's date of 1790; he also made attempts to decode the strange addition to the title. Commenting on the ode's history, the scholar has interpreted the poet's ironic phrase on his tipsy condition as an obvious intention to hide his real goal and soften the satirical arrows towards his powerful enemies; Derzhavin's dismissal from the governance in Tambov and the prosecution by the Moscow Senate made the poet more cautious in his ridicule and therefore lead to a kind of masquerade.[5]

Meanwhile, Derzhavin's playful remarks on his tipsy condition must be understood neither as a peculiar account of the poet's real circumstances, nor as an attempt to avoid criticism from angry courtiers. Derzhavin would seem to be pursuing some literary goal by mentioning the carnival and his own drinking. Moreover,

---

[5] *Sochineniia Derzhavina s ob"iasnitel'nymi primechaniiami Ia. Grota*, 9, 238.

it makes obvious the poet's need to declare the ironic mode of his poem as indicative of a specific genre. The ode instantly acquires features of an absurdist panorama of modern politics that deals with an acute international crisis of early 1789.

Anna Lisa Crone calls the poem an "anti-ode," meaning that Derzhavin had reversed his flattering image of Catherine as Felitsa and proclaims, instead, the poet's superior status.[6] Actually, the ode is not less flattering toward Catherine than his other works of the time. The setting of Catherine's representation, however, is different. Derzhavin depicts modern times as a mad carnival. In his panorama of Europe just on the eve of the French Revolution, absurdity reigns, kings are engaged in inappropriate dealings, while Catherine (Wisdom) turns out to be the only stronghold of reason:

> In those days, when Wisdom among the thrones
> Alone desists from making macaroni;
> And from going to the forge... [7]

She alone confronts this mad world in her domestic, international, and cultural policy. Only she, as the poet suggests, can restore rationality and justice, and only she can reinstate the poet's status at court.

Meanwhile, Derzhavin's ode, clearly absorbing some carnivalesque elements, does not contain any specific traits which refer to the Russian tradition of carnival festivities. Instead, at every turn, the poem reflects a thoroughly Western carnival viewpoint. The ode develops an impressive picture of a totally mad and topsy-turvy universe, devoid of its regular hierarchy and order. The author depicts the world in utter confusion as to all the usual structural definitions of "high" and "low," "rich" and "poor," etc. Kings, nobles, slaves, and jesters quickly ascend and suddenly descend,

---

[6] Anna Lisa Crone, *The Daring of Derzhavin. The Moral and Aesthetic Independence of the Poet in Russia*, 172. See also her special article: Anna Lisa Crone, "Na scchast'e as the Undoing of Felitsa," in *Russian Literature*, 44 (1998), 17–40.

[7] *Sochineniia Derzhavina s ob'iasnitel'nymi primechaniiami Ia. Grota*, I (Saint Petersburg, 1868), 173. Further page references to the *Ode to Fortune* are given in the text in brackets.

according to the will of capricious Fortune. Ambivalence pervades the world, thus abolishing reason and order, and indulges in chaos and the hazardous play of fate. The poet figures contemporary society and mankind in general as a foolish globe which dances in the tipsy whirlwind of a universe-carnival, while politicians, kings, the clergy, and common folk frantically play cards, bidding for human life and death:

> In those days, the whole world makes merry,
> Politics and justice,
> Reason, conscience and sacred law
> And logic celebrate feasts,
> At cards they stake the Golden Age,
> They gamble with the fates of men,
> They bend the universe into a card game;
> Poles, meridians,
> The sciences, Muses, gods are tipsy,
> One and all gallop, dance, and chant. (172–173)

Referring to the tipsy and carnivalesque background of the ode, Derzhavin emphasizes its stylistic strategy, poetics, and literary sources. The culture of laughter occupied a central role in the civilization of the Enlightenment. The discourse of witticism, as well as a tolerant attitude toward ridicule, and even satire, constituted the qualities of a "man of the Enlightenment."[8] Catherine II considered herself to belong to this group of people and counted herself as a full member of the European "republic of letters."[9]

In fabricating Catherine's image, Derzhavin, in his poems, presents Catherine-Felitsa not only as his patron, teacher, the model of decency and wisdom, but *as an initiator of his amusing style, and — in his ode To Fortune — as his literary ally, a proponent of this amusing style.* While kings indulge in shameful occupations that signified, as many contemporaries stated, the collapse of the Ancien Regime, the Russian Empress is engaged in noble and enlightened activities:

---

[8] Antoine de Baecque, *Les éclats du rire. La culture des rieurs au XVIII-e siècle* (Paris, 2000), 7.

[9] Dena Goodman, *The Republic of Letters. A Cultural History of the French Enlightenment*, 112.

> Meanwhile, in times of boredom,
> She calls the Muses to attend,
> Equipped with a skillful pen,
> Never arguing with anyone ever,
> To amuse everyone and herself,
> She crafts comedies, distills mores,
> And sings her "hem, hem, hem." (173)

In his account of Catherine's literary works, Derzhavin, quite consciously, presents the Russian Empress as a writer who shares his own aesthetic tastes. Derzhavin endows the Empress with a "skillful pen" which symbolizes her belonging to the same "amusing style." If the "pen" means a literary "style," the adjective "skillful" signifies a "witty" and "light" type of style. This formula became a tool to distinguish the new generation of modern writers from the old didactic ones who were not able to entertain and amuse. The Empress, as the poet implies, puts her "skillful" pen to paper "to amuse everyone and herself" as well as to "distill mores." Combining "useful" with "pleasant," she also played the role of Derzhavin's ally, or rather the exemplary model of Derzhavin's esthetic credo.

Moreover, speaking about Catherine's literary tastes, Derzhavin interprets them as the ideal model of his own poetic aspirations. The Empress, as Derzhavin suggests, fosters a refined, gallant, and enlightened laughter which does not destroy reputations or severely condemn others ("never arguing with anyone ever"). This kind of laughter, a good-natured joking, a mild teasing, or a gallant ridiculing (the meaning of the French term "persiflage") served as a sign of belonging to the most enlightened and fashionable society.

The term "persiflage" appeared in France around 1734 and vanished at the beginning of the French revolution.[10] It proved popular not only among the salons' witty libertines, but among such writers and philosophers as Voltaire, Denis Diderot, Claude Prosper

---

[10] On the evolution of laughter in the eighteenth century, see: Antoine de Baecque, *Les éclats du rire. La culture des rieurs au XVIII-e siècle* (Paris, 2000); Anne Richardor, *Le rire des Lumières* (Paris, 2002).

Jolyot de Crébillon, Choderlos de Laclos, Antoine de Rivarol. What were the characteristics of this kind of laughter?

First of all, the style introduced the cult of nonsense, as well as fragmentary narratives which ridicule some close-knit circle belonging to society's upper crust, but the allusions are always foggy. The participant in the circle remained in doubt as to the real object of ridicule's true identity. It was difficult even to make conclusions about whether the saying was serious or ironic. Compliments and ridicule were so tightly intertwined that one had to guess how to react properly.

Catherine's essays *Truths and Fables* (*Были и небылицы*), which came out in 1783 in her *Interlocutor*, were supposed to serve as a literary platform for elaborating this type of laughter. Not by accident, in her letter to Grimm on 16 August 1783, she boasts that the magazine "constituted the happiness of the city and the court," and that "the readers were dying of laughter."[11] After finishing the publication of the essays, she left her *Will* (*Завещание*), where she reveals her esthetic canon which she recommends to other writers. The Empress affirms that "joyful things are the best," that "laughter, witticisms, and metaphors" should "flow like streams."[12] Forbidding boring moralistic works, Catherine encourages "pleasant turns," and a "light style"; she advises authors to "look at different thoughts in different ways," and eventually, she suggests that "the author should hide his presence" inside the text, and "leave no trace that he had acted here."[13]

Catherine's work, however, differs a great deal from her esthetic credo, and the imperial presence in the text was always tangible. On the other hand, when Derzhavin implied persiflage-like jokes in his odes, the reaction of Catherine's courtiers was rather hostile, and the amused style brought the poet quite real persecution, right after his ode *Felitsa*, the most eloquent manifesto of a new style in poetry. Thus, Princess Dashkova recalled the appearance of the magazine the *Interlocutor* (which opened with Derzhavin's ode), and

---

[11] *Sochineniia imperatritsy Ekateriny II*, 5 (Saint Petersburg, 1903), 117–118.
[12] Ibid, 104.
[13] Ibid, 105.

the apparent resentment of Derzhavin's superior, A. A. Viazemskii. Dashkova writes:

> The Russian Academy started a new magazine for which the Empress and I were among the contributors... When Viazemskii came into the knowledge that Derzhavin published his verses in the magazine, he took the poet's satiric poems as referring to him as well as to his wife. For some time, he acted against Derzhavin and made him lose the post of vice-governor; therefore, he assumed that Derzhavin would take revenge by portraying him in his poems which were in great demand, as Derzhavin was a very famous and talented poet.[14]

According to Derzhavin, as he put it in his ode to Fortune, his persecution by Viazemskii and then by I. V. Gudovich (instigated by Viazemskii) was a sign of a violation of the norms of gallantry and an uncultured paradigm of behavior as well.

The Invocation of Fortune

The extended title (*"Written during Shrovetide"*) is an indication of the specific genre of his text: its genesis and poetics. What is the meaning of Derzhavin's appeal to Fortune in his ode of 1789? Fortune has been the goddess of chance, luck, and fate since the time of the early Roman Empire. Odes to Fortune constitute a whole tradition, beginning with the first and most famous ode by Horace. Images of Fortune on a whirling wheel or ball became very popular.[15]

However, starting in the Medieval Ages, the incantation of Fortune, the pagan goddess of chance, became linked with drinking songs in the lyrics of students and clergy, such as those that have been collected in the *Carmina Burana*, in the section of "drinking

---

[14] Ekaterina Dashkova, *Zapiski*, 1743–1810 (Moscow, 1990), 152. Dashkova combines here two episodes of persecution against Derzhavin; first, in 1783, after *Felitsa*'s publication Viazemskii fired the poet who served as his aide; second, in 1788-89, when Viazemskii indirectly forced the poet to be removed from the post of vice-governor in Tambov.

[15] See: Howard Rollin Patch, *The Tradition of the Goddess Fortuna in Roman Literature and in the Transitional Period* (Northampton, MA, 1922).

songs." The first one has the expressive title *Fortune, the Empress of the World.* These songs contain lamentations on capricious fate which oppresses and soothes, which makes kings and kingdoms and then destroys them. The smart and educated plebeians blame the rich and dull aristocrats, complain about social injustice, and chant drinking and games as the most adequate measures of surviving a malicious fate. They were written in macaronic language, a mixture of Latin and the German or French vernacular of the time.[16] Such lyrics formed a specific genre of European (mostly German) poetry which existed and flourished for centuries.

The songs were not known in Russia, but they influenced the flourishing of burlesque odes in Europe, especially in Germany at the beginning of the eighteenth century. The primary example in this tradition, the *Ode to Fortune* (*A die Gelegenheit*) by Johann Christian Günther (1695–723), was very well known to Derzhavin.

Lev Pumpianskii has already discovered that Derzhavin was very familiar with Günther's ironic and even burlesque ode. Pumpianskii writes:

> *Ode to Fortune* is one of the most ingenious works by Derzhavin, containing sharp conclusions on truly Russian material ... but the genre and its theme, the most appropriate for an amusing ode, come from the ode *A die Gelegenheit*. The title aquires its meaning from Günther's ode: its does not mean *bonheur,* but chance, fortune, that is just *Gelegenheit.* The well-known note that the poem was written when the author was tipsy does not refer to any personal context. It's a genre feature.[17]

Not accidentally, and approximately at the same time, Derzhavin composed another poem, entitled *Drunk and Sober Philosophers* (*Философы, пьяный и трезвый*), that even more openly exhibits its membership in the tradition.

Pumpianskii believes that Derzhavin relied on some Russian "soldier songs" while composing his ode. The scholar was aware

---

[16] Howard Rollin Patch, *Fortune in Old French Literature* (Northampton, MA, 1923).

[17] L. V. Pumpianskii, "Lomonosov i nemetskaia shkola razuma,", in *XVIII vek*, 14 (Leningrad, 1983), 10.

of the presence of some intrinsic blasphemous or even obscene contents, but he did not know yet about the so-called "barkoviana," the corpus of texts written by Ivan Barkov and some other poets.[18] Derzhavin's ode, therefore, acquires ironic and even obscene implications. On one hand, the poem could be interpreted as the poet's complaint about the injustice of Fortune and the loss of his social status. At the same time, the ode contains an interior text about a "Sovereign" and refers to "barkovian" poems that were addressed to a close circle of friends.

Meanwhile, the title, as well as the recurrent pleas to Fortune, makes uncertain the addressee of Derzhavin's caustic ode. At every turn the poet challenges the reader to guess whether or not he should associate Fortune with Catherine. Following the poetics of the previous odes to Catherine, this new ode, at first glance, pretends to be a playful appeal to Catherine-Felitsa, disguised as Fortune: the poet jokingly asks his former protector to grant him a new portion of happiness — to dismiss all unjust accusations and to restore his social status. Iakov Grot, in his commentary on this poem, takes for granted Derzhavin's crafty "explanations," and, as a result, he assumes that "Fortune represents Catherine here."[19]

When commenting on the famous "international" strophes of the ode, Grot believes that the two couplets "enclose allusions to Russia's successful military affairs and to very advantageous alliances that enabled the Empress to gain political dominance over Europe."[20] Hence Grot interprets the goddess Fortune of 1789 and Felitsa of 1782 as two analogous lyric names for the same Empress. The scholar does not express any doubts when, all of a sudden, apart from Fortune, Minerva appears in some central strophes (from 9 to 12), and she alone is clearly associated with Catherine:

> In those days, when Wisdom among the thrones... (173)

---

[18] See Vera Proskurina, "Mezhdu Felitsei i Fortunoi: Derzhavin i barkoviana," in *Permiakovskii sbornik*, II (Moscow, 2009), 128–143.

[19] *Sochineniia Derzhavina s ob'iasnitel'nymi primechaniiami Ia. Grota*, I, 246.

[20] Ibid.

Moreover, Derzhavin embodies his Fortune in a masculine figure in contradiction to the main tradition where the Goddess Fortune is presented as a woman. The poet does so on purpose and quite consciously. Later, his friend, the artist A. N. Olenin, provided the ode with illustrations: a joyful boy sitting on a whirling ball. Derzhavin, in his poem, stresses the difference between the gallant and respectable Felitsa and a "carnavalesque" and even wicked young god (not goddess!) named Fortune:

> A son of time, circumstance, fate,
> Or some unknown cause,
> A strong, playful, gentle, wicked God!
> On a ball-like chariot,
> Crystal, slippery, fatal,
> Following a shining dawn
> Across mountains, steppes, seas, forests
> You gallop about the globe all day,
> You are waving a magic towel,
> And work miracles. (171)

Derzhavin makes a distinction between Catherine as Minerva and the "wicked god" Fortune, and even implies the gender difference to underscore this point. The author's play with both figures as well as with two associated contexts — his usual half-joking reverence for Minerva-Catherine and his half-playful indignation for the mad and unpredictable god named Fortune — constitute the main counterpoint of the ode.

Ambivalent, unclear allusions that correspond very well with the strategy of persiflage have resulted in quite opposite conclusions. If Grot, who does not perceive the distinction between Catherine and Fortune, interprets the ode as a description of Catherine's triumphs, other scholars have been forced to presume that Derzhavin, in this "anti-ode," "cancels out" the positive image of Catherine, and instead, begins criticizing her deeds.[21] However, the caustic arrows target his enemies among the boyars, while the ironic mode takes aim at Fortune, not Catherine. The strategy of

---

[21] Anna Lisa Crone, *The Daring of Derzhavin. The Moral and Aesthetic Independence of the Poet in Russia*, 172.

the poem does not consist of either polemics with the Empress, or the refutation of her image. The ode is a carefully crafted play with, and even a profanation of, the Felitsa myth which Derzhavin had created before.

Political metaphors versus Real Politics

Assuming that the image of Fortune was a new embodiment of Catherine, Grot considers all the "deeds" described in the poem as Catherine's real strategy for success. This interpretation obfuscates the understanding of this poem and contradicts all real facts pertaining to Catherine's diplomacy. Grot's commentary is based on the presumption that Derzhavin's "explanations" and "notes" are absolutely truthful and straightforward. Thus, Grot believes that an ironic panorama of political events depicts the successful diplomacy of the Empress:

> You tweak Istanbul's beard,
> You ride piggyback on the Taurus,
> You want to pepper Stockholm's pot,
> And smear wax on Berlin's mustaches.
> You dress the Thames in crinolines,
> You fluff Warsaw's tuft of hair,
> And smoke sausage for the Dutch.
> In those days, when you assure Vienna,
> And muss Paris's wig,
> You turn your nose up at Madrid,
> You seed frost on Copenhagen,
> You give a bucket of roses to Gdansk,
> You don't show solicitude for Venice or Malta,
> And order Greece to gape;
> To prevent Rome's legs from swelling,
> When they drop their sacred shoes,
> You forbid kings to kiss them. (172)

Grot tries to connect each line in these "international" strophes to some diplomatic effort of the Russian court. Meanwhile, Derzhavin has no intention to display successful achievements in these fragments; on the contrary, he is depicting the mad features of a mad world. It was not Catherine who generated the political carnival, but a capricious and irresponsible, blind and unfair god named Fortune.

These strophes consist of satiric aphorisms that describe sovereigns and their countries as a grotesque body exposed to Fortune's attacks. The high politics usually symbolized in odes via images of the beautiful or strong body of the sovereign (Lomonosov's odes picture Russia as a beautiful Elizaveta Petrovna) are desacralized and deconstructed here. Instead of the symbolic body of the emperors, the poet introduces the parts of the body or clothes related to them: a beard (the Turks), mustaches (Prussia), a crinoline (England), a wig (France), a nose (Spain), a tuft of hair (Poland), shoes (the Roman Pope). Additionally, these countries are involved in some dishonorable or carnivalesque actions, similar to street puppet-theater where they muss wigs, tweak beards and ride piggyback. Moreover, Derzhavin associates each word with physical activities or gestures using specific idioms related to fighting or harm — in their comic and deflated versions.

Derzhavin's satirical overview gives a detailed and well-informed account of several topsy-turvy political events that confronted Catherine's regime in 1788–89. It is not a poetic story of her success. On the contrary, 1787–89 turned out to be the most difficult and hectic time for Russian politics under Catherine. Moreover, this period brought a very grave international crisis that threatened Russia and all of Catherine's previous achievements. All of a sudden, soon after a triumphant journey to the Crimea, Catherine found herself in an even worse situation than on the eve of her first war with the Turks (1768–1775).

What was perhaps the most successful accomplishment of the previous war with the Porte, the annexation of the Crimea (Taurus) in 1783, even became an object of new and controversial negotiations and threats. At the beginning of August 1787, the Russian minister in Constantinople, Iakov Bulgakov, was interrogated and imprisoned in the Castle of the Seven Towers. On 13 August 1787, the Turkish sultan Abdul-Khamid (who ruled 1774–1789) declared war on Russia. The Turks made a claim to get the Crimea back under their control. The Turkish army occupied the town of Kinburn in an attempt to cut the Crimea off of the mainland. The protracted

Kinburn-Ochakov operation started, and ended only in December of 1788, after the capture of the Turkish fortress Ochakov. As Derzhavin writes, his Fortune played games with the most painful geo-political areas of Russia's interests:

> You tweak Istanbul's beard,
> You ride piggyback on the Taurus... <...> (172)

The first line refers to the fight against the Turks: Fortune helps to "tweak" the "beard" of the Turks. The second line has to be considered more closely. It relates to the Crimea and its ancient name of Taurida (Tavrida in Russian) or Taurus (Tavr). Derzhavin used the name Taurus (Tavr) in his poem *On the Acquisition of the Crimea* (*На приобретение Крыма*, 1784):

> Russia put her hand
> Upon the Taurus, the Caucasus, and the Chersoneses <...> [22]

By invoking the metaphor of "riding piggyback," the poet defines the current status of the Crimea as unstable. Grigorii Potemkin, the commander-in-chief of the Russian army, spent the autumn of 1788 in great difficulty. The court believed that his actions were too slow and indecisive. By the end of September 1788, after bad news about the Sevastopol fleet, which had been partially destroyed by a storm, Potemkin fell into a deep depression, asked to retire from his post, and even suggested returning the Crimea to the Turks.[23] Catherine was also anxious, as the failure could lay open to the Turks the way to the "heart of the Empire."[24]

Circumstances worsened in mid-1788 when Russia became involved in war on two fronts — with the Ottoman Porte and

---

[22] *Sochineniia Derzhavina s ob"iasnitel'nymi primechaniiami Ia. Grota*, I, 127.

[23] A. N. Petrov, *Vtoraia turetskaia voina v tsarstvovanii Ekateriny II*, I (Saint Petersburg, 1880); Olga Eliseeva, *Grigorii Potemkin* (Moscow, 2006), 420–421; *Ekaterina II i G. A. Potemkin: Lichnaia perepiska 1769-1791* (Moscow, 1997), 311–329. See also the detailed account of the struggles around the Crimea by Albert Sorel: *Europe and the French Revolution. The Political traditions of the Old Regime* (London, 1969), 548–549.

[24] *Ekaterina II i G. A. Potemkin: Lichnaia perepiska 1769-1791*, 790. For more on this question, see: V. N. Vinogradov, "Diplomatiia Ekateriny Velikoi," in *Novaia i noveishaia istoriia*, 4 (2001).

Sweden. Gustav III, the King of Sweden, took advantage of the Russian army's preoccupation with their southern frontiers and started a campaign in the Northern Sea.[25] He threatened to revenge his grandfather's defeat of 1709 at Poltava and restore Sweden's power over the northern lands. For several days in 1788, the cannonade from the fighting was clearly heard in Tsarskoe Selo (near Saint Petersburg), where Catherine spent her summers. Gustav III received political and financial support from England and Prussia, and announced his plan to enter Saint Petersburg and pull down the Bronze Horseman, a famous monument to Peter the Great built by Catherine in 1783. However, in July 1788 the Russian fleet, under the command of admiral S. K. Greig, destroyed the Swedish ships in the Finnish gulf. Derzhavin's verse on Stockholm refers to the ill-fated attack by the Swedes:

> You want to pepper Stockholm's pot <...> (172)

Derzhavin talks about Gustav III a few times more in his ode:

> She does not let heroes in armor or without
> Squeeze lemons in their paws <...> (173–174)

Then, the reference to Gustav is made by alluding to the biggest theatrical hit of the Saint Petersburg season 1789-90, Catherine's comic opera *The Unfortunate Hero Kosometovich* (*Горе-богатырь Косометович.*) Derzhavin's lyric hero laments his fifty-year anniversary as well as his recent misfortunes:

> And now I have turned fifty,
> Fortune has flown away from me,
> I am an unfortunate hero without armor. (175)

In mentioning armor, Derzhavin makes clear references to both — to Catherine's opera and Gustav's fascination with the accoutrements of the medieval knight. Catherine constantly mocked her "cousin" and his peculiar manners. Thus, she wrote to Potemkin on 3 July 1788:

---

[25] Ia. K. Grot, "Ekaterina i Gustav III," in *Trudy Ia. K. Grota*, IV (Saint Petersburg, 1901), 262–266.

The King of Sweden has had himself forged suits of armor, a cuirass, a breastplate, and a helmet with awful feathers. Having left Stockholm, he promised the accompanying ladies that he would give them a breakfast in our Petergof… He has announced to his army in Finland and to the Swedish people that he intends to surpass the deeds of Gustavus Adolphus, to eclipse him, and to complete the endeavors of Charles XII of Sweden… In addition, he claimed that he would force me to renounce the throne… The behavior of this treacherous sovereign looks like madness.[26]

From September to December 1788, Catherine, together with her secretary (and Derzhavin's friend) A. V. Khrapovitskii, had been working on the comic opera which would first appear in January of 1789 in theaters in Moscow and Saint Petersburg. Catherine made special suggestions to the actors in her Hermitage Theater: "The opera is burlesque; therefore, you have to play it livelier and without stinting."[27] At the beginning of 1789, the text of the opera was published. Potemkin (who returned from the army to the capital in February) just barely succeeded in persuading the Empress not to stage the piece in a public theater in front of foreign diplomats. For a time performances of this "burlesque" were suspended. Therefore, discussions surrounding the opera hit their peak at the beginning of February, which also coincides with the most plausible time when Derzhavin could have composed his ode *To Fortune*, full of the most recent political, literary, and everyday-life phenomena.

"Mad World! Mad Kings! Mad Composition!"

These lines taken from Shakespeare's chronicle *King John* correspond very well to the political circumstances described in the ode. England and Prussia signed a treaty that announced a defensive union against Russia. They made their union known, invited Holland to join, and threatened Russia from all directions: by supporting the Turks' intention to take back the Crimea, by

---

[26] *Ekaterina II i G. A. Potemkin: Lichnaia perepiska 1769-1791*, 299–300.
[27] *Pamiatnye zapiski A. V. Khrapovitskogo*, 143.

augmenting their influence in Poland, and by backing Gustav's military campaign.

By the end of 1788, Russia faced a severe threat that had been constituted by a coalition of four countries, the so-called "quadruple union": Prussia, England, Sweden, and Holland. The union intended to support any anti-Russian military action from the North or from the South. Of course, the union pulled every string to advance Turkey's cause, and the coalition made all possible efforts to ignite riot against Russia in Poland. Meanwhile, in her turn, Russia also strove to build her own quadruple union which proposed to include Austria, France, and Spain.

The unions and coalitions, kings who die and go mad, as well as their depraved occupations and their political impotence, represent, in Derzhavin's ode, the symptoms of the total confusion of a world which was teetering right at the edge of a precipice. Derzhavin writes:

> In those days, when Wisdom among the thrones
> Alone desists from making macaroni;
> And from going to the forge. (173)

Derzhavin, in this fragment, juxtaposes the Russian Empress and the house of Bourbon in the person of Ferdinand I, the King of Naples, and the Two Sicilies (1751–1825), as well as Louis XVI of France. The first was notorious for his ill-mannered nature, and his fervent love for macaroni and their manufacture. According to memoirs of his contemporaries, this "King-Falstaff" spent a lot of time in markets, often in dirty company; he also was obsessed with ordering the most technically advanced machines for making macaroni.[28] The other personage in the satirical fragment, Louis XVI, adored carpentry and metallurgy, and had a turning shop. He collected the most peculiar locks, and was even given a nickname: the "locksmith" ("le serrurié").[29]

---

[28] *Lady Emma Hamilton: From New and Origin sources & Documents* (London, 1905), 117.

[29] P. P. Cherkasov, *Ekaterina II i Ludovik XVI* (Moscow, 2004).

Both kings married sisters — the two daughters of the Austrian Queen Maria Theresa: Maria Carolina (Ferdinand I) and Marie Antoinette (Louis XVI). Derzhavin stresses the insolence of Ferdinand I as well as a lack of enlightenment as preventing him from fulfilling his duties. He seemed intent on keeping out of state affairs which became the responsibility of his energetic wife. The last king of pre-revolutionary France, Louis XVI, also avoided his royal obligations; he preferred going to his forge than to other kingly sites, such as his throne and his wife's boudoir. Louis's sexual impotence was perceived by the people as a significant symbol of the declining monarchy.[30] The peculiar features of the king became the constant object of libels and political caricatures which circulated across Europe.[31]

However, the events in England proved to be the most perplexing. The Prime Minister William Pitt the Younger (1759–1806) was a long-time enemy of Catherine; he could not forgive her clandestine support of the North American revolution against Great Britain, or her politics of the so-called *military neutrality* that, in fact, prevented England from receiving aid. Pitt made clear to the Russian Minister to London, Count Semen Vorontsov, that he considered the Russian position to be a betrayal of a former alliance, when Britain collaborated with Russia during the first war with the Turks (1768–1775).

In addition, England's membership in the anti-Russian union was especially dangerous for Russian politics. Catherine was enormously preoccupied with the constant threat from Britain to send their navy against Russia to support Sweden. All of a sudden, in autumn of 1788, some extraordinary news came to Russia from the shores of the Thames. At first glance, the one sentence of Derzhavin's international strophe which refers to England looks like a commonplace of carnival discourse:

> You dress the Thames in crinolines <...> (172)

---

[30] Robert Darnton, *The Literary Underground of the Old Regime* (Cambridge, MA; London, 1982), 203.
[31] Baecque Antoine de. *La caricature revolutionnaire*. Paris, 1988.

Meanwhile, the phrase reflects the culmination in a chain of events which took place in London, on the shores of the Thames, at that time. Starting in November 1788, rumors about the sudden insanity of the British King George III (1738–1820) had begun to reach the Russian court. There were rumors circulating about his poisoning. Modern scholars claim that he had a rare blood disorder (porphyria) which could be provoked by prescribed medications containing arsenic. The affairs in London became an extremely important topic, especially for the Empress who nervously followed the development of the plot during November 1788–March 1789. Starting at the end of November 1788, Catherine began to discuss with increasing frequency the madness of King George with members of her close circle, including her state-secretary A. V. Khrapovitskii, the close friend and constant correspondent of Derzhavin. Khrapovitskii carefully recorded Catherine's statements in his diary:

> 30 November [1788]. After reading German newspapers, she (Catherine II. — V. P.) said that the King of England fell ill with madness.... During the Empress's hairdressing there was received a post from Count Vorontsov in which the King's madness was confirmed...[32]
>
> 3 December [1788]. We worked with British newspapers, and translated into French everything related to the King's madness. — Count Vorontsov writes that he is better, and begins to recognize people, but that there is no sense in his speech; they are still delaying to convene Parliament, which has to approve the Regent.[33]
>
> 7 December [1788]. Before her hairdressing, she (Catherine II. — V. P.) spoke, with fervor and firmness, about the much anticipated change in England that could prove very profitable....[34]

At the beginning of 1788 the situation in England became even more tense. Catherine's preoccupation with the affairs in London

---

[32] *Pamiatnye zapiski A. V. Khrapovitskogo*, 141.
[33] Ibid, 142.
[34] Ibid, 143.

was so intense that she felt her own head spinning with madness. The Russian minister to London Count Semen Vorontsov quickly informed Catherine of the King's condition as well as the growing struggle surrounding his successor.

> 5 January [1789]. [She said]: "From following what is going on in the Kingdom of England, it would be possible to go mad myself; I am under difficult circumstances".[35]

Iakov Grot, commenting on the ode, interprets Derzhavin's sentence as an adulation of a new triumph of Russian diplomacy. He writes that Queen of England, Charlotte, (Charlotte of Mecklenburg-Strelitz, 1744–1818) attempted to ascend the throne and sought Catherine's support. Meanwhile, diplomatic and political relations between Russia and England are too far removed from Grot's statements. All hopes of Catherine II were connected not with Charlotte, but with Charlotte's opponents in England.

Moreover, Catherine expressed her hatred toward Queen Charlotte, who was plotting to deprive her own son, the Prince of Wales and the Regent, of power. To the contrary, the Russian Empress Catherine II supported the Prince Regent, and his *party of patriots*. She hoped that the Regent would appoint his proponent Charles James Fox as his Prime Minister.[36] Fox was the most suitable candidate, according to Catherine. It was Fox who struggled against Queen Charlotte and her ally, the current Prime Minister Pitt, Catherine's longtime enemy. Thus, it was not Catherine, but a wicked Fortune who "dressed the Thames in crinolines."

At that time, Catherine frequently and intensively discussed diplomatic issues with Grigorii Potemkin, who not only headed the army combating the Turks, but also advised the Empress in her political affairs. On 27 November 1788 Catherine wrote to Grigorii Potemkin:

---

[35] Ibid, 156

[36] Grant C. Robertson, *England under the Hanoverians* (New York; London, 1911), 323–326; Herbert Kaplan, *Russian Overseas Commerce with Great Britain During the Reign of Catherine II* (Philadelphia, 1995), 154.

> The English King is dying now, and if he drops dead then perhaps we'll have success establishing concord with his son (who till now has been obeying Fox and the English patriotic party, and not the Hanoverians).[37]

Khrapovitskii's notes also confirm Catherine's position in the British struggle and her disapproval of Charlotte's character:

> 11 January [1789]. She has read to me from the post about the Regent. The Queen of England, together with the ministers, opposes the party of her son, the Prince of Wales; moreover, they wish to diminish his power in order to force him not to claim the throne and to leave the Kingdom. Count Vorontsov writes this.[38]
>
> 14 January [1789]. She said that there are reports that the Queen of England has accepted the regency: "She is unintelligent and greedy"....
>
> 18 January [1789]. Discussions on the regency in England yet continue....
>
> 19 January [1789]. Continuation of the discussion about the King of England. Hopes now are on the Crown Prince. Ségur knows him well; he (the Prince. — V. P.) is a little rascal, but smart, and when he enters into the Cabinet of the Duke of Portland and the true patriots, it would be advantageous for us....Six posts from England are now missing, and it is quite possible that the revolution has taken place.[39]

Catherine was passionately waiting for any news from England. She read newspapers, and seems to have believed in any political movement that held out hope. The absence of reliable information kept her in ignorance: she blamed Queen Charlotte for her greediness, and suspected her of spreading false rumors about the King's health. Khrapovitskii writes:

> 21 January [1789]. It was noticed (by Catherine. — V. P.) that the seventh post from England is missing. Berlin's newspapers, in their reports on Parliament, suggest that the navy and the army have sided with the Crown Prince; is this not the revolution?

---

[37] *Love Conquest. Personal Correspondence of Catherine the Great and Prince Grigory Potemkin.* Edited and translated by Douglas Smith (DeKalb, 2004), 272–273.

[38] *Pamiatnye zapiski A. V. Khrapovitskogo*, 158–159.

[39] Ibid, 163.

> 25 January [1789]. She spoke about the vile character of the Queen of England, for Vorontsov writes that money is her deity; in circulating a false medical report about the King's recovery, she strengthened the party of the Ministers; they took measures to deprive her son of regency; but all things are being revealed now.[40]

Finally, at the beginning of March, London made an official statement about the King's improvement. Catherine refused to believe it, but had to reconcile herself to the restoration of active (and even more adversarial) politics in Britain. Khrapovitskii writes:

> 4 March [1789]. She read to me from the German press Pitt's announcement on the King's recovery, which provoked protests from the Duke of York in Parliament (who was not admitted to the King); il est ci malade qu'il été; all these are intrigues originating from Pitt and the Queen; she is terribly avaricious, and completely infected with a base passion.[41]

The events in England can clarify more precisely when Derzhavin's ode *To Fortune* was composed: it could have happened only before March 1789 when all the newspapers announced the convalescence of King George III. Officially, the crisis was over, and it is very doubtful that Derzhavin would have alluded to Queen Charlotte and her intrigues afterward. In fact, the poem does not contain references to the later events, including the storming of the Bastille on 14 July 1789 that marked the beginning of the French Revolution. If the poem had still been in progress later in the year, it is most unlikely that Derzhavin would have omitted such an important event. Personal facts, and Derzhavin's constant reference to his poor circumstances (the lingering trial, which was over by July 1789) as well as literary self-references (mentioned above) all support the conclusion about the date of the poem's composition. In dismissing Derzhavin's later report that the poem was written in 1790 as an apparent contradiction to all known political and personal circumstances, we will take for granted the poet's constant appeal to the Russian Carnival week (12–18 February 1789). The

---

[40] Ibid, 164, 166.
[41] Ibid, 175.

poet's decision to bring into play carnivalesque motifs could be motivated by the actual festivities.

...*And smears wax on Berlin's mustaches*....

The phrase literally means that Fortune applies wax to Berlin's mustaches to prevent them from drooping. This mocking metaphor was a genuine creation of Derzhavin, and later, dictionaries (Vladimir Dal', Ushakov) would cite this quotation from the poem to explain the meaning of the word "fabrit'" (to smear). The poet suggests that Prussian emperor Frederick William II, who succeeded his famous uncle Frederick II in 1786, has increased the level of his predecessor's active and rather aggressive politics. This figure of speech also implies mockery, reveals the bellicose character of the country, and corresponds to a comic literary image of a dull, warlike, boastful soldier. It is interesting that the Russian court mocked the mustaches of Berlin's two other allies: Gustav III and his brother Charles, the Duke of Södermanland. Khrapovitskii made a note in his diary on 7 October 1788: "The Count V. P. Musin-Pushkin has arrived; during [Catherine's] toilette, he related that the King of Sweden and his brother Charles wear mustaches, like cats' whiskers."[42]

In Derzhavin's poem, this deconstructive metaphor aimed to ridicule — most of all — the King of Prussia, one of the most dangerous enemies of Catherine II. Therefore, it is difficult to accept Grot's commentary on this phrase that advocates another Russian "success": Catherine's attempt to make Prussia her ally.[43] The circumstances were quite different.

In 1788, the King of Prussia, supported by his union with England and Holland, attempted to force political mediation on Catherine II in her war with Turkey. The conditions of the proposed treaty between Russia and Turkey, according to Berlin, required Catherine to give back practically all territories annexed after the first war with the Ottoman Porte, including the Crimea and

---

[42] Ibid, 117.
[43] *Sochineniia Derzhavina*, 1, 178.

Moldova. Berlin also was deeply involved in Polish affairs, plotting against Russian influence there and threatening to send an army to Poland. Besides supporting Gustav III in his aggression toward Russia, Frederick William II threatened to unleash war along the whole western frontier of Russia, from Finland to the Black Sea. At the same time, Prussia attempted to break the alliance between Russia and Denmark and to send an army to the Danish province of Holstein (the province was given to the Danes by Catherine in 1762 in exchange for peaceful relations). Being engaged in war with Sweden, Russia pushed Denmark to fulfill the requirements of their alliance, while Berlin made all possible efforts to prevent the Danish court from supporting Russia. Catherine II wrote to Grigorii Potemkin on 19 October 1788 about the Prussian intrigues: "The Prussian King has made two declarations — one to Poland against our alliance with the Poles... the other to the Danish court, threatening to send thirty thousand troops into Holstein should the Danish court, in our aid, enter Sweden."[44]

When Derzhavin mentioned Copenhagen in his humorous panorama, he meant the situation with Denmark and Berlin's threat to occupy Holstein (the situation remained very ominous throughout the winter months):

> You seed frost on Copenhagen <...> (172)

Catherine was so annoyed by Prussia's provoking and dictatorial tone, that she — for a few months — was about to announce war with Berlin. She wrote to Potemkin on 19 October 1788: "Day after day more is coming to light about their [the Prussians'] intentions and adopted plan not only to cause us all manner of harm, but also to provoke us at the present time, which is already difficult enough for us."[45]

The letter was treated at Potemkin's headquarters as an injunction to prepare for war with Prussia.[46] War was a hot-button

---

[44] *Love Conquest. Personal Correspondence of Catherine the Great and Prince Grigory Potemkin*, 265.
[45] Ibid, 265–266.
[46] M. A. Garnovskii, "Zapiski. 1786–1790," in *Russkaia starina*, 16 (1876), 224.

issue at the time, as the Danish court, having been knocked down by Prussia, had stopped military actions against Sweden. Potemkin tried to persuade Catherine to refrain from a fight with Prussia, while Catherine's advisers (Zavadovskii included) pushed her forward and argued against Potemkin's plan. In November — December of 1788 her intense correspondence with Potemkin slightly cooled down, as Catherine accused him of following Nikita Panin's geopolitical strategy of having Prussia as an ally. At practically the same time, both Potemkin and Derzhavin found themselves wrongly castigated for offenses they did not commit -- by the same group of people (Zavadovskii and Bezborodko). Potemkin had to clarify his position and to dismiss the calumnies of his court enemies; in his letter to Catherine II on 26 December 1788, he explains:

> Matushka, you expressed your anger in your last letters in vain. My zeal does not merit this. I do not base my ideas on the arguments of Count Panin, but on the state of affairs. I'm not in love with the Prussian King, I don't fear his troops... I am not one who would want your honor tarnished. But to begin anything without first making peace with the Turks cannot bring you glory. And this must be avoided in every possible way, for we surely shall lose if we poke our noses in everywhere.[47]

Catherine took Potemkin's side and avoided war with Berlin. Frederick William II was a dangerous enemy. He was a Mason, and — in addition to the direct military threat, he was an ideological opponent. His uncle, Frederick II, an enlightened king, friend and correspondent of Voltaire, as well as the author of *Antimachiavell* (1740), preferred to maintain reasonably pragmatic relations with the Russian Empress. His nephew was conservative, religious, and devoid of "enlightened" sentiments. Catherine felt insulted, especially by his open and passionate anti-Russian attitude. The king proclaimed Russia a constant threat to Europe and made every effort to isolate her. Catherine compared these two kings, expressed her sympathy toward Frederick the Great and explained, in a letter

---

[47] *Love Conquest. Personal Correspondence of Catherine the Great and Prince Grigory Potemkin*, 276.

to her constant correspondent I. G. Tsimmerman that the King of Prussia wanted to follow the old model of the balance of powers, but in reality he only desired to dominate all of Europe.[48]

Polish affairs were closely connected with the tense relations between the Russian court and Prussia. Grigorii Potemkin attempted to persuade Catherine to conclude an alliance treaty with her former lover and King of Poland, Stanislaw Poniatowski. According to the conditions for the alliance, Poland had to raise military troops to join the Russian army in combating the Turks. However, in autumn of 1788, after the announcement of the Swedish war against Russia, the Poles felt reluctant to pursue Russian directives. The dispersed groups of nobles looked toward Prussia and strove to bolster Poland against Russian aggression.[49] Both Russia and Prussia, in their effort to adjoin Poland to their adversarial coalitions, had virtually guaranteed autonomy to the Polish town of Danzig (Gdansk in Polish), a constant place of geo-political clashes between European powers. Thus, right at that moment, Fortune was very amiable toward the disputed city on the Baltic Sea, and Derzhavin's ode reflects this favorable course of events:

> You give a bucket of roses to Gdansk <…> (172)

Soon, however, Poniatowski, in his turn, began changing the terms of his loyalty to Catherine II. First, he started negotiating new proceedings in the law of succession to the throne for the sake of his nephew. Second, he refused to furnish the troops to fight against the Turks. Third, besides Gdansk, the Poles asked Russia to cede to them too many new territories. Finally, the so-called Four-Year Sejm (1788-1792), began its session in Warsaw. Catherine II awaited with apprehension the opening of the Polish parliament, but did not protest its conduction in order to "prevent social disturbances," as she wrote to her emissary in Poland.[50] Meanwhile, influenced by

---

[48] "Pis'ma imperatritsy Ekateriny II k I. G. Tsimmermannu. 1785–1791," in *Russkaia starina*, 7 (1887), 305–306.

[49] Albert Sorel, *Europe and the French Revolution* (London, 1969), 537–540.

[50] Lord Robert Howard, *The Second Partition of Poland. A Study in Diplomatic History* (Cambridge, 1915), 95; P. V. Stegnii, *Razdely Pol'shi i diplomatiia Ekateriny II* (Moscow, 2002), 211.

Prussian promises to return all Polish lands annexed in 1772 (during the first partition of Poland), the Sejm simply vetoed Stanislaw's provisions that were based on Catherine's project.

The majority of the Sejm consisted of the "patriots" headed by Ignatii Pototsky. This party of "patriots" represented different social strata of the Polish gentry and exhibited nationalistic feelings and hatred toward Russia as well. The party immediately required all Russian troops be removed from Poland, and they ordered that the pro-Russian Department of military affairs be abolished. The gatherings of the Sejm incited enormous enthusiasm in society.[51] It was a serious political failure, and Catherine had the courage to admit it.

Derzhavin's verse reflects the rise of anti-Russian ecstasy in Warsaw:

> You fluff Warsaw's tuft of hair <…> (172)

This sarcastic line provides an image of a famous attribute of the Polish military uniform, a cap with a quadrangular top, a cloth crown, and a huge tuft of feathers. The cap first appeared during the Bar Confederation in Poland in 1768–1772, and became a symbol of the Polish struggle for independence from Russia.

"You spit in the eyes of patriotism…"

Derzhavin's sentence on patriotism, placed in an unexpected context, remains puzzling and misinterpreted. Who spits in eyes of patriotism? What does Derzhavin mean to say? The ode's grotesque style has partially contributed to the false impression that the poet juxtaposes true and false patriotism, that the poet declares his own true patriotic feelings and claims his independence from the regime.[52] Meanwhile, the word "patriotism," in the modern sense of its meaning, was not very popular in Russia at that time: it was associated mostly with foreign affairs and politcal parties. Quite

---

[51] *Ekaterina II i G. A. Potemkin, Lichnaia perepiska*, 327.

[52] Anna Lisa Crone, *The Daring of Derzhavin. The Moral and Aesthetic Independence of the Poet in Russia*, 162.

"patriotic" Russian odes of the eighteenth century hardly employ this word at all. Derzhavin refers here to the specific political events abroad. Hence, it does not seem correct to believe that the phrase "is a kind of motto for the entire piece," whereby Derzhavin reveals his "true patriotism." Derzhavin's usage of the expression is strictly historical, and it does not stand for his own beliefs.

First of all, the poet makes allusions to the bad luck that plagued all "patriotic parties" which then existed in Poland, England, and Holland. The "patriots" headed by the Prince of Wales did not obtain power and failed in their political game with Pitt's ministerial party. The Polish "party of patriots", as Derzhavin implied, guided the country to disaster and to German invasion.

The events in Holland were even more dramatic. By the second half of the eighteenth century, the "party of patriots" had been formed from the remains of an old republican party, and it included representatives of the middle class. They were in some way influenced by France and by the ideas of the French Enlightenment. The "patriots" harshly criticized all aristocratic hereditary privileges and embraced the objective to abolish the power of the monarch (the stadholder). In 1785, the "patriots" incited a civil war against the monarch William IV, Prince of Orange and seized power.

However, Catherine's adversary, the Prussian King Frederick William II, sent troops to Holland, brutally put down a revolution, and restored his proponent and relative William IV as ruler. Holland was forced to become an ally of the union between England and Prussia. Many "patriots" fled to France. Thus, Fortune spat in eyes of "patriots" who had to leave their *"patria."*

Catherine II was very much concerned with the affairs in Holland: they weakened the influence of France, her current ally, and strengthened the entire anti-Russian coalition. Derzhavin means the Prussian involvement in Holland's affairs when he writes:

> And smoke sausage for the Dutch <...> (172)

Right at that time, Holland (like Poland) became the intersection of a severe struggle between different European powers — Prussia, England, France, and even Russia. Meanwhile, Catherine II, even in 1788, considered the possibility of a new wave of "patriots'" struggles in Holland. On 26 February 1788 she informed Potemkin: "Holland's affairs are not finished yet. The Prince of Orange is trying to be an absolute monarch, his wife is also gathering her party close at hand, and the patriots, in spite of everything, are once again gaining in strength."[53]

Derzhavin's sentence is apparently ironic towards the failed "patriotic parties," though the poet did not sympathize at all with their opponents. The combination of a colloquial form (to spit) with the abstract and ideological term "patriotism" produced a comic effect and created a grotesque atmosphere that imbued both the political discourse and the politics of the age alike.

Catherine II, Joseph II,
and the Plot against Grigorii Potemkin

Catherine made every effort to build a coalition against the powerful tripartite union of England-Prussia-Holland. First, the Russians counted Joseph II (1780–1790) of Austria, the Holy Roman Emperor, as an old friend. An enlightened ruler who abolished serfdom and capital punishment in Austria, he turned toward Catherine at the beginning of the 1780s, after the death of his mother and co-ruler Maria Theresa. Possessing a very skeptical attitude toward religion, and nurturing reforms in the Catholic church, Joseph refused to be influenced by the Pope. In 1782, he forced Pius VI to go against tradition and to come to visit him in Vienna — in person. Joseph's brother Peter Leopold II, Grand Duke of Tuscany, even more openly conducted policy to put the local clergy under his control. Their demonstrative gestures of independence marked a new course of relations between the pontiff and the archbishops, which were proclaimed in 1786 at a congress in Ems. Both royal brothers succeeded in some antipapal resolutions: the right to

---

[53] *Ekaterina II i Potemkin. Lichnaia perepiska. 1769–1791*, 272.

appoint local clergy, and freedom from papal inauguration of their power. Derzhavin's verses on Rome reflect these events:

> To prevent Rome's legs from swelling,
> When they drop their sacred shoes,
> You forbid kings to kiss them. (172)

Instead, Joseph paid a visit to Russia in 1783, and then in 1787, he joined Catherine during her trip to the Crimea. They signed a compact, and Joseph took Russia's side when the Ottoman Porte declared war in autumn of 1787. In 1788 Austria conducted military campaigns in close contact with the Russian army. The military operations of Austria went slowly, and were rather unsuccessful. In November 1788, Joseph II returned to Vienna from the front seriously ill, and would soon die, in 1790.

In autumn of 1788, the Austrians aggressively tried to involve Russia in the war with Prussia. They pushed the Empress to remain with Austria against Prussia, while Potemkin strove to convince the Empress to adopt a more cautious position toward the Prussians, and not to embark on war. In his letter on 3 November 1788, Potemkin writes:

> The Emperor [of Austria, Joseph II] has conducted an odd war, he has exhausted his army with its defensive position, and everywhere he has taken part himself he's been beaten up along with his best troops.... But if he sends some troops against the Prussian King, then you can be assured that the Turks will march into Vienna, and the Prussian King will grow even stronger.... Just think in what state of complete lethargy the Bourbons are — they'll betray us too, just as they did the Dutch. It is a powerful league: England, Prussia, Holland, Sweden, Saxony. And many Imperial Princes will join them. Poland will burden us more than the other states. Instead of starting a new war, for which we lack the strength, do everything possible to make peace with the Turks and direct your cabinet to lessen the number of Russia's enemies.[54]

---

[54] *Love Conquest. Personal Correspondence of Catherine the Great and Prince Grigory Potemkin*, 267–268.

Several members of Catherine's cabinet — A. Vorontsov, P. Zavadovskii, and A. Bezborodko — advised the Empress to side with Austria against Prussia. They hoped, most of all, to diminish Potemkin's influence. Taking advantage of Potemkin's absence, the pro-Austrian cabinet attempted to sabotage him at court by spreading rumors about his poor strategy and reluctance. At the same time, they encouraged Austria to vigorously confront Prussia as well. Derzhavin, in his panorama, devotes a brief line to Austria:

> In those days, when you assure Vienna <...> (172)

Derzhavin's Fortune takes care of Austria, like Catherine's pro-Austrian cabinet, which, making use of Potemkin's criticisms of Austrian maneuvers, plotted against the former favorite at exactly the same time. Derzhavin spent the autumn of 1788 in the closest contact with the family of Count S. F. Golitsyn, the major-general in Potemkin's army; hence he was very well informed on the military affairs of that time. His poem *An Autumn during the Siege of Ochakov* ("Осень во время осады Очакова") was dedicated to Varvara Engelgardt, Golitsyn's wife (and Potemkin's niece). Undoubtedly, Derzhavin considered Russia's support of Joseph's exhausted and disorganized army in order to enlist its services in the war against Prussia to be a strategic mistake. He includes this "support" ("when you assure Vienna") in his list of the political "scheming" of the Goddess Fortune who meddled in Russian domestic and international affairs.

However, after the capture of Ochakov, the grumbling against Potemkin quieted down, and on 16 December 1788, Catherine informed Potemkin of the change:

> "My true friend, you've silenced everyone, and this happy occasion provides you another opportunity to show magnanimity to your blind and empty-headed critics."[55]

The boyars' plot against Potemkin was no secret to Derzhavin. At the beginning of 1789, on the occasion of the celebration of

---

[55] *Love Conquest. Personal Correspondence of Catherine the Great and Prince Grigory Potemkin*, 275.

the siege of Ochakov, Derzhavin created his poem *To the Hero* ("Победителю"), which was addressed to Potemkin, based on the 90th Psalm, and therefore, constituted a kind of rescue from the nets of ill-wishers. The poet apparently associated the anti-Potemkin conspiracy with his own misfortunes, seeing that they both had become victims of intrigues and slander issued from the same group surrounding Catherine. A real plot against Potemkin started in September of 1788. Potemkin, disheartened by a severe storm on the Black Sea that partially destroyed the fleet at Sevastopol Bay, sent the General Field-Marshal P. A. Rumiantsev a desperate letter in which he practically requested to withdraw from command. Rumiantsev immediately mailed a copy to his protégée Zavadovskii, who handed it over to Catherine. [56]Potemkin's aide in Saint Petersburg Mikhail Garnovskii thoroughly collected the court rumors and related them to his superior. On 15 October 1788, Garnovskii conveyed his conversation with Catherine's current and well-informed favorite A. M. Dmitriev-Mamonov, who dispatched a warning to Potemkin: "Loving Your Excellence as a true father and my benefactor, I wish, on one hand, to advise him against engaging in very harmful correspondence which only helps the intrigues of his adversaries."[57]

At first, Zavadovskii seemed to have achieved his goal when the outraged Empress broke off her correspondence with Potemkin. Only the successful siege of Ochakov averted the plot's further development. Derzhavin was sure that his misfortunes came from the same camp, as he wrote in his *Memoirs*:

> The Senate, after having received a second complaint, though they could not consider it convincing, but being influenced by the general-prosecutor Viazemskii, and also by the Count Petr Vasilievich Zavadovskii (who had the powerful Count Bezborodko as his supporter), who, in his turn, was compatriot, relative, and old friend to Gudovich… decided to hand the report over to Catherine without waiting

---

[56] Olga Eliseeva, *Potemkin*, 425–426.
[57] *Russkaia starina*, 15:3 (1876), 477.

for Derzhavin's answer... The Empress having received such a tendentious report, rushed to persecute Derzhavin...[58]

Derzhavin's and Potemkin's lives turned out to be linked by spiteful scheming: the poet purposely combined allusions to his miserable status with Potemkin's fall into disfavor. In the ode, the poet mentions that he had turned fifty years old when, in reality, he was only forty-six. Right at that same time, Potemkin celebrated his fiftieth birthday — this method of complex allusions which referred to various real prototypes had already been elaborated in *Felitsa*.

France and others

The social and financial crisis in France provoked the French monarchy to seek an alliance with Russia in order to counterbalance British trade expansion as well as Prussia's aggression in Holland. Starting in 1787, Louis XVI attempted to forge close ties (political and commercial) with Russia. Tension began to mount in the negotiations with France at that time, and even Catherine's friend, the French diplomat Count Ségur, who actively promoted a new trade contract with Russia, was unable to remedy the situation. Catherine, meanwhile, suspected that France, her longtime enemy, was much more preoccupied with England and Prussia, and had plans to involve Russia in this confrontation. Catherine did not rush to sign any treaty, as it was quite clear that pre-revolutionary France was, little by little, losing strength and facing an escalating social and political crisis. On 6 November 1787 Catherine II wrote to Potemkin: "No doubt, France is apparently weakening, and seeks a union with us, but we should delay and continue talks as long as we can."[59]

The French monarchy was exhibiting the first indications of decline. In 1787, Louis XVI had to restore the French Parliament. In June 1788 a powerful social uprising in poor suburbs of Paris forced

---

[58] G. R. Derzhavin, *Zapiski. 1743–181* (Moscow, 2000), 118.
[59] *Ekaterina i Potemkin. Lichnaia perepiska. 1769–1791*, 250.

the French King to send the army to suppress the rebels. In 1788 and even at the beginning of 1789, not only Derzhavin, but many politicians could not yet anticipate the Revolution. Meanwhile, some gloomy forebodings that the French monarchy and aristocracy were in danger already existed. "France is weak" was a permanent motif in the correspondence of Catherine, Potemkin and the Russian minister in Paris, I. M. Simolin.[60]

Derzhavin's caustic sentence reflects the first symptoms of evaporation of the monarch's power in France — his capricious Fortune "musses Paris's wigs." The wig, as an old regime symbol of aristocracy, privilege, or simply status, serves here as a mocking reference to France, where wig production had become one of the main industries.

Derzhavin includes a line which concerned two other countries — the Venetian Republic and Malta:

> You don't show solicitude for Venice or Malta <...> (172)

The Venetian Republic, governed by its last Doges Paolo Renier (1779–1789) and Lodovoco Manin (1789–1797), besides displaying clear signs of economic and political decline, had become a territory of real and imagined expansionist plans.[61] As early as 1782, Joseph II, the Austrian emperor, was striving to occupy Dalmatia, while, at the same time, he proposed to Catherine II that she acquire Cyprus and several Greek islands. Russia also elaborated plans to embed its presence in the Mediterranean Sea, and hence looked upon Venice and Malta as potential strongholds in the enduring struggle against the Ottoman Porte. In its turn, France was worried about the rumors circulating that Russia, exerting its power, had signed a treaty with the Kingdom of Naples to take Malta. In 1797, Venice passed under the control of Napoleon, and later, in 1815, Dalmatia became the territory of Austria. However, already on the eve of the international

---

[60] "Frantsuzskaia revolutsiia 1789 v doneseniiakh Simolina, in *Literaturnoe nasledstvo*, 29 -30 (Moscow - Leningrad, 1937), 388–389.

[61] W. Carew Hazlitt, *The Venetian Republic, its Rise, its Growth, and its Fall, 421–1797* (London, 1900); Horatio Forbes Brown, *The Venetian Republic* (London, 1902); Larry Wolff, *Venice and the Slavs. The Discovery of Dalmatia in the Age of Enlightenment* (Stanford, 2003).

crises of 1789, both Venice and Malta could be considered as the first and most susceptible victims of malicious Fortune, an embodiment of imperialistic intrigues. Derzhavin's line on Greece's status among European powers coincides with the first two, Venice and Malta. According to Derzhavin's grasp of events, the fate of modern Greeks was in hands of other powers — Russia, Austria, and the Ottomans. The only role they could play in the contemporary international arena was to stare and await their destiny. As Derzhavin puts it in his ode:

> And order Greece to gape <...> (172)

The last potential ally of the quadruple union (besides Russia, Austria, and France) was Spain. Derzhavin's portrait of Spain was a reaction to the unexpectedly increasing role of a country which had been losing its greatness and its territories throughout the eighteenth century:

> You turn your nose up at Madrid <...> (172)

One of the most important lands, Gibraltar, had gone to Britain. The Spaniards strove to regain it and to retain control over the entire Mediterranean. Siding with France, Spain began to establish communication with Russia. The King of Spain, Charles III, in autumn of 1788, proposed diplomatic mediation to Russia in order to prevent a global European conflict. Catherine II, as Khrapovitskii's diary attests to, was rather appalled by such an offer from a country which already could not prove its influence. Khrapovitskii writes in an entry for 19 October 1788: "I brought downstairs a confidential communication in which the King of Spain, fearing an international war, proposed his mediation with complete self-assurance."[62]

Derzhavin's verse refers to the events of autumn of 1788 when Russia faced a serious crisis, and — for the first time in recent history — all the countries of Europe found themselves involved in a conflict of interests. At that time, Catherine II received many letters from different courts suggesting negotiations with different parties involved in the conflict.

---

[62] *Pamiatnye zapiski A. V. Khrapovitskogo*, 122.

Meanwhile, the King of Spain, Charles III, died on 1788, 14 December, and the treaty of alliance was postponed. The new king, Charles IV, was not experienced in political affairs, and, all along, relied on his much more knowledgeable ministers, such as Count Florida Blanca. Khrapovitskii, on 9 February 1789, made a brief account on the status of the treaty:

> The Spanish court is going to enter into a proposed alliance with the Emperor [of Austria], France and us. Count Florida Blanca feels it is risky to involve the new King in a union which is likely to provoke a war with England; the minister is not so powerful as he was under the late King; in addition, he is disposed to be influenced by the Prussian Court.[63]

The union with two Bourbon courts — French and Spanish — never came to fruition. The impending French revolution would change all of Catherine's strategic plans dramatically.

Again Felitsa: a Happy End

In his ode *To Fortune*, Derzhavin depicts the Tambov trial as a brutal violation of existing literary relations that had been established between him and Catherine-Felitsa. The poet demonstrably expresses, though with a bit of irony, rhetorical disappointment in his "amusing style" which contains jokes towards the "boyars" but leads only to disaster. He claims that he followed the rules of his and her (Felitsa's) mutual game, but as a result, he was fired from his post and taken to court. Instead of civilized literary polemics or witty and stylish satiric duels, the "boyars" organized a vicious, and quite real, persecution. They broke the rules of the convention of a "republic of letters," and exhibited their backwardness and lack of taste. Derzhavin writes:

> In those days, when she, to all incomparable,
> Is allied with you,
> It cannot be told in a fairy tale,
> Nor described beautifully with the pen,

---

[63] Ibid, 170–171.

> How she loves to pour out grace,
> How justly she rules,
> She does not burn people at the stake
> Or behead them without a trial.
> But only the Boyars somehow
> Or other screw up their mugs
> And beat someone now and then. (173)

By choosing a low-style vocabulary for depicting "the boyars," Derzhavin points toward the uncivilized and unenlightened behavior of his persecutors. By contrast, he and the Empress turned out to be "allied" by a unity of humanism (she is fair and merciful) and a branch of the humanities (she is a writer with good taste.)[64] Hence, the poet persistently intertwined both his and Catherine's literary occupations into his administrative affairs. He asked her, half-seriously and half-jokingly, to judge him by taking into account the new and mutually accepted esthetics: good and fashionable taste reflects a merciful and enlightened character.

Derzhavin performed his literary gambit quite flawlessly. As a result, the Empress not only accepted the rules of his game (established already by his *Felitsa* in 1783), but, following the Senate's favorable conclusion, completely acquitted him from all legal charges. Catherine stressed her understanding of their mutual game when, right at the moment of signing the acquittal, she declaimed a few sentences from Derzhavin's *Felitsa* and stated that it would be hard for her to accuse the author of the poem.[65] Khrapovitskii, an eyewitness to the episode, recorded on 27 June 1789:

> I have read the report on Derzhavin, who was acquitted by the 6th Department. Asked to retrieve a copy of the ode to Felitsa... I read Derzhavin's petition and presented the ode to Felitsa; in my presence she recited:
>
> > They also say, without falsehood,

---

[64] In his poem *To the Admirer of Arts* (*Любителю художеств*, 1791), Derzhavin links bad taste to cruelty and despotic rule. He calls the bearer of "vulgar taste" an "enemy" of "the common good" (*Sochineniia Derzhavina s ob"iasnitel'nymi primechaniiami Ia. K. Grota*, I, 256).

[65] *Pamiatnye zapiski A. V. Khrapovitskogo*, 198 (11 July 1789).

> That it is always possible for anyone
> To approach you, and speak the truth.

I was ordered to tell Derzhavin that his report and his petition were read, and that it was difficult for Her Highness to indict the author of the ode to Felitsa, *celà le concolera*. I have conveyed to her Derzhavin's gratitude — *on peut lui trouver une place*.[66]

This solemn and apparently theatrical episode proved that Catherine understood the rules of a "republic of letters," and she made her imperial decisions in accordance with these literary strategies. These two parties finished the Tambov trial not only as the Empress and her subject, but as participants in a literary scenario which had been developed in Derzhavin's odes. Once again, Catherine played along with their joint plot and confirmed that she was a true Felitsa.

---

[66] Ibid.

Chapter Eight

Ridiculing the Monarch

*I*n the October issue of the magazine *Saint Petersburg Mercury* (Санкт-Петербургский Меркурий) published in 1793 by two literary allies Ivan Krylov (1769–1844) and Alexander Klushin (1763–1804), perceptive readers might stumble upon an anonymous poem which has not attracted the attention of modern scholars. The authorship of this satiric vignette or verse fable, written quite soundly in bold iambic verses, remained concealed for centuries. The text had the provoking title *A Dying Coquette (Умирающая кокетка)*, as well as a most enigmatic subtitle, "Sent by an unknown person," and described a certain elderly lady who strove to seduce men while being already half-dead:

> One cannot count the follies
> Of our amazing Nature:
> It seems that men and women
> Fell into madness.
> The dying beauty is already covered with ash
> And only in the heat of the moment
> Is not buried in the ground.
> She espied a piece of flannel from her coffin
> Which had been prepared the week before
> In order to ornament her dead body as appropriate.
> "I don't want," she said
> "This black cloth to enfold me,
> It does not suit me at all,
> I wish you would dress me as for a wedding,
> In pearl-colored satin,
> And adorn my pale face with a lace cap.

> Give me a bit of red for my cheeks.
> No need to frighten men even from the grave."
>
> If she wished to please men so in death,
> What sort of woman had she been in life? <...>¹

The poem provides an image of a coquette, epitomizing one of the most popular personages of ridicule, which was widespread in verse tales, comedies, and satirical prose. At first glance, the text represents a traditional satire on the excusable "vice" of coquetry, and its content revolves around the customary mockery of women's passion for fashion and dress that saturated satirical magazines since the 1760s.[2] Moreover, the poem apparently refers to Alexander Pope's epistle *Of the Knowledge and Characters of Men*, written at the beginning of the 1730s and included in his *Moral Essays*. One of the epistle's fragments describing some Narcissa might be considered as a literary source of *A Dying Coquette*:

> 'Odious! in woollen! 'twould a saint provoke,'
> (Were the last words that poor Narcissa spoke),
> 'No, let a charming chintz and Brussels lace
> Wrap my cold limbs, and shade my lifeless face:
> One would not, sure, be frightful when one's dead —
> And, Betty, give this cheek a little red.'[3]

Both Pope and the anonymous Russian author describe a certain lady who asks for some fashionable clothing and cosmetics and does not want to frighten men while preparing for a funeral. Alexander Pope (1688–1744) was one of the most well-known poets in eighteenth-century Russia, and translations of his work began to appear in 1749.[4] Besides Russian translations, many French editions of Pope's work were popular among his Russian readers. Characterizing social morals, Pope emphasized the significance

---

[1] *Sankt-Peterburgskii Merkurii*, 4 (1793, October), 34–36.

[2] L. O. Zaionnts, "Khvoraniia po mode Nikolaia Strakhova, ili ob odnom neosushchestvlennom zamysle Iu. M. Lotmana", in *Antropologiia kul'tury*, 2 (Moscow, 2004), 171–186.

[3] *The Works of Alexander Pope in 9 volumes*, III (London 1822), 201–202.

[4] See *Russko-evropeiskie literaturnye svizi. XVIII vek. Entsiklopedicheskii slovar'* (Saint Petersburg, 2008), 173–175.

of human follies or, as he formulated, of the "Ruling Passion," a concept he first examined in his major work, *An Essay on Man*. The Narcissa of Pope's epistle was a satiric portrait of the famous British actress Mrs. Anne Oldfield (1683–1730), the daughter of a soldier who became not only a theatrical star, but also a recognized society celebrity.[5] The appearance of the Russian poem referring to Pope was not accidental. The magazine *Saint Petersburg Mercury* in 1793 frequently included materials connected with Alexander Pope: in the April issue they published Voltaire's note on Alexander Pope, and in the August and September issues Pope's *Essay on Man* appeared, translated by Ivan Martynov. Some of the magazine's poetic output (for example, P. M. Karabanov's *Theft of Locks of Hair for my Ring to Aniuta* (Похищенные волоски в перстень к Анюте) in the September issue) displayed obvious references to Pope's poetry (*The Rape of the Lock*, first of all). Overall, the authors and editors of the magazine *Saint Petersburg Mercury* could have been called disciples of Alexander Pope's satirical and philosophical work.

Meanwhile, the poem *A Dying Coquette*, like Pope's epistle, not only comprises some eloquent speculations on women's coquetry, but it contains at the same time a good deal of allusions. The Russian author even crossed the border of blameless ridicule and added much more offensive features to his verses. The final sentences reveal something more than a general portrait of an elderly coquette and introduce a malicious satire on a very particular person:

> If she wished to please men so in death,
> What sort of woman had she been in life?[6]

The irritation and even rage of the anonymous poet could not escape the reader who had some grounds to deduce that the poem belonged to the editor of the magazine Ivan Krylov, while the prototype of a dying coquette implied Krylov's personal adversary and persecutor Catherine II.

---

[5] Joanne Lafler, *The Celebrated Mrs. Oldfield: the Life and Art of an Augustan Actress* (Carbondale, IL 1989).

[6] *Sankt-Peterburgskii Merkurii*, 4 (October 1793), 35.

Scenarios of Publishing:
Literary Magazines against Power

Scholars usually depict the early Krylov's journalistic endeavors as well as his relationship with the authorities as a kind of a diagram which indicates a gradually declining sharpness of criticism. They assume that the young editor of satirical magazines was, step by step, forced by the government to reduce the level of his denunciation of the late Catherine's regime. Krylov's first magazine, *Mail for Spirits* (*Почта духов*), which appeared in January of 1789, evidently proved his political radicalism when he (and his contributors, such as Alexander Radishchev) dared to criticize the tangible facts of Russian society by the end of Catherine's rule. This edition proved to be popular even in diplomatic circles; as Charles Masson recalled in his memoirs, the magazine was "the most philosophical and poignant that ever ventured to appear in Russia."[7] This edition ceased publication after several months, in August of that same year, presumably under pressure from "above." Krylov had to resign from all journalistic activity for two years.[8]

The political atmosphere stirred by the French revolution of 1789 was not favorable to satirical enterprises. In 1789, the censorship banned the tragedy *Vadim of Novgorod* (*Вадим Новгородский*) by Iakov Kniazhnin, a loyal playwright who took the liberty of presenting a half legendary rebellion of 864. In 1790, Alexander Radishchev, the author of *A Journey from Saint Petersburg to Moscow* (*Путешествие из Петербурга в Москву*), which sharply criticized the current political and social system, was exiled to Siberia. In 1792, Nikolai Novikov, the most prominent editor at the time and the leader of the Russian Enlightenment, was arrested and imprisoned in the Shlisselburg Fortress.

---

[7] Charles Masson, *Mémoires secrets sur la Russie, et particulièrement sur la fin du règne de Catherine II et le commencement de celui de Paul I* (Paris, 1800), 189.

[8] Iu. M. Lotman brought up evidence of the existing continuation of Krylov's *Mail for Spirits*, after it was banned by the censorship: Iu. M. Lotman, "O tretiei chasti *Pochty dukhov* I. A. Krylova," in *XVIII vek*, 3 (Moscow- Leningrad, 1958), 511–512.

Despite malevolent political circumstances, in 1792, Ivan Krylov began publishing a new magazine. His *Spectator* (*Zritel'*) continued for a whole year in spite of caustic remarks toward the authorities in his stories *Nights* (*Ночи*), *Каиб*, as well as in his prose grotesque *A Laudatory Speech in Memory of My Grandfather* (*Похвальная речь в память моему дедушке*). This edition survived even the most tumultuous event in Krylov's political biography. On 12 May 1792 Krylov's publishing house became the subject of a police search which was initiated, according to rumor, by Platon Zubov, the last of Catherine's favorites. They looked for Krylov's story *My Fevers* (*Мои горячки*) and Klushin's poem *Turtle-doves* (*Горлицы*). Krylov was interrogated, and the story was confiscated and sent to Zubov; it still remains unknown what happened to the manuscript.[9]

As for Klushin, he managed to destroy the manuscript whose written synopsis he had had to provide to police. Examining a brief outline, Grigorii Gukovskii was able perhaps to restore the main plot of the poem: "From a brief description, it is clear that the poem *Turtle-doves* was about the French (disguised as 'turtle-doves') who found a new life in their revolution as well as about the Austrian and Russian governments (disguised as 'crows') that were ready for an intervention against a revolutionary France."[10] The authorities, meanwhile, did not prohibit the magazine, though they did put Krylov's publishing house under secret surveillance. Gossip about the occurrence widely circulated in literary circles.[11]

Since 1793 a new magazine, *Saint Petersburg Mercury*, made a start in the same publishing house. The last journalistic endeavor by Krylov and Klushin, as some scholars assumed, proved to be not as provocative and radical in its treatment of political and social

---

[9] G. Rozhdestvenskii, *Krylov i ego tovarishchi po tipografii i zhurnalu v 1792 godu* (Moscow, 1899), 11.

[10] G. A. Gukovskii, *Russkaia literatura XVIII veka*, 481.

[11] Later, on 3 January 1793, Nikolai Karamzin, in a letter to his friend and literary ally Ivan Dmitriev, made inquires about the incident: "I was told that the editors of the *Spectator* were arrested, is it true? Why?" in *Pis'ma N. M. Karamzina k I. I. Dmitrievu* (Saint Petersburg, 1866), 33.

matters.[12] Gukovskii gave the following explanation of the evident change in the magazine's strategy: "It had already ceased to be an efficient weapon of a group of writers on the offensive. It was undoubtedly the result of pressure of the authorities. They made it clear to Krylov and Klushin what they could do and what they could not, and both editors had to concede to power. It was 1793, the year of revolutionary dictatorship in France."[13]

However, even a cursory glance at the magazine's material stirs controversy with the scholar's remark. The *Saint Petersburg Mercury* provides evidence that it was not less sharp than the previous two magazines. In the January and April issues, Krylov included his two satirical speeches *A Sycophantic Speech on the Art of Killing Time* (Похвальная речь науке убивать время) and *A Laudatory Speech to Ermalafid* (Похвальная речь Ермалафиду). His July issue came out with a translation of the Abbot Raynal's *On the Discovery of America* (Об открытии Америки). The Abbot Raynal was one of the thinkers who inspired the leaders of the French Revolution (as well as Alexander Radishchev),[14] and the publication was meant to attract attention. Krylov and Klushin consciously provoked a scandal. They published Voltaire's translations (Voltaire was already considered, in the context of the Revolution, to be a dangerous writer) in the August issue, Iakov Kniazhnin's tragedy *Vadim of Novgorod* was discussed, and Klushin wrote a panegyric to the accused author.[15] The editors at every turn challenged the regime: they filled the magazine with forbidden names, addressed the most painful topics to their audience, and attempted to engage the regime in a direct dialog.

Some scholars presumed that Krylov and Klushin relied on their prominent supporters, representatives of the so-called "party of the heir," Pavel Petrovich.[16] Meanwhile, at the beginning of

---

[12] G. A. Gukovskii, *Russkaia literatura XVIII veka*, 481.

[13] Ibid.

[14] P. N. Berkov, *Istoriia russkoi zhurnalistiki XVIII veka* (Moscow-Leningrad, 1952), 492.

[15] *Sankt-Peterburgskii Merkurii*, I (February 1793), 141–142.

[16] A. M. Gordin, M. A. Gordin, "Krylov: real'nost' i legenda, in *I. A. Krylov v*

the 1790s, there was not a distinct "party," although some of the high-ranking officials began expressing their disappointment with Catherine II. Ekaterina Dashkova was among them. In 1793–1794 Dashkova published four of Krylov's plays in the newly established magazine *Russian Theater* (*Российский Театр*). Eventually Krylov enjoyed appreciation from a powerful supporter who had counted his works amongst the "best Russian plays": the tragedy *Philomela* (*Филомела*, 1786), the comic opera *A Wild Family* (*Бешеная семья*, 1786), and the two comedies *Mischievous Persons* (*Проказники*, 1788), and *A Writer in the Ante-Chamber* (*Сочинитель в прихожей*, 1786.)

Moreover, since August 1793, Dashkova arranged the production of the *Saint Petersburg Mercury* in the publishing house of the Russian Academy under her supervision. Dashkova moved yet further to an open scandal when she published the tragedy *Vadim of Novgorod* by Kniazhnin: the tragedy came out in September 1793 in the same volume (№ 39) of *Russian Theater* in which Krylov's plays were printed. Platon Zubov, Catherine's favorite, having been informed of the publication, reported back to Catherine, who requested that the pages with the text of the play be torn out of that issue of the magazine, as well as that a separate edition of Kniazhnin's tragedy be burned. Soon after that, Dashkova would be forced to resign from her post as the President of the Russian Academy.

The *Saint Petersburg Mercury* also became subjugated. At the same time, in September 1793, both co-editors Krylov and Klushin were dismissed from the magazine, and, as many memoirists presumed, were personally interrogated by Catherine. Catherine obviously did not want a public scandal and made some arrangements for the two disgraced editors. The young writer and translator Ivan Martynov was appointed chief editor of the magazine in order to fulfill the annual commitment to subscribers. The October issue of 1793 turned out to be the last one completed by Krylov and Klushin. Only in April 1794 did readers receive the last

---

vospominaniiakh sovremennikov (Moscow 1982), 16; see also: M. Gordin, Ia. Gordin, *Teatr Ivana Krylova* (Leningrad 1983), 20–23.

two issues (November's and December's), prepared by Martynov and equipped with a polite announcement about the end the publication:

> "The year of the *Mercury* is over, and since the editors have taken a leave of absence, it cannot be continued."[17]

In his memoirs, Martynov cautiously described an official version of the events, avoiding detailed commentary: "Around the middle of this year <1793> Klushin, who wished to go abroad, left the magazine, and the empress Catherine the Great granted him his salary of 300 rubles for 5 years in advance, in total 1500 rubles; after that I had no knowledge of where he went; and Krylov also left to stay with some countryman. Therefore, I was charged with the administration of the *Mercury*."[18]

Hence, the poem *A Dying Coquette* appeared on the pages of the last issue of the *Saint Petersburg Mercury*, prepared by Krylov and Klushin, right in time for this outlandish and thoroughly veiled turmoil. The role of Catherine, who stopped the edition's publication but provided money to both editors to send them away from the capital, appears quite unusual. The circumstances of such personal involvement on the part of the empress and her evident efforts to carry out the dismissal as secretly as possible stir up controversy around Krylov and stress the importance of the real addressee of the poem decrying a dying coquette.

Creating a Russian Libertine: Ivan Krylov and His Circle

At first sight, it is rather difficult to associate the later Krylov, a famous Russian fabulist, author of numerous fables, the "Russian Aesop," "Krylov the grandfather," as he was called, with any kind of libertinage. The glossy image of a calm wizard who proclaims mutual consensus between differences, common sense and the

---

[17] *Sankt-Peterburgskii Merkurii*, IV (1793 December), 257–258.

[18] I. I. Martynov, "Zapiski," in *Pamiatniki novoi russkoi istorii*, 2 (Saint Petersburg, 1872), 88.

peaceful coexistence of men and monarch did not correspond too well with the bawdy, naughty, cheeky world of French libertinism. However, one title Krylov has been endowed with, "the Russian La Fontaine," sounded ambiguous, for the reason that La Fontaine with his *Contes et Nouvelles en vers* (1665–1666) belonged to the libertine trend and composed erotic verse tales.

Meanwhile, young Ivan Krylov, as he presented himself during the final decades of the eighteenth century, was a rather disturbing and cheeky person who created lampooning comedies and grotesque speeches, as well as, with his friend and literary ally Alexander Klushin, magazines of exceptional satirical resonance. Some scholars (for example, Grigorii Gukovskii and Pavel Berkov) have contextualized Krylov's extravagant literary image within the framework of a satiric writer decrying the "vices" and exposing the "follies" of Russia's corrupted gentry.[19] They considered Krylov to be a social and literary parvenu who consistently attacked the most powerful and respectable group of the so-called "gentry writers" (such as Kniazhnin, Derzhavin, and Karamzin).

In fact, since the mid-1780s, Krylov began constructing his literary and journalistic stance by aggressively rejecting the existing Russian stereotypes. He did not wish to cultivate the normative role of a "writer in the ante-chamber" of a powerful boyar, as he put it in the title of his comedy. Krylov as well as his friend Klushin insistently embarked on ridiculing Catherine's best singer Gavrila Derzhavin, scorning his image of a poet who playfully conducted a soulful and sincere dialogue with a "good monarch." Derzhavin's ode *A Vision of Murza* (*Видение Мурзы*), which was printed in the first issue of the *Moscow Journal* (*Московский Журнал*) in 1791, became the prime target of their attacks. Derzhavin always repudiated any accusation of flattery towards Catherine but was not successful in persuading the two young journalists of there being any political or literary grounds for adulation.

First, in his poem *To Happiness* (*К Счастию*, 1793), Krylov, while referring to Derzhavin's odes (including *To Fortune*) and saturating his poem with Derzhavin's reminiscences, blamed his

---

[19] G. A. Gukovskii, *Russkaia literature XVIII veka*, 473.

humble destiny and ironically juxtaposed the luxurious feasts in Derzhavin's *Felitsa* to his more than modest dinner:

> Why do you tender your favorites,
> Like a grandmother her grandsons,
> Always indulging their whims?
> To spite envious minds,
> You raise to heaven their homes,
> Like miraculous palaces,
> As we hear in tales <...>
> Whilst, my friend, we don't have
> Even preserved apples
> For our modest dinner <...>...[20]

Krylov addressed his sarcastic invectives to the monarch when he mentioned a "grandmother" and her "tales." If the first referred to Catherine's well-known pseudonym under which she had published her magazine *All Sorts and Sundries* (*Всякая всячина*), the latter alluded to Catherine's didactic tales on Chlor and Fevei. Krylov, like Derzhavin, chose the genre of the ode to Fortune, but rewrote it according to his own strategy, stressing the point that Derzhavin's self-contented complaints to Fortune are merely a way to improve one's social status.

Krylov's poem was printed in the November issue of the *Saint Petersburg Mercury*, together with Klushin's poem entitled *In Gratitude to Catherine the Great for my Most Kind Dismissal Abroad with a Pension* (*Благодарность Екатерине Великой за всемилостивейшее увольнение меня в чужие краи с жалованием.*) At first glance, the poem seemed to be a complimentary ode to Catherine, if taken out of context. However, Klushin purposely shaped his poem as a collage of reminiscences from Derzhavin's *A Vision of Murza*, and the poet evidently and deliberately accentuated his mass borrowings from Derzhavin. Klushin applied Derzhavin's formulas and poetic turns, and an absurd density of quotations transformed praise into parody:

> Through dark blue-grey clouds
> A silver moon was glimpsing;

---

[20] I. A. Krylov, *Polnoe sobranie sochinenii*, III (Moscow, 1946), 254.

> Casting light down from up above
> Her horns silvered the air.
> Upon light blue waves
> Corals and purples gamboled
> Tracing stars on the water. [21]

The beginning of Klushin's poem referred to the famous opening of Derzhavin's poem *A Vision of Murza*:

> Upon the dark-blue sky
> The golden moon was floating;
> With a silver porphyry,
> Gleaming from above, she
> Brought light through windows to my house;
> And her pastel rays
> Painted golden glows
> On my polished floor.[22]

Like Alexander Sumarokov, whose *Mock Odes* (Вздорные оды) parodied Lomonosov by tightly and absurdly connecting most impressive quotations, Klushin turned worship into mockery and completely deconstructed the complimentary ode as a genre. At the same time he made every effort to demonstrate the hyperbole and ludicrousness of his distorted quotations. Combining the plot of Derzhavin's *Vision of Murza* and the ode *The God*, Klushin made his lyrical hero suddenly perceive himself as a "grain of sand" or mere "dust" before the great "wife" or the "gentle Goddess" came down and resurrected him.

By the end of the poem *A Vision of Murza*, Derzhavin, referring to Horace, glorified the empress and proclaimed his poetic immortality as bound up with the immortality of the monarch whom he has chanted. Addressing Catherine, Derzhavin concluded:

> Among the sun or the moon
> I will place your image for future days;
> I will extol and glorify you;
> I will be immortal through you. [23]

---

[21] *Poety XVIII veka*, 2, 356.
[22] *Sochineniia Derzhavina s ob"iasnitel'nymi primechaniiami Ia. Grota*, I, 106–107.
[23] *Ibid*, I, 111.

Klushin parodied the poem by including Derzhavin's most eloquent speculations on his mystical association with Catherine and their mutual immortality:

> Everything can change in the universe,
> Can be glimpsed, vanish, be extinguished,
> But my gratitude will last forever
> For you, my immortal one!
> My progeny will read in my verses
> That your deeds are great and sound;
> Through you, I will be immortal, too. [24]

Klushin was not a well-known or highly acclaimed poet, and out of context, his verses sounded far too pompous and inadequate. Klushin demonstrably implied an appeal to his progeny, introduced too many verbs with the same semantics of vanishing, and affectedly declared his immortality, linking it to the immortality of the object of his praise (Catherine II). For both writers, mock poetry and political rebellion were closely aligned.

Some scholars, in attempting to bolster Krylov's image as an indefatigable combatant, have even characterized the writer as a tireless plotter against Catherine II and a hidden member of the so-called "Panin opposition," a group that worked for the interests of Catherine's son, Paul.[25] However, both the sociological and conspiratorial approaches need to be seriously reexamined, insofar as they obscure Krylov's more complex political and literary strategy.

In constructing his authorial stance, Krylov primarily oriented himself on the models of French libertinage. Among the most characteristic features of a typical French libertine of the eighteenth century were freethinking, an anti-clerical (even atheistic) outlook and an emancipated (even Bohemian) mode of behavior. Nicolas Boileau in his *Fourth Satire* defined libertines as people "without soul and faith," as people who "make their pleasure the superior law."[26]

---

[24] *Poety XVIII veka*, 2, 358–359.

[25] M. Gordin, Ia. Gordin, *Teatr Ivana Krylova*, 64.

[26] "Un Libertin d'ailleurs, qui sans âme et sans foi, / Se fait de son plaisir une suprême loi," see: Boileau, *Oeuvres complètes* (Paris, 1966), 26.

Chapter Eight

The libertines' literary life was full of scandals, and lampooning was their preferred way of communicating with literary opponents. Their works combined metaphysical themes (which revealed a diversity of beliefs and opinions that differed from traditional norms) with conspicuously pornographic motifs.

Among the most well-known were Crébillion fils with his novel *Le Sopha* (1742), Diderot's novel *Les Bijoux indiscrets* (*Speaking Jewelry*, 1748; in 1749 the novel was translated into English in 1749 as *The Talking Pussy*). One of the most popular was the English novel by John Cleland, *Memoirs of a Woman of Pleasure* (1748-49), called in short *Fanny Hill* and translated into French as *Fille de Joye* (1751). Among the most famous was also a pornographic novel, *Thérèse philosophe* (1748), by Marquis d'Argents. Jean-Baptist de Boyer, marquis d'Argents (1704–1771), and Louis-Sébastien Mercier (1740–1814) would soon become very popular in Russia. This kind of literature was international: all works were immediately translated, though the distribution of such literature was very difficult.[27] These novels had enormous success throughout Europe, irrespective of the borders of language or social position. It was a very significant moment when such works burst into print and started a new epoch in which "everything was held up to question and nothing was sacred."[28] Russian writer Ivan Krylov was an exemplary apprentice of this movement.[29]

First of all, Krylov was very well acquainted with this tradition: his *Mail for Spirits* was inspired by the prose of d'Argents and another French writer, Louis-Sébastien Mercier. Almost half the letters of Krylov's novel was a very close transposition (sometimes a mere translation) of works by d'Argents and Mercier.[30]

---

[27] Robert Darnton, *The Forbidden Best-Sellers of Pre-Revolutionary France* (New York, 1995), 118.

[28] Ibid, 90.

[29] Mark Altshuller, "Krylov i volterianstvo", in *Russia and the World of the Eighteenth Century*. Ed. R. P. Bartlett, A. G. Cross, Karen Basmussen (Columbus, Ohio, 1988), 347–359.

[30] M. V. Razumovskaia, "*Pochta dukhov* A. Krylova i romany markiza d"Arzhana" in Russkaia literatura, 1 (1978), 103–115.

The "Voltairian" and atheistic atmosphere of early Krylov is also very characteristic. Krylov's closest friends and literary allies were two inveterate free-thinkers. First, Ivan Rakhmaninov (mid 1750s–1807) was a translator of Voltaire and Mercier, as well as the editor of two journals, *Medicine for Boredom and Troubles (Лекарство от скуки и забот, 1787)* and *Morning Hours (Утренние часы, 1788–89)*. He was a convinced Voltairian and gave Krylov books to read and money to print journals. Krylov himself appreciated very much Rakhmaninov's erudition and strong libertine principles and wrote about him: "Voltaire and modern philosophers were his deities."[31] Rakhmaninov successfully published a three volume edition of Voltaire in 1785–1789 and planned to publish the complete works by his favorite author. However, in 1794, by Catherine's ordinance, the edition was bunged, and his publishing house was closed. Krylov's second close friend was his co-editor Alexander Klushin, a satirical writer, poet, and journalist. According to the famous A. T. Bolotov's *Memoirs*, Klushin was "very clever, a good writer, <...> but he had a nasty heart, he was a great atheist," "a foul-mouthed person," "he swears and uses foul language especially when he talks about priests and saints."[32] So the immediate environment of young Krylov exhibited some pretty peculiar qualities: an atheistic outlook, a tendency to oppose any compliance with the authorities, freethinking, an orientation toward French liberal literature, and independence in one's personal life. They did not agitate for any kind of revolt against the monarchy, but the group differentiated itself from other circles of writers by their provocative nature and non-conformist position.

Exposing Cleopatra on the Throne

Erotic plots and portraits of the "desacralized king" were among the most popular topics in the French libertine tradition. The peculiarities of the Russian situation allowed Krylov to combine both topics. Catherine the Second, having had, during the 34 years

---

[31] *Krylov v vospominaniiakh sovremennikov* (Moscow 1982), 113.
[32] A. T. Bolotov, *Pamiatnik protekshikh vremen* (Moscow 1875), 69.

of her reign, 21 official favorites (and an innumerable quantity of temporary partners) thus acquired not only a reputation for being a "philosopher on throne." European writers placed Catherine in the most piquant context: Rudolph Raspe's famous Baron Munhausen asked the empress for a night, and the Marquis de Sade depicted her in his pornographic *A History of Juliette*. Moreover, French poet Sénac de Meilhan in 1775 composed an epic poem in six chapters entitled *La Foutromanie* (*A Passion for Copulation*.) It was an imitation of the most well-known pornographic poem *Ode a Priape* by Alexis Piron. Among the heroes of *Foutromanie* were Greek gods and… Catherine the Second.[33]

Even the diplomatic memoirist Charles Masson, in depicting the empress's nocturnal bacchanalias in the company of Zubov and his brother, caustically noticed: "Catherine was as much a philosopher as was Thérèse."[34] The sentence refers to *Thérèse philosophe* by marquis d'Argents, the bestseller of French literature and the best example of libertine philosophical pornography. The heroine of this novel appears occupied exclusively with love affairs that are entwined together with metaphysical speculations that regard sexual desire as a kind of philosophy. The comparison of Catherine to Thérèse openly mocked Catherine's well-known pretension of being a "philosopher on throne."

In the last years of her reign the dissipation of Catherine the Great acquired grotesque forms. The young cornet Platon Zubov (who was twenty-two years old) entered the bedroom of the aging empress in 1789 and he would leave it only after her death in November of 1796. His swift ascent as well as his improbable power (he had been assigned the rank of field-marshal) provoked discord even among Catherine's retinue. Memoirs of contemporaries depict his intellectual and political debility and the total mediocrity of

---

[33] Alexandrian, *Histoire de la littérature érotique* (Paris, 1989), 166; Larry Wolff, "The Fantasy of Catherine in the Fiction of the Enlightenment: From Baron Munchausen to the Marquis de Sade" in *Eros and Pornography in Russian Culture*. Ed. by M. Levitt and A. Toporkov (Moscow, 1999), 249–261. See also: Oliver Gajda, *Katharina II von Russland im Diskurs der Sexualitat. Mittelbare Einflusse narrativer Fiktion auf Geschichtsschreibung* (Berlin 2002).

[34] Ch. Masson, *Mémoires secrets sur la Russie* (Paris, 1800), 163.

his personality as well. Prince Mikhail Shcherbatov expressively describes the court environment in his book *On the Corruption of Morals in Russia* (*О повреждении нравов в России*):

> "To add to the corruption of women's morals and all decency, she has set other women the example of the possession of a long and frequent succession of lovers <...> Seeing a shrine erected to this vice in the heart of the Empress, women scarcely think it a vice in themselves to copy her <...> Although she is in her declining years, although grey hair now covers her head and time marked her brow with indelible signs of age, yet her licentiousness still does not diminish."[35]

Young Krylov was not indifferent to the peculiar customs of the royal court. His tragedy *Cleopatra* (*Клеопатра*; 1785) became the earliest confirmation of Krylov's preoccupation with the depraved ways of the imperial house. The precise content of the vanished play remains unknown. However, the despotic Egyptian queen, full of love, is easily associated with her Russian counterpart. The mere title of Krylov's tragedy (a genre which presupposed political allusions) was very provocative. Mikhail Pogodin in his *Diary* recounts a brief but expressive story told by Krylov himself about his most recent meeting with Catherine's hated son, the Russian Emperor Paul the First. The episode took place soon after Paul's accession. Pogodin stated: "Paul met him and said: 'Hello, Ivan Andreevich. How are you?' Krylov gave him the tragedy *Cleopatra*."[36] The presentation of the tragedy appears senseless without the anti-Catherinian context of Krylov's play.

In Krylov's comedy *A Wild Family*, all female characters, regardless of their age, are completely engulfed in love affairs. The playwright depicted their "love fevers" focusing, in particular, on the elderly grandmother, named Gorbura, who happened to be madly in love as well. The same character and name would appear soon thereafter in a few works by Krylov. His comedy about

---

[35] Prince M. M. Shcherbatov, *On the Corruption of Morals in Russia*. Edited and translated by A. Lentin (Cambridge, 1969), 245.
[36] *I. A. Krylov v vospominaniiakh sovremennikov*, 245.

depraved social customs, by the end, transcends mere ridicule and becomes a buffoonish travesty.[37] It was not by accident that Krylov focuses on topics of love's obsession, and specifically, on the elderly ladies' "wildness" in love. He deliberately emphasized such "love fevers" as he tried to demonstrate to his readers which personalities and scenarios were the most emblematic of their age. It was also quite characteristic that later, in 1792, the police, sent by the order of Platon Zubov, would search for his story entitled *My Fevers*. The topic of "love fevers" was easily associated with the Russian court.

Krylov's next comedy, *Mischievous Persons* (1788), again centers on the depraved behavior of well-known personages, and love affairs constitute the main intrigue of the play. The comedy was a clear libel of Krylov's theatrical rival Iakov Kniazhnin and his wife who recognized themselves in the two main characters Rifmokrad and Taratora and even complained about the public slander. Both personages were endowed with equally immoral features and meaningful names: "a person who steals rhymes" (Rifmokrad) and "a person who chatters" (Taratora.) Krylov did not depict a single positive hero, and turned every traditional comic trope into a grotesque. Like "love fevers," the word "mischievous persons" pointed towards to their adultery. The comedy *A Writer in the Antechamber* did not avoid similar grotesque and politically evocative episodes. In the culmination of the plot, the main hero, Count Dubovoi, who was supposed to read a laudatory poem, was given instead a wrong piece of paper which contained a list of his fiancée Novomodova's 44 lovers. This hint gets directly to the point, thereby challenging the regime to an extent never before experienced in Catherine's time.

A number of allusions to the empress's "love fevers," which Krylov habitually staged to ridicule the "vices" and "follies" of the gentry, contributed to the continuing desacralization of the monarchy in a much more personal way. In Krylov's prose work

---

[37] G. A. Gukovskii, Russkaia literature XVIII veka, 473. See also a detailed examination of early Krylov's theatrical works: L. Kiseleva, "Nekotorye osobennosti poetiki Krylova-dramaturga (vzaimootnosheniia s literaturnoi traditsiei)" in *Klassitsizm i modernism. Sbornik statei* (Tartu 1994), 55–83.

Mail for Spirits, women's coquetry and depravity came under the scrutiny of fictional gnomes who are corresponding with each other. The naïve and straightforward spirits exchange letters in which they make a detailed account of the prevailing customs of some "unknown" country. In particular, they describe a passion for masquerades, unbridled adultery, and the precarious nocturnal adventures of emancipated society women. Krylov's text features an endless procession of elderly beauties, provided with "talking names," such as "Besstyda" ("Shameless") and "Neotkaza" ("An Easy Woman").[38]

As many memoirists relate, Catherine adored masquerades and was frequently in attendance, being concealed by a mask and a loose-fitting domino-cape. Her disguise did not constrain courtiers, and she also could take pleasure in the performance-intrigue quite uninhibitedly. The masqueraded balls took place in her Hermitage Palace each Friday, and the number of guests could reach as many as 5,000.[39] The empress enjoyed visiting select private or even public masquerades that were organized in designated houses, such as the house of the director of the Italian opera in Saint Petersburg, Giovanni Battista Locatelli. A note in the court journal, dated 19 January 1791, recounts that after the dinner Catherine "went to the billiard room where masquerade dresses were prepared for Her Imperial Majesty and Their Royal Highnesses as well as for guests of both genders; after all had donned the dresses and covered their faces with masks, they proceeded toward the entrance hall on the Neva embankment; there Her Imperial Majesty took her place in a 4-seated carriage of His Excellency Platon Aleksandrovich Zubov and went to a masquerade."[40]

It is clear that the night adventures of the aged empress, accompanied by her favorite Platon Zubov, were the topic of ridicule among the capital's youth.

---

[38] I. A. Krylov, *Polnoe sobranie sochinenii*, 1, 217.

[39] "During the masquerades in Hermitage, quite often, Her Highness and the Grand Dukes changed clothes several times a night, forcing courtiers to guess [their identities anew]," in N. V. Soloviev, *Pridvornaia zhizn' 1613–1913. Koronatsii, feierverki, dvortsy* (Saint Petersburg, 1913), 30.

[40] Ibid, 31.

The Desacralization of the Empress:
the technique of prose slander

Meanwhile, Krylov in his writing sought out more piercing and at the same time more camouflaged means of anti-Catherinian scurrility. In this search, the libertine literary tradition proved the most appealing to the young ruffler. Krylov imbued all his works with a combination of eroticized elements and audacious attacks against the empress that centered on her senile appearance and depraved behavior. Krylov's most powerful weapon was the use of French erotic argot which became very popular among society people of the time. Krylov's stylistic and linguistic game was based on the jargon of French libertine and pornographic literature, on the most popular terms of French erotic argot. This very risky politico-linguistic game became a way "to say everything and not be imprisoned in the Bastille." Hidden but quite decipherable slander against the throne and court customs saturated Krylov's journalistic prose to an extent like never before.

Thus, Krylov's story *Nochi* (1792), published in the first part of *The Spectator (Зритель)*, was especially striking.[41] Nikolai Karamzin shrewdly perceived the actual subtext of the story and the direction of its polemical arrows when he rhetorically inquired of his friend and young poet Ivan Dmitriev on June 12, 1792: "What do you think about Saint-Petersburg's *Spectator* which harshly smites Saint-Petersburg's actors of low ranks and *Venus's priestesses?*"[42] If the first part of the sentence took aim at Klushin's theatrical reviews, the last part (Karamzin put it in italics) made a reference to Krylov's story.

The plot of the story reveals a series of adventurous episodes, intensely flavored with erotic connotations and tied together by the narrator's ironic meditations. However, the perceptive reader found

---

[41] The story was influenced by the French novel by Louvet de Couvray, Les amours du chevalier de Faublas (Love Adventures of Faublas), see: N. D. Kochetkova, "Satiricheskaia proza Krylova," in *Ivan Andreevich Krylov. Problemy tvorchestva* (Leningrad, 1975), 100-103. Krylov took part in translation of the book (S. M. Babintsev, "I. A. Krylov. Novye materialy. Iz arkhivnykh razyskanii"), in *Russkaia literatura* 3 (1969), 112–114.

[42] *Pis'ma N. M. Karamzina k I. I. Dmitrievu*, 26.

without difficulty a lampooning episode which maliciously stung the aging Empress. Krylov, as usual, described the elderly coquette who has returned home after her night activities:

> "She sleeps, and all her charms are laid out on her dressing table: her perfect teeth are placed in order near the mirror, her head is as smooth as a turnip, and her wonderful hair hangs down, cautiously thrown over the mirror; her delicate flush and her charming whiteness are standing ready for her morning at the shoals <…> Don't think, however, my reader, that this madam lacks sense. If somebody happened to steal her charms, she would have at least one charm left. No heart in the world can resist it: the eloquence of it is her most powerful weapon; she exceeds the author of *New Eloise* in it. Her letters to her lovers are very convincing, though, truth be told, they are all written after one pattern, because they all start like this: "The State Credit Bank pays the holder of this, etc."[43]

The allusions were all too easy to recognize. Firstly, Catherine generously compensated her favorites for their love. Her claims to be a writer and a philosopher also were well-known. By the 1790s, Catherine's passion for cosmetics, especially for rouge ("rumiana"), became the target of malicious jokes. Charles Masson recounts an incident in the Hermitage Palace when somebody put rouge on the cheeks of the marble bust of Catherine. The empress refused to punish anybody and said: "Most likely some of my pages wanted to ridicule the fact that sometimes I apply rouge on my face; let's wash it off."[44] Jean-Henri Castéra, in his memoirs, paid a lot of attention to Catherine's excessive rouge as an attempt to cover her age.[45] Count Shternberg, in his memoirs, also made a notable description of the empress right at the time of Krylov's magazines: "She concealed traces of her advanced age by a brilliant and sophisticated dress. Her stout cheeks are powdered by artificial rouge."[46]

---

[43] I. A. Krylov, *Polnoe sobranie sochinenii*, I, 284.

[44] Ch. Masson, *Mémoires secrets sur la Russie*, 118.

[45] Jean-Henri Castera, *La vie de l'imperatrice* (Paris, 1797), 231.

[46] I. Shternberg, "Russkii dvor v 1792–1793 godakh. Zametki grafa Shternberga," in *Russkii arkhiv*, 3: 11–12 (1880), 263.

Krylov's strategy, meanwhile, was to avoid direct political accusations and to focus on personal features. He did not ridicule the blunders of high politics; he did not touch any political errors. He was concerned only with his senile and depraved heroine. It was a very intricate game with the Empress who could not respond with any direct acts of repression. To do otherwise would be to verify the identity of the exhibited portrait.

Meanwhile, Catherine did not rush to act against the young writer. Krylov's literary libertinage did not threaten her absolute power. For many years, dating back to the age before the French Revolution, Catherine, in her circle, cultivated witty repartee, sharp jokes (including the ridicule of women!), and the Voltairian tradition. She confessed in her letter to Grimm on 1 October 1778, right after the death of Voltaire:

> "I am obliged to him (Voltaire. — V. P.), or, more precisely, to his work towards the enlightenment of my mind and sense. I told you several times that I am his pupil. When I was younger, I liked to earn his praise. I was content when I could accomplish something that was worthy of relating to him <...>"[47]

The atmosphere of the court encouraged Catherine's opponents to consider her in terms of French freethinking and even libertinage. Thus, Prince Mikhail Shcherbatov, in his book *On the Corruption of Morals in Russia*, granted Catherine a very eloquent characteristic: "<...> Delighted by a senseless reading of modern writers, she thinks nothing of the Christian religion, though she pretends to be quite devout. However much she conceals her thoughts, these are frequently revealed in her conversation, and her deeds prove it even more. Many books by Voltaire, undermining religion, have been translated by her order, such as *Candide*, *The Princess of Babylon*, and others; and Marmontel's *Belisaire*, which makes no distinction between pagan and Christian virtue, was not merely translated by a society at her order, but she herself took part in translating it."[48]

---

[47] Pis'ma Ekateriny Vtoroi k baronu Grimmu, in *Russkii arkhiv*, 3 (1878), 53.

[48] Prince M. M. Shcherbatov, *On the Corruption of Morals in Russia*, 257 (corrections in the translation are mine).

Even in 1794, according to memoirists' testimonies, the rooms of the Hermitage were packed with pictures and life-sized sculptures of Voltaire.[49]

Meanwhile, Krylov's strategy was rather successful. In May of 1792 when there was a search of Krylov's publishing house, the police took the manuscript of Krylov's story entitled *My Fevers*. Nevertheless, the journal continued to come out and Krylov remained unpunished. Moreover, the disobedient author paid back Zubov and Catherine by publishing his new story *Kaib* in the 12th (the last) issue of his journal *Zritel'*.

The genre of oriental tale was deeply linked with Voltaire's name in Russia (Voltaire's *White Bull* and the *Princess of Babylon* were well-known among enlightened readers). The "oriental story" *Kaib* contains all the main paradigms of the genre, but these oriental trappings do not quite veil the Russian reality.[50] Though the text sounded very defiant, it was difficult to find the satirical elements of the story. Vissarion Belinskii, the well-known literary critic of Pushkin's time, pointed out that "Kaib's true merit lies in its satirical mood, sometimes unusually well-aimed and malicious."[51] Where was the satire? The ruler, Kaib, was not so bad. He is described according to typical standards of the genre and is presented as a naive prince who is far removed from life and people, but decides to enlighten himself by traveling incognito around his kingdom. Kaib's three advisers are pictured with a good touch of satire, but its intensity could not be compared to that of a fable or verse tale of the eighteenth century. Two of his advisers are Grabilei and Osloshid: the first name is derived from the word "robber" while the second name is derived from "ass." They are traditional examples of satirical masks of the time. The third — Dursan — is not so typical. Krylov described him:

---

[49] I. G. Georgi, *Opisanie rossiisko-imperatorskogo stolichnogo goroda Sankt-Peterburga i dostopamiatnostei v okrestnostiakh onogo, s planom* (Saint Petersburg, 1996), 338-339.

[50] V. N. Kubacheva, "Vostochnaia" povest' v russkoi literature XVIII–nachale XIX veka, in *XVIII vek*, 5 (1962), 310.

[51] V. G. Belinsky, *Sobranie sochinenii*, 7 (1981), 276.

"The first was Dursan, a man of great virtues: chief among them was that his beard reached his knees and resembled a bunchuk (a stick with a horsehair tail-end, very popular in Turkey. – V. P.) in his pomposity. The kaliph himself, though he did not have a big beard, knew that such enormous beards attached importance to the divan (a kind of sofa and the name of the Turkish Council of State. — V. P.) That was the reason he elevated him as high as the beard grew long. Finally, once Dursan's beard had grown to waist-length, the kaliph admitted him to his divan. Dursan, for his part, was not careless. He understood his fortune in serving his fatherland by the beard, and so he looked after his beard with more care than did the gardener after his cucumbers <...>"[52]

Scholars tried to find a real prototype for the hero. For example, M. and Ia. Gordin found that the famous prince Potemkin had been ridiculed under the name of Dursan.[53] However, the description of Dursan in Krylov's story does not seem to bear any likeness, in appearance or in mentality, to Grigorii Potemkin. Krylov did not have any reason to allude to Catherine's former lover. While Potemkin died in 1791 (one year before the story was written), he had lost the status of a favorite much earlier. Most importantly, Potemkin, even according to the opinions of his enemies, was an outstanding politician, very clever, and his reputation far superseded the implied satiric associations. Meanwhile, Dursan means "durak" (a fool) with an orientalized ending.

This fragment contains obvious erotic connotations which suggest Platon Zubov. All memoirists depict the intellectual weakness of Catherine's last favorite. The Empress's secretary A. V. Khrapovitskii in his *Memoirs* called him "duraleiushka Zubov" ("the little fool Zubov").[54] Zubov was mediocre and had no talent excepting his status as the empress' lover. According to Charles Masson, French diplomat and memoirist, "Potemkin, in his majesty, was almost completely indebted to himself, while Zubov — to Catherine's weakness for him."[55]

---

[52] I. A. Krylov, *Polnoe sobranie sochinenii*, I, 355.
[53] M. Gordin, Ia. Gordin, *Teatr Ivana Krylova*, 85.
[54] *Pamiatnye zapiski A. V. Khrapovitskogo*, 252.
[55] Ch. Masson, *Mémoires secrets sur la Russie*, 276.

Kaib's adviser "Dursan" is endowed with only one admirable feature: he has a big and very well-maintained "beard" by which he served the fatherland. The beard (as well as a comparison with "bunchuk" or "a cucumber") refers to the phallic semantic field. The sentence about the divan was especially striking and also contained erotic meanings: "Finally, once Dursan's beard had grown to waist-length, the kaliph admitted him to his divan."[56] Krylov ironically juxtaposes two meanings of the word "divan": "the state council" in oriental countries (Zubov was enormously promoted by Catherine and was even appointed field-marshal); a sofa, which became very popular and very chic right at that time. Ivan Dmitriev, in his narrative poem *A Fashionable Wife* (Модная жена, 1792) hailed the sofa as a fashionable accessory essential for every society woman and her amorous adventures.

Krylov's "oriental story" *Kaib* (1792), while giving an account of the customs and morals of some eastern court, enclosed many erotic hints, and apparently portrayed Platon Zubov (under the name "Dursan") as a purely pornographic hero. The fragment about Dursan's "beard" derived in part from French erotic poetry (as in the poem *The Power of the Beard* (*Le pouvoir de la barbe*) by d'Offerwille.[57] At the same time, Krylov also could rely on the Russian tradition: Mikhail Lomonosov's *A Hymn to the Beard* (Гимн бороде, 1756–1757) already played with the sexual connotations of the beard:

> O my dear priceless beard!
> A pity you are not baptized,
> And a shameful part of the body
> Is given preference over you <…>[58]

In Lomonosov's poem, the beard and the phallus, both parts of the body, are equalized; the one may serve as a substitution for the other. The next fragment from *Kaib* clarifies the semantics of the beard. Dursan gives advice to the caliph:

> "As to the question of who is to rule during your absence, you may give a commission to the most trustworthy person;

---

[56] I. A. Krylov, *Polnoe sobranie sochinenii*, I, 355.
[57] *Parnasse satyrique du XVIII-e siècle* (Paris, 1912), 111–112.
[58] M. V. Lomonosov, *Polnoe sobranie sochinenii*, 8, 624.

it would not be intemperate if your preference were to go to a respectable person with a considerable beard, the length of which proves the breadth of his wisdom and experience. Since, your highness, even disobedient hearts look upon a long beard as an auspicious credential granted by nature <...> After that Dursan felt silent and started to smooth out his long beard."[59]

The discussion about the length of the beard also referred to some erotic undertones. The sentence about "the hearts" that "look" at "a long beard," at first glance, seems strange and stylistically awkward. However, in French erotic argot (as well as in French erotic literature) the word "heart" ("le coeur") signified "vulva."[60] The poem *The Heart* (*Le Coeur*, 1763) written by the well-known French poet Chevalier De Boufflers revealed the meaning quite plainly.[61] The verses even provoked the appearance of a poem written by Voltaire, *A Response by Voltaire on the piece entitled The Heart* (*Réponse de Voltaire la pièce intitulée Le Coeur*)[62] as well as two poems by Ch. Bovie, *That's girls' hearts for you!* (*Ce que c'est que le coeur des filles*) and *That's boys' hearts for you!* (*Ce que c'est que le coeur des garçons*)[63]

These poems as well as the argot meaning of the word "heart" (le coeur) were well known in Russian high society.[64] One incident that took place in the royal palace of Catherine II testifies to this. The ex-favorite Potemkin successfully introduced a new lover to Catherine's bedroom. It was the charming, handsome, and witty A. M. Dmitriev-Mamonov. Appointed, as usual, as an aide-de-camp, and approved as a new official favorite, Mamonov decided

---

[59] I. A. Krylov, *Polnoe sobranie sochinenii*, I, 357.

[60] See: Alfred Delvau, *Dictionnaire erotique moderne* (Amsterdam, 1865), 94.

[61] *Parnasse satyrique du XVIII-e siècle*, 20–23.

[62] Ibid, 23–24

[63] Ibid, 24–30.

[64] Ivan Barkov's manuscript tragedy *Durnosov and Farnos* as well as a fable *The Fire* (*Пожар*) operated with the same argot meaning: see *Devichia igrushka, ili Sochineniia gospodina Barkova* (Moscow, 1992), 285; 153. Derzhavin's poem *Some crazy man ran down the street* <...> (*Какой-то бешеный по улице бежал*), written around 1776, proved the popularity of erotic language and metaphors in Russian society.

to show his gratitude to Potemkin. He presented him with the gift of a golden teapot with an inscription in French: "Plus unis par le coeur que par le sang" ("Linked more through the heart than by blood").[65] This gallant slogan played with the idea of high friendship and, at the same time, it contained an obscene metaphor of the union of two favorites (previous and current) at the Empress' bosom. Thus, when Krylov saturated his texts with erotic expressions, he knew perfectly well that his readership was equal to the task.

Krylov's use of French argot as well as his play with pornographic texts of French libertine literature allowed him to conduct a very twisted and complicated game with the empress Catherine the Great. Young Krylov and the empress both knew the language of this game. Both were raised on the same literary tradition. This explains the reason why Krylov was not punished like Kniazhnin, Novikov or Radishchev. The consequences Krylov faced were very mild indeed, especially in comparison with others. Kniazhnin in his serious tragedies, Novikov in his didactic (and Masonic) propaganda, and Radishchev in his social and ideological novel *A Journey from Saint Petersburg to Moscow* did not touch upon the Empress's personal life, appearance or behavior. Krylov did, and very skillfully at that. To punish him seriously and openly would have been tantamount to Catherine putting her royal signature on the portrait he had painted.

The Behest of the Monarch in Libertine Fashion

Not only Krylov's prose, but also his poetry revolved around the themes of women and their follies. Besides stories, in the *Saint Petersburg Mercury* in 1793, he published a series of poems addressed to a lyric heroine called Aniuta (she was apparently a fictional character.) These satirical poems once again displayed his distaste for elderly coquettes. Krylov even pretended, quite ironically, to give an explanation for his extraordinary fixation on this one topic; he composed a poem entitled *My Apology, to Aniuta*

---

[65] N. I. Pavlenko, *Ekaterina Velikaia*, 382.

(*Мое оправдание, к Анюте*) and printed it in the June issue of the magazine. There he wrote:

> You are not at all content,
> When I condemn women
> And denounce their follies <...>
> Let the one-hundred-year-old Venus
> Grit her false teeth,
> Looking sullen, grinning her wilt lips!
> She can curse me,
> And I am guilty
> As I look too harshly upon her toilette.[66]

Despite the ironic attitude, the author, in the poem, showed his insecurity, and an indistinct foreboding of an approaching threat. By the end, he implied some dissonant overtones in his satiric verse:

> If everything is in vain here,
> Maybe, some law of nature
> Put an end to my freedom.
> Very soon, it seems,
> I will pay a great price
> For the crime of daring
> To struggle against women.[67]

His lyric hero foresaw some "thunder" or "severe storms," and the words became rather popular linguistic clichés for alluding to political trouble. Krylov, by that time, had already presumed that his literary war against old coquettes would prove too dangerous:

> It is gloomy, but you can't avenge evil,
> You can't dismiss clouds with your sorrow,
> You can't send away the thunder.[68]

Krylov's poem *My Apology* (*Мое оправдание*), in fact, was a satire enveloped into the formal frame of the genre of epistle. The real context endowed the image of a depraved coquette with

---

[66] I. A. Krylov, *Polnoe sobranie sochinenii*, III, 241.
[67] Ibid, 240.
[68] Ibid.

a topical meaning alluding to a very dangerous target, the elderly Catherine and her last favorite Platon Zubov. The anonymous poem *A Dying Coquette*, published in Krylov's magazine in 1793, displayed a similar image and might be understood as belonging to the same pen.

The mere title was quite provocative: in 1793 Catherine was terminally ill; she would die in three years. She almost completely lost the ability to work, though she made every effort to appear younger and stronger. She was severely frightened by the unexpected deaths of three European monarchs in a row, the Austrian emperor Leopold II, King Gustav III of Sweden (both died in March of 1792), and finally, at the beginning of 1793, the execution of Louis XVI. Most probably, at that time, prompted by tragic reports from Europe, Catherine II composed a document outlining instructions for her funeral in case of a sudden death.

The extraordinary document became known to her secretary A. V. Khrapovitskii,[69] and circulated in scholarly works under the title *The Strange Will of Catherine* (Странное завещание Екатерины). In this statement, she designated the possible places of her burial (dependent upon her last residence) and gave instructions to her courtiers on how to behave:

> "Only horse-guardsmen should carry my coffin. Put my body in a white dress, and cover my head with a golden crown, with my name engraved on it. Go into mourning for half a year, the shorter the better. Open all public entertainment after six weeks. Allow engagements, weddings, and music right after my funeral."[70]

The will contains many deviations from the regular ritual of funerals for Russian tsars. It was the brave gesture of an enlightened and even libertine-like person. The testament corresponded very

---

[69] A. V. Khrapovitskii, in the entry for 28 April 1792, described the document that he had found on a nightstand in Catherine's bedroom (*Pamiatnye zapiski A. V. Khrapovitskogo*, 265).

[70] *Sochineniia imperatritsy Ekateriny II*, 12 (2), 702–703. Already in 1774, Catherine had invented her libertine-like end in a letter to Grimm: "I want to be surrounded at this moment only by brave hearts and inveterate wits": *Russkii Arkhiv*, 3 (1878), 7.

well with Catherine's freethinking spirit, her desire to remain herself even post-mortem — to be dressed in her favorite color and to be surrounded by young brave officers.

On the other hand, gossip circulated very quickly, and A. V. Khrapovitskii was a very close friend of many writers. Such a peculiar will by Catherine could have encouraged the anonymous author to compose *A Dying Coquette*, the poem which applied Alexander Pope's formulas to the Russian context. Ivan Krylov could be considered the first candidate for the authorship of the poem published in his magazine. Catherine's order to Krylov (and Klushin) to resign from the magazine (a new editor, I. I. Martynov, was appointed to replace them), to leave Saint Petersburg and go abroad, meant, in fact, the end of Krylov's career as a journalist. After that, Klushin took the money provided by the empress and went to Revel (modern Tallinn) in Estonia. Krylov left the capital for eight years and spent the remainder of Catherine's rule as well as Paul I's at the country estates of his friends and protectors. In fact, the relatively soft punishment of two rather scandalous authors was puzzling, and a number of questions continue to surround the incident. Charles Masson recalled that Catherine was very tolerant of any personal slander. When the French newspaper *The Monitor* (*Le Moniteur*) printed some satires on Catherine and her court, she ordered that all issues be closely examined. After reading a paragraph in which she was styled the depraved Messalina of the North, Catherine said: "As this concerns only myself, let it be distributed."[71]

Meanwhile, more than extraordinary circumstances might have forced Krylov, a disobedient writer, to seek revenge. While Klushin responded with his ironic *In Gratitude to Catherine the Great for my Most Kind Dismissal Abroad with a Pension*, Krylov also had to act in response. Most probably, the libelous satire *A Dying Coquette* was his answer to the dismissal. Having been fired, Krylov threw his poem in the face of the empress who had demolished his literary, journalistic, and personal life. He printed the poem in the last issue of the magazine he had to leave forever. By publishing the verse

---

[71] Ch. Masson, *Mémoires secrets sur la Russie*, 187.

pamphlet on the dying imperial coquette during a time of scandal, Krylov penned his final, but resonant conclusion to the whole story of desacralization of the monarchy in Russia.

Bibliography

Primary Sources

Barkov I. S., *Devichia igrushka, ili Sochineniia gospodina Barkova*. Ed. A. Zorin & N. Sapov. Moscow: Ladomir, 1992.

Bogdanovich I. F., *Sochineniia*, I—VI. Ed. P. Beketov. Moscow: Tipografiia Moskovskogo universiteta, 1809–1810.

_____, *Sochineniia*, I–II. Saint Petersburg: Izdatel'stvo A. Smirdina, 1848.

Boileau N., *Oeuvres complètes*. Paris: Gallimard, 1966.

Bolotov A. T., *Zhizn' i prikliucheniia Andreia Bolotova, opisannye samim im dlia svoikh potomkov. 1738-1793*, 1–3. Saint Petersburg: V. I. Golovin, 1872.

_____, *Pamiatnik protekshikh vremen*. Moscow: P. S. Kiselev, 1875.

_____, *Zapiski 1737–1796*. 1–2. Tula: Priokskoe knizhnoe izdatel'stvo, 1988.

Castera Jean-Henri, *La vie de l'impératrice*. Paris: F. Buisson, 1797.

Catherine II, "Pis'ma Ekateriny Vtoroi k baronu Grimmu," in *Russkii arkhiv*, 3 (1878).

_____, "Pis'ma imperatritsy Ekateriny II k I. G. Tsimmermannu. 1785–1791," in *Russkaia starina*, 7 (1887).

_____, *Sochineniia imperatritsy Ekateriny II na osnovanii podlinnykh rukopisei s ob''iasnitel'nymi primechaniiami akademika A. N. Pypina*, I–X. Saint Petersburg: Imperatorskaia Akademiia nauk, 1901–1907.

_____, *Zapiski Imperatritsy Ekateriny Vtoroi*. Saint Petersburg: Imperatorskaia Akademiia nauk, A. S. Suvorin, 1907.

_____, *Documents of Catherine the Great. The Correspondence with Voltaire and the Instruction of 1767 in the English text of 1768*. Ed. W. F. Reddaway. Cambridge: Cambridge University Press, 1931.

_____, *The Memoirs*. Transl. M. Budberg. New York: McMillan Company, 1955.

_____, *Ekaterina II i ee okruzhenie*. Ed. A. I. Iukht. Moscow: Pressa: 1996.

_____, *Ekaterina II i G. A. Potemkin: Lichnaia perepiska 1769–1791*. Ed. V. S. Lopatin. Moscow: Rossiiskaia Akademiia nauk, 1997.

_____, *Love Conquest. Personal Correspondence of Catherine the Great and Prince Grigory Potemkin.* Ed. and transl. D. Smith. DeKalb: Northern Illinois University Press, 2004.

Engel'gardt L. N., *Zapiski*. Ed. I. I. Fedukin. Moscow: Novoe literaturnoe obozrenie, 1997.

Corberon Marie Daniel Bourrée (baron de), *Un diplomate français à la court de Catherine II. 1775–1780. Journal intime du chevalier de Corberon*, I–II. Paris: Plon-Nourrit, 1901.

Dashkova E. R., *Memoirs of the Princess Dashkova, Lady of Honour to Catherine II, Written by herself*. 1–2 (London: Henry Colburn, 1840).

_____, *The Memoirs of Princess Dashkov*. Transl. Kyril Fitzlyon. London: J. Calder, 1958.

_____, *Zapiski. 1743–1810*. Ed. G. N. Moiseeva. Moscow: Nauka, 1990.

_____, *O smysle slova vospitanie. Sochineniia. Pis'ma. Dokumenty*. Ed. G. I. Smagina. Saint Petersburg: D. Bulanin, 2001.

Derzhavin G. R., *Sochineniia. S ob"iasnitel'nymi primechaniiami Ia. Grota*. 1–9. Saint Petersburg: Akademiia nauk, 1868–1878.

_____, *Zapiski. 1743–1816*. Ed. Iu. V. Sokortova. Moscow: Mysl', 2000.

_____, *Poetic Works. A Bilingual Album*. Ed. A. Levitsky. Providence: Brown University Press, 2001.

_____, *Sochineniia*. Ed. G. N. Ionin. Saint Petersburg: Akademicheskii proekt, 2002.

Diderot Denis, *Correspondance*. Ed. G. Roth & J. Valoot, 6. Paris: Éditions de Minuit, 1961.

Dolgorukii I. M., *Sochineniia*, 1–2. Ed. A. Smirdin. Saint Petersburg: Imperatorskaia Akademiia nauk, 1849.

"Doneseniia frantsuzskikh poslannikov pri russkom dvore," in *Sbornik imperatorskogo russkogo istoricheskogo obsh'estva*, 86. Saint Petersburg, 1893.

Falconet E. - M. *Correspondance avec Catherine II. 1767-1778*. Ed. L. Réau. Paris: E. Champion, 1921.

Fonvizin D. I., *Sobranie sochinenii.*, 1–2. Ed. G. P. Makogonenko. Moscow: Gosudarstvennoe izdatel'stvo khudozhestvennoi literatury, 1959.

"Frantsuzskaia revolutsiia 1789 g. v doneseniiakh russkogo posla v Parizhe I. M. Simolina". Ed. N. Lukin, O. Starosel'skaia & E. Alexandrova, in *Literaturnoe nasledstvo*, 29–30. Moscow — Leningrad: Zhurnal'no-gazetnoe ob"edinenie, 1937, 343–538.

Georgi I. G., *Opisanie rossiisko-imperatorskogo stolichnogo goroda Sankt-Peterburga i dostopamiatnostei v okrestnostiakh onogo, s planom.* Saint Petersburg: LIGA, 1996.

Golenishchev-Kutuzov Pavel, *Oda na vseradostnyi den' vosshestviia na Vserossiiskii prestol Pavla I* (Moscow, 1796).

Golovina V. N., *Istoriia zhizni blagorodnoi zhenshchiny.* Ed. V. M. Bokova. Moscow: Novoe literaturnoe obozrenie, 1996.

Gribovskii Adrian, *Zapiski o imperatritse Ekaterine Velikoi.* Moscow: Universitetskaia tipografiia Katkov & K, 1864.

Hamilton Emma, *From New and Origin sources & Documents.* Ed. W. S. Sichel. London: Archibald Constable & Company, Ltd., 1905.

Herbert Mary (Sidney), Countess of Pembroke, *The Collected Works*, 1. Ed. M. P. Hannay, N. J. Kinnamon & M. G. Brennan. Oxford: Clarendon Press, 1998.

Karamzin N. M., *Sochineniia*, 8. Saint Petersburg: A. Smirdin, 1835.

_____, *Pis'ma k I. I. Dmitrievu.* Ed. Ia. Grot & P. Pekarskii. Saint Petersburg: Imperatorskaia Akademiia nauk, 1866.

_____, *Polnoe sobranie stikhotvorenii.* Ed. Iu. Lotman. Moscow — Leningrad: Sovetskii pisatel', 1966.

_____, *Izbrannye stat'i i pis'ma.* Ed. A. Smirnov. Moscow: Sovremennik, 1982.

Kheraskov M. M., *Tvoreniia*, I–XII. Moscow: Universitetskaia tipografiia, Khr. Ridiger, 1796–1803.

Kheraskov M. M., *Izbrannye sochinenia.* Ed. A. Zapadov. Leningrad: Sovetskii pisatel', 1961.

Khrapovitskii A. V., *Pamiatnye zapiski.* Ed. G. Gennadi. Moscow: Universitetskaia tipografiia, 1862..

Krylov I. A., *Polnoe sobranie sochinenii*, I–III. Ed. N. Stepanov, N. Brodkii & D. Blagoi. Moscow: Gosudarstvennoe izdatel'stvo khudozhestvennoi literatury, 1945–1946.

Krylov v vospominaniiakh sovremennikov. Ed. A. Gordin & M. Gordin. Moscow: Khudozhestvennaia literatura, 1982.

The Literature of Eighteenth-Century Russia. An Anthology of Russian Literary Materials of the Age of Classicism and the Enlightenment from the Reign of Peter the Great (1689-1725) to the Reign of Alexander I (1801-1825). Ed. and trans. by H. Segel, 1–2. New York: Dutton, 1967.

Ligne Charles Joseph (Prince de), *Lettres à la Marquise de Coigny*. Ed. H. Lebasteur. Paris: E. Champion, 1914.

———, *Mémoires et mélanges historique et littéraire*, 1–2. Paris: Dupont, 1827–1829.

Lomonosov M. V., *Polnoe sobranie sochinenii*, 8. Ed. V. Vinogradov, A. Andreev, G. Blok. Moscow — Leningrad: Akademia nauk SSSR, 1959.

Maikov, V. I. *Sochineniia i perevody*. Ed. P. Efremov. Saint Petersburg: Tipografiia I. Glazunova, 1867.

———, *Izbrannye proizvedeniia*. Ed. A. Zapadov. Moscow — Leningrad: Sovetskii pisatel', 1966.

Martynov I. I., "Zapiski," in *Pamiatniki novoi russkoi istorii*, 2 : 2 (Saint Petersburg, 1872), 68–182.

Masson Charles François P., *Secret Memoirs of the Court of Petersburg, particularly towards the end of the reign of Catherine II and the commencement of that of Paul I*. London: C. Pougens, 1800 & 1801.

Montesquieu Ch.-L., *Considérations sur les causes de la grandeur des romains et de leur decadence*. Paris: Firmin-Didot, 1879.

Novikov N., *Opyt istoricheskogo slovaria o rossiiskikh pisateliakh* . Saint Petersburg; Tipografiia Akademii nauk, 1772.

Panegiricheskaia literatura petrovskogo vremeni. Ed. V. Grebeniuk & O. Derzhavina Moscow: Nauka, 1979.

Parnasse satyrique du XVIII-e siècle. Ed. G. Apollinaire. Paris: Bibliothèque des curieux, 1912.

Petr v russkoi literature XVIII veka. Ed. S. Nikolaev. Saint Petersburg: Nauka, 2006.

Petrov Vasilii, *Oda vsepresvetleishei, derzhavneishei, velikoi Gosudaryne Imperatritse Ekaterine Vtoroi, samoderzhitse vserossiskoi na vziat'e Ias I pokorenie vsego moldavskago kniazhestva*. Saint Petersburg, 1769.

_____, *Oda na pobedy rossiiskogo flota, oderzhannaia nad turetskim, pod predvoditel'stvom grafa Alekseia Grigor'evicha Orlova, v Arkhipelage, pri Khiose*. Saint Petersburg, 1770.

_____, *Poema na pobedy Rossiiskogp voinstva, pod predvoditel'stvom generala fel'dmarshala Grafa Rumiantseva, oderzhannyia nad Tatarami I Turkami, so vremeni ego voenachal'stva nad pervoiu armieiu do vziatiia goroda Zhurzhi*. Saint Petersburg, 1771.

_____, *Sochineniia*, I–II. Saint Petersburg: Vol'naia tipografiia Shnora, 1782.

Pis'ma russkikh pisatelei XVIII veka . Ed. G. Makogonenko. Leningrad: Nauka, 1980.

Poety XVIII veka. I–II. Ed. G. Makogonenko, I. Serman, N. Kochetkova. Leningrad: Sovetskii pisatel', 1972.

Pope Alexander, *The Works in 9 volumes*, III. London: J. F. Dove, St. John's Square, for R. Priestley, 1822.

Potemkin Pavel, *Rossy v Arkhipelage*. Saint Petersburg, 1772.

Prokopovich Feofan, *Sochineniia.* Ed. I. P. Eremin. Moscow-Leningrad: Akademiia nauk SSSR, 1961.

Pushkin A. S., *Sobranie sochinenii v 10 tomakh*, 7. Ed. Iu. Oksman, T. Tsiavlovskaia. Moscow: Gosudarstvennoe izdatel'stvo khudozhestvennoi literatury, 1962.

Put' k tronu. Istoriia dvortsovogo perevorota 28 iunia 1762 goda. Ed. G. A. Veselaia. Moscow: Slovo, 1997.

Ruban Vasilii, *Oda na den' vseradostneishego torzhestva na predpriniatyi i blagopoluchno sovershivshiisia k neopisannomu schastiiu vseia Rossii, Eia imperatorskogo velichestva I Ego imperatoeskago vysochestva v privitii ospy, 22 noiabria 1768 goda*. Saint Petersburg, 1768.

Rulhière Claude Carloman de, *The History, or Anecdotes of the Revolution in Russia, in the year 1762*.Transl. from French by M. de Rulhière. London: T. N. Longman, Paternoster-Row, 1797).

Rumiantsev S. P., "Avtobiografiia grafa S. P. Rumiantseva," in *Russkii arkhiv*, 7 (1869), 839–854.

Samoilovich D., *Mémoirs sur la peste, qui, en 1771, ravagea l'empire de Russie, surtout Moscou, la capital*. Paris: Leclerc, 1783.

Sankt-Peterburgskii Merkurii (serial), 1793–1794.

Ségur L.-Ph., *Memoirs and Recollections of Count Ségur, ambassador from France to the court of Russia and Prussia, written by himself*, II. London: Henry Colburn, 1826.

Sobesednik liubitelei russkogo slova, serial. Saint Petersburg, 1783–1784.

Shcherbatov M. M. (Prince), *On the Corruption of Morals in Russia*. Ed. and transl. by A. Lentin. Cambridge: Cambridge University Press, 1969.

Shternberg I., "Russkii dvor v 1792–1793 godakh. Zametki grafa Shternberga". Ed. L. Maikov, in *Russkii arkhiv*, 3 : 11–12 (1880), 261–266.

Suetonius, *The Lives of the Caesars*. Ed. Molly Dauster. New York: Barnes & Noble Publishing Inc., 2004.

Sumarokov A. P., *Polnoe sobranie vsekh sochinenii v stikhakh i prose*, I–X. Ed. N. Novikov. Moscow: Universitetskaia tipografiia N. Novikova, 1781–1782.

Théâtre de l'Hermitage de Catherine II, impératrice de Russie, composé par cette princess, par plusieurs personnes de sa societé intime, et par quelques ministres etrange, 1–2 (Paris: Buisson, 1799).

Virgil, Enei. *Geroicheskaia poema Publiia Vergiliia Marona. Perevedena s latinskago Vasil'em Petrovym*, 1. Saint Petersburg, 1770.

_____, *Geroicheskaia poema*, translated by Vasilii Petrov. Saint Petersburg, 1781.

_____, *Works: The Aeneid, Eclogues, Georgics*. Transl. by J. W. Mackail. New York: The Modern Library, 1934.

Voltaire, *A Philosophical Dictionary*, I–II. London: W.Dugdale, 1843.

_____, *Oeuvres completes*, 8–10. Paris: Garnier, 1877.

_____, *The Princess of Babylon*. London: S. Bladon, 1768.

Voltaire and Catherine the Great. Selected Correspondence. Transl. and ed. A. Lentin. Cambridge, UK: Oriental Research Partners, 1974.

Young Edward, *Night Thoughts*. Boston: E. Littlefield, 1841.

Zhukovskii V. A., *Polnoe sobranie sochinenii v 12 tomakh*. Ed. A. Arkhangel'skii. Saint Petersburg: Izdatel'stvo A. F. Marksa, 1902.

_____, *Polnoe sobranie sochinenii i pisem*, I. Ed. O. Lebedeva & A. Ianushkevich. Moscow: Iazyki russkoi kul'tury, 1999.

Zolotoi vek Ekateriny Velikoi: Vospominaniia. Ed. V. M. Volkova & N. I. Thimbaev. Moscow: Prosveshenie, 1996.

Secondary Literature

Alekseeva N. Iu. *Russkaia oda. Razvitie odicheskoi formy v XVII–XVIII vekakh.* Saint Petersburg: Nauka, 2005.

Alexander John T., *Bubonic plague in early modern Russia: public health and urban disaster.* Baltimore: Johns Hopkins University Press, 1980.

_____ , *Catherine the Great. Life and Legend.* New York — Oxford: Oxford University Press, 1989.

_____ , "Amazon Autocratrixes: Images of Female Rule in the Eighteenth Century," in *Gender and Sexuality in Russian Civilization.* Ed. Peter I. Barta. London: Taylor & Francis Books Ltd., 2001, 33–54.

Alexandrian S., *Histoire de la littérature érotique.* Paris : Seghers, 1989.

Altshuller Mark, "Krylov i volterianstvo," in *Russia and the World of the Eighteenth Century.* Ed. R. P. Bartlett, A. G. Cross, Karen Rasmussen (Columbus, Ohio, 1988), 347–359.

_____ , *Beseda liubitelei russkogo slova. U istokov russkogo slavianofil'stva.* Moscow: Novoe literaturnoe obozrenie, 2007.

Anisimov E. V., *Rossiia bez Petra: 1725–1740.* Saint Petersburg: Lenizdat, 1994.

Apostolidès Jean-Marie, *Le roi-machine. Spectacle et politique au temps de Louis XIV.* Paris: Les Editions de Minuit, 1981.

Astrury Katerine, *The Moral Tale in France and Germany 1750-1789.* Oxford: Voltaire Foundation, 2002.

Babintsev S. M., "I. A. Krylov. Novye materialy. Iz arkhivnykh razyskanii," in *Russkaia literatura,* 3 (1969), 114–116.

Baecque Antoine de, *La caricature revolutionnaire.* Paris: Presses du CNRS, 1988.

_____ , *The Body Politic. Corporeal Metaphor in Revolutionary France, 1770–1800.* Stanford: Stanford University Press, 1997.

_____ , *Les éclats du rire. La culture des rieurs au XVIII-e siècle.* Paris: Calmann-Lévy,, 2000.

Baehr Stephen Lessing, *The Paradise Myth in Eighteenth-Century Russia. Utopian Patterns in Early Secular Russian Literature and Culture.* Stanford: Stanford University Press, 1991.

Barran Thomas, *Russia Reads Rousseau, 1762-1825.* Evanston: Northwestern University Press, 2002.

Bartlett R. P., "Russia in the Eighteenth Century European Adoption of Inoculation for Smallpox," in *Russia and the World of the Eighteenth Century* (Columbus, OH, 1988), 193–213.

Bekasova A. V., "Istoriia o tom, kak privivali ospu Rossiiskomu dvoru," in *Ekaterina Velikaia: epokha rossiiskoi istorii. Tezisy dokladov* (Saint Petersburg, 1996), 18–22.

Berkov P. N., "Khor ko prevratnomu svetu i ego avtor," in *XVIII vek*, 1 (Moscow –Leningrad, 1935), 181–202.

_____ , *Istoriia russkoi zhurnalistiki XVIII veka* . Moscow — Leningrad: Akadeniia nauk SSSR, 1952.

Bil'basov V. A., "Nikita Panin i Mercier de la Rivière, 1762-1767," in *Russkaia starina* 72: 11-12 (1891), 283–324; 507–529.

Bogdanov K. A., *Vrachi, patsienty, chitateli: patograficheskie teksty russkoi kul'tury XVIII–XIX vekov*. Moscow: O. G. I. , 2005.

Brikner A., "O chume v Moskve 1771 goda," in *Russkii Vestnik*, 173: 9–10 (1884), 5–48; 502–568.

Brown Horatio Forbes, *The Venetian Republic*. London: J. M. Dent & Co, 1902.

Burke Peter, *The Fabrication of Louis XIV*. New Haven & London: Yale University Press, 1998.

Carcopino Jerome, *Virgile et le mystère de la IV eclogue*. Paris: L'Artisan du livre, 1943.

Castle Terry, *Masquerade and Civilization. The Carnivalesque in Eighteenth-Century English Culture and Fiction*. Stanford: Stanford University Press, 1986.

Cherkasov P. P., *Ekaterina II i Liudovik XVI*. Moscow: Nauka, 2001.

Chernov S. N., "Lomonosov v odakh 1762 g.," in *XVIII vek*, I (Moscow — Leningrad, 1935), 178–180.

Conant Marta Pike, *The Oriental Tale in England in the Eighteenth Century*. New York: The Columbia University Press, 1908.

Craveri Benedetta, *The Age of Conversation*. New York: New York Review Books, 2005.

Crone Anna Lisa, "Na scchast'e as the Undoing of Felitsa, in *Russian Literature*, 44 (1998), 17–40.

_____, *The Daring of Derzhavin. The Moral and Aesthetic Independence of the Poet in Russia* Bloomington: Slavica, 2001.

Cross Antony G., "Vasilii Petrov v Anglii (1772–1774)," in *XVIII vek*, 11 (Leningrad, 1976), 229–246.

Cross Anthony, "Professor Thomas Newberry's Letter from St. Petersburg, 1766, on the Grand Carousel and Other Matters," in *Slavonic & East European Review*, 76:3 (1998), 487–493.

Dan'ko E. Ia., "Izobrazitel'noe iskusstvo v poezii Derzhavina," in *XVIII vek*, 2 (Moscow-Leningrad, 1939), 166–247.

Darnton Robert, *The Literary Underground of the Old Regime*. Cambridge, MA: Harvard University Press, 1982.

_____, *The Forbidden Best-Sellers of Pre-Revolutionary France*. New York: W. W. Norton, 1995.

Delvau Alfred, *Dictionnaire erotique moderne*. Amsterdam, 1865.

Dieckmann H. and J. Seznec, "The Horse of Markus Aurelius. A Controversy between Diderot and Falkonet," in *Journal of the Warburg and Courtauld Institutes*, 15 (1952), 198–228.

Donnels O'Malley Lurana, *The Dramatic Works of Catherine the Great. Theater and Politics in Eighteenth Century Russia*. Burlington: Ashgate, 2006.

Druzhinina E. I., *Kuchuk-Kainardjiiskii mir 1774 goda, ego podgotovka i zakliuchenie*. Moscow: Academiia nauk SSSR, 1955.

Eliseeva Olga, *Grigorii Potemkin*. Moscow: Molodaia gvardiia, 2006.

Faggionato Raffaella, *A Rosicrucian Utopia in Eighteenth-Century Russia. The Masonic Circle of N. I. Novikov* (Dordrecht: Springer, 2005).

Folz R., *L'idée d'empire en Occident du V-e au XIV-e siècle*. Paris: Aubier, 1953.

Foucault Michel, *Discipline and Punish: the Birth of the Prison*. New York: Vintage Books, 1995.

Gajda Oliver, *Katharina II von Russland im Diskurs der Sexualitat. Mittelbare Einflusse narrativer Fiktion auf Geschichtsschreibung*. Berlin: Verlag für Wissenschaft und Forschung 2002.

Ganulich A. K., "Pridvornaia karusel' 1766 goda i ee otrazhenie v literature i iskusstve," in *Ekaterina Velikaia: Epokha Rossiiskoi istorii. Tezisy dokladov* (Saint Petersburg, 1996), 234–237.

Gardzonio Stefano, "Librettistika Ekateriny II i ee gosudarstvenno-natsional'nye predposylki," in *Rossia/Russia. Kul'turnye praktiki v ideologicheskoi perspective. Rossiia, XVIII — nachalo XX veka*, 3 (11) (Moscow — Venice, 1999), 82–90.

Garnovski M. A. i, "Zapiski. 1786–1790," in *Russkaia starina*, 16: 5–7 (1876), 1–32; 207–238; 399–440.

Gasparov M. L., *Ocherk istorii russkogo stikha*. Moscow: Fortuna Limited, 2000.

Greenleaf Monika, "Performing Autobiography: The Multiple Memoirs of Catherine the Great (1756-96)." in *The Russian Review* 63:3 (2004)., 407–426.

Goodman Dena, *The Republic of Letters. A Cultural History of the French Enlightenment*. Ithaca & London: Cornell University Press, 1994.

Gordin A. M., Gordin M. A., "Krylov: real'nost' i legenda, in *I. A. Krylov v vospominaniiakh sovremennikov*. Moscow: Khudozhestvennaia literatura, 1982, 5–36.

Gordin M., Gordin Ia., *Teatr Ivana Krylova*. Leningrad: Iskusstvo, 1983.

Grot Ia., *Zhizn' Derzhavina*. Saint Petersburg: Imperatorskaia Akademia nauk, 1880.

———, "Ekaterina i Gustav III," in *Trudy Ia. K. Grota*, IV (Saint Petersburg, 1901), 262–266.

Gukovskii G. A., "O 'Khore ko prevratnomu svetu. Otvet P. N. Berkovu," in *XVIII vek*, 1 (Moscow — Leningrad, 1935), 203–217.

———, *Ocherki po istorii russkoi literatury XVIII veka: Dvorianskaia fronda v literature 1750-kh — 1760-kh godov*. Moscow — Leningrad: Akademiia nauk SSSR, 1936.

Jackson Richard, *Vive le roi! A History of the French Coronation from Charles V to Charles X*. Chapel Hill, N.C.: University of North Carolina Press, 1984.

Harris Jane, "Derzhavin i Iung: K voprosu o vliianii perevodov na literaturnyi protsess," in *Gavrila Derzhavin. Simposium devoted to his 250th Anniversary* (Norwich, 1995), 202–223.

Hart Pierre R., *G. R. Derzhavin: A Poet's Progress*. Columbus, OH: Slavica 1978.

Hazlitt W. Carew, *The Venetian Republic, its Rise, its Growth, and its Fall, 421–1797*. London: Adam & Charles Black, 1900.

Hopkins Donald R., *Princes and Peasants. Smallpox in History*. Chicago and London: University of Chicago Press, 1983.

Howard Robert, *The Second Partition of Poland. A Study in Diplomatic History*. Cambridge, MA: Harvard University Press, 1915.

Ikonnikov V. S., "Arsenii Matseevich, mitropolit Rostovskii," in *Russkaia starina*, 24–26 (1879), 24: 731–752; 1–34; 25: 577–608; 26: 1–34; 177–198.

Isksul' S. N., *Rokovye gody Rossii. God 1762. Dokumental'naia khronika*. Saint Petersburg: LIK, 2001.

Kaganovich A., *Mednyi vsadnik. Istoriia sozdaniia monumenta*. Leningrad: Iskusstvo, 1975.

Kahn Andrew, "Reading of Imperial Rome from Lomonosov to Pushkin," in *The Slavic Review* (1993), 52:4, 745–768.

____, *Pushkin's The Bronze Horseman*. London: Bristol Classical Press, 1998.

Kaganov G. Z., *Peterburg v kontekste barokko*. Saint Petersburg: Stella, 2001.

Kantorowicz Ernst H., *The King's Two Bodies. A Study in Medieval Political Theology*. Princeton: Princeton University Press, 1957.

Kaplan Herbert, *Russian Overseas Commerce with Great Britain During the Reign of Catherine II*. Philadelphia: American Philosophical Society, 1995.

Kermode Frank, *The Classic: Literary Images of Permanence and Change*. Cambridge, MA — London: Harvard University Press, 1983.

Khodasevich V. F., *Derzhavin*. Paris: Sovremennye zapiski, 1931.

Kirichenko Evgeniia, "Sviashchennaia toponimika rossiiskikh stolits: vzaimosviaz' i vzaimovliianie," in *Rossia/Russia. Kul'turnye praktiki v ideologicheskoi perspective. Rossiia, XVIII — nachalo XX veka*, 3 (11) (Moscow — Venice, 1999), 20–35.

Kiseleva L., "Nekotorye osobennosti poetiki Krylova-dramaturga (vzaimootnosheniia s literaturnoi traditsiei" in *Klassitsizm i modernism. Sbornik statei* (Tartu 1994), 55–83.

Klein Yoakhim, *Puti kul'turnogo importa. Trudy po russkoi literature XVIII veka*. Moscow: Iazyki slavianskoi kul'tury, 2005.

Kliuchevskii V. O., *Sochineniia v deviati tomakh*. Moscow: Nauka, 1987–1990.

Knabe G. S., *Russkaia antichnost'*. Moscow: RGGU, 2000.

Kobeko D., *Tsesarevich Pavel Petrovich (1754–1796): Istoricheskoe issledovanie*. Saint Petersburg: Tipografiia M. M. Stasulevicha, 1882.

Kochetkova N. D., "Satiricheskaia proza Krylova," in *Ivan Andreevich Krylov. Problemy tvorchestva* (Leningrad: Nauka, 1975), 53–112.

Kubacheva V. N., "Vostochnaia" povest' v russkoi literature XVIII — nachale XIX veka, in *XVIII vek*, 5 (1962), 295–315.

Kuchariants A., *Antonio Rinaldi*. Saint Petersburg: Iskusstvo, 1994.

Lafler Joanne, *The Celebrated Mrs. Oldfield: the Life and Art of an Augustan Actress*. Carbondale, IL: Southern Illinois University Press, 1989.

Lastochkin S. Ia., Rubezhanskii Iu. F., *Tsarskoe Selo — rezidentsiia rossiiskikh monarkhov*. Saint Petersburg: Voennyi inzhenerno-tekhnicheskii universitet, 1998.

Levin Eve, *Sex and Society in the World of the Orthodox Slavs. 900-1700*. Ithaca & London: Cornell University Press, 1989.

Levin Iu. D., "Angliiskaia poeziia i literatura russkogo sentimentalizma," in *Ot klassitsizma k romantizmu* (Leningrad: Nauka, 1970), 210–223.

Levitt Marcus C., *Early Modern Russian Letters: Texts and Contexts. Selected Essays*. BostonAcademic Studies Press, 2009.

Longinov M., *Novikov i moskovskie martinisty*. Saint Petersburg: Lan', 2000.

Iu. M. Lotman, "O tretiei chasti Pochty dukhov I. A. Krylova," in *XVIII vek*, 3 (Moscow- Leningrad, 1958), 511–512.

_____ , "Simvolika Peterburga i problemy semiotiki goroda," in *Semiotika goroda i gorodskoi kul'tury: Peterburg* (Tartu, 1984), 30–45.

_____ , *Kul'tura i vzryv*. Moscow: Gnozis, 1992.

_____ , Uspenskii B. A., "Otzvuki kontseptsii "Moskva — tretii Rim" v ideologii Petra Pervogo: K probleme srednevekovoi traditsii v kul'ture barokko," in Lotman Iu. M., *Istoriia i tipologiia russkoi kul'tury* (St. Petersburg: Iskusstvo — SPb, 2002), 349–361.

Lovejoy Arthur O., *The Great Chain of Being. A Study of the History of an Idea*. Cambridge: Cambridge University Press, 1948.

Madariaga Isabel de, "Tsar into emperor: the title of Peter the Great," in *Isabel de Madariaga, Politics and Culture in Eighteenth-Century Russia. Collected Essays* (London and New York: Longman, 1998), 15–39.

Matveev V. Iu., "K istorii siuzheta Petr I, vysekaiush'ii statuiu Rossii," in *Kul'tura i iskusstvo Rossii XVIII v. Novye issledovaniia i materially* (Leningrad: Iskusstvo, 1981), 26 –43.

Ocherki po istorii russkoi kul'tury XVIII — nachala XIX veka. In Iz istorii russkoi kul'tury. Vol IV (XVIII — naschalo XIX veka). Moscow: Iazyki russkoi kul'tury, 2000.

Ospovat A. L., R. D. Timenchik, *Pechal'nu povest' sokhranit'*. Moscow: Kniga, 1987.

Ospovat A. L., "K preniiam 1830-kh gg. O russkoi stolitse," in *Lotmanoskii sbornik*, 1 (Moscow: ITS-Garant, 1995), 476–487.

Panchenko A. M.. ""Potemkinskie derevni" kak kul'turnyi mif ," in *XVIII vek*, 14 (Leningrad, 1983), 93–104.

Patch Howard Rollin, *The Tradition of the Goddess Fortuna in Roman Literature and in the Transitional Period*. Northampton, MA: Smith College, 1922.

_____ ,*Fortune in Old French Literature*. Northampton, MA: Smith College, 1923.

Pavlenko N. I., *Ekaterina Velikaia*. Moscow: Molodaia gvardiia, 1999.

Petrov A. N., *Vtoraia turetskaia voina v tsarstvovanii Ekateriny II*. Saint Petersburg: P. Golike, 1880.

Pogosian Elena, *Vostorg russkoi ody I reshenie temy poeta v russkom panegirike 1730-1762 gg*. Tartu: Tartu University Press, 1997.

_____ , "Ot staroi Ladogi do Ekaterinoslava (mesto Moskvy v predstavleniiakh Ekateriny II o stolitse imperii," in *Lotmanovskii sbornik* , 2 (Moscow: OGI-RGGU, 1997), 511–522.

_____ , "Momus i Prevratnyi svet v maskarade Torzhestvuiushchaia Minerva," in *I vremia I mesto. Istoriko-filologicheskii sbornik k shestidesiatiletiiu A. L. Ospovata* (Moscow: Novoe izdatel'stvo, 2008), 55–71.

Pozdneev A. V., "Rannie masonskie pesni," in *Scando Slavica*, 8 (1962)., 26–64.

Proskurin Oleg, "Burlesknyi kulachnyi boi I bor'ba za epopeiu: Elisei, ili Razdrazhennyi Vakkh V. Maikova i Poema na pobedy Rossiiskogo voinstva V. Petrova," in *Jews and Slavs*, 14 (2004)., 91–102.

Proskurina Vera, "Ot Afin k Ierusalimu," in *Lotmanovskii sbornik*, 1 (Moscow: ITS-Garant, 1995), 488–502.

_____ , "Mezhdu Felitsei i Fortunoi: Derzhavin i barkoviana," in *Permiakovskii sbornik*, II (Moscow: Novoe izdatel'stvo, 2009), 128–143.

Pumpianskii L. V., "Lomonosov i nemetskaia shkola razuma," in *XVIII vek*, 14 (Leningrad, 1983), 3–44.

_____, *Klassicheskaia traditsiia. Sobranie trudov po istorii russkoi literatury* (Moscow: Iazyki russkoi kul'tury, 2000.

Pyliaev M. I., *Zabytoe proshloe okrestnostei Peterburga*. Saint Petersburg: A. S. Suvorin, 1889.

Pypin A. N., *Russkoe masonstvo XVIII i pervoi chetverti XIX veka*. Petrograd: Ogni, 1916.

Rasmussen Karen, "Catherine II and the Image of Peter I," in *Slavic Review*, 37:1 (1978), 51–69.

Razumovskaia M. V., "Pochta dukhov A. Krylova i romany markiza d'Arzhana" in *Russkaia literatura*, 1 (1978), 103–115.

Revard Stella P., *Pindar and the Renaissance Hymn-Ode: 1450-1700*. Tempe: Arizona Center for Medieval and Renaissance Studies, 2001.

Riazanovsky Nicholas, *The Image of Peter the Great in Russian History and Thought*. New York-Oxford: Oxford University Press, 1985.

Riazantsev I. V., "Ekaterina v zerkale antichnoi mifilogii," in *Russkaia kul'tura poslednei treti XVIII veka — vremeni Ekateriny Vtoroi* (Moscow, 1997), 127–142.

Richardor Anne, *Le rire des Lumières*. Paris: Champion, 2002.

Robertson Grant C., *England under the Hanoverians*. New York; London: G. P. Putnam's Sons, 1911.

Rossiia XVIII stoletiia v izdaniiakh Vol'noi russkoi tipografii A. I. Gertsena i N. P. Ogareva. Spravochnyi tom k Zapiskam E. R. Dashkovoi, Ekateriny II, I. V. lopukhina. Moscow: Nauka, 1992.

Rothery G. C., *The Amazons in Antiquity and Modern Times*. London: F. Griffiths, 1910.

Rovinskii D. A., *Podrobnyi slovar' russkikh gravirovannykh portretov*, 2. Saint Petersburg: Imperatorskaia Akademiia nauk, 1887.

Rozhdestvenskii G., *Krylov i ego tovarishchi po tipografii i zhurnalu v 1792 godu*. Moscow, 1899.

Russkaia epigramma vtoroi poloviny XVII — nachala XX v. Leningrad: Sovetskii pisatel', 1975.

Russko-evropeiskie literaturnye sviazi. XVIII vek. Entsiklopedicheskii slovar'. Saint Petersburg: Fakul'tet filologii i iskusstv SPbGU, 2008.

Semeka A., *Russkie rozenkreitsery i sochineniia imperatritsy Ekateriny II protiv masonstva*. Saint Petersburg: Senatskaia tipografiia, 1902.

Schenker Alexander M., *The Bronze Horseman: Falconet's Monument to Peter the Great*. New Haven & London: Yale University Press, 2003.

Serman Ilia, "Derzhavin v krugu druzei-poetov," in *Gavrila Derzhavin. Simposium devoted to his 250th Anniversary* (Norwich, 1995), 318–329.

Shil'der N. K., *Imperator Pavel Pervyi: Istoriko-biograficheskii ocherk*. Saint Petersburg: A. Suvorin, 1901.

Shumigorskii E. S., "Imperator Pavel i masonstvo," in *Masonstvo v ego proshlom i nastoiashchem*, II (Moscow: IKPA, 1991), 135–152.

Shmurlo E., *Peter Velikii v otsenke sovremennikov i potomstva*, 1. Saint Petersburg: Senatskaia tipografiia, 1912.

Sokolovskaia Tira, "Dva portreta Imperatora Pavla s masonskimi emblemami," in *Russkaia starina*, 136:10 (1908), 85–95.

Soloviev N. V., *Pridvornaia zhizn' 1613–1913. Koronatsii, feierverki, dvortsy*. Saint Petersburg: Kruzhok liubitelei iziashchnykh izdanii, 1913.

Soloviev S. M, *Istoriia Rossii s drevneishikh vremen*, 28. Moscow: AST, 2002..

Sorel Albert, *The Eastern Question in the Eighteenth Century. The Partition of Poland & the Treaty of Kainardji*. New York H. Fertig, 1969.

_____, *Europe and the French Revolution. The Political traditions of the Old Regime*. London: The Fontana library, 1969.

Stegnii P. V., *Razdely Pol'shi i diplomatiia Ekateriny II*. Moscow: Mezhdunarodnye otnosheniia, 2002.

Stepanov V. P., "Ubiistvo Pavla I i vol'naia poeziia," in *Literaturnoe nasledie* (Leningrad, 1975), 78–86.

_____, "Zabytye stikhotvoreniia Lomonosova i Sumarokova," in *Russkaia literatura*, 2 (1978), 111–115.

_____, "Polemika vokrug D. I. Fonvizina v period sozdaniia Nedoroslia," in *XVIII vek*, 15 (Leningrad, 1986), 204–229.

Strong Roy, *A Splendor at Court. Renaissance spectacle and illusion*. London: Weidenfeld and Nicolson, 1973.

_____, *The Cult of Elizabeth: Elizabethan portraiture and pageantry*. London: Thames and Hudson, 1977.

Tanner Marie, *The Last Descendant of Aeneas. The Hapsburgs and the Mythic Image of the Emperor*. New Haven-London: Yale University Press, 1993.

Tarle E. V., *Chesmenskii boi i pervaia russkaia ekspeditsiia v Arkhipelag. 1769–1774*. Moscow –Leningrad: Akademiia nauk SSSR, 1945.

Teatral'naia zhizn' Rossii v epokhu Elizavety Petrovny. Ed. L. Starikova, 2. Moscow: Nauka, 2005.

Thyret Isolde, *Between God and Tsar. Religious Symbolism and the Royal Women of Muscovite Russia* (DeKalb, 2001).

Toporov V. N., "Peterburg I peterburgskii tekt russkoi literatury: vvedenie v temu," in *Semiotika goroda i gorodskoi kul'tury: Peterburg. Trudy po znakovym sistemam*, XVIII (Tartu 1984), 4–29.

Tyrrell Wm. Blake, *Amazons. A Study in Athenian Mythmaking* (Baltimore & London, 1984).

Uspenskii B. A., "Iazyk Derzhavina," in *Lotmanovskii sbornik*, 1 (Moscow, 1994), 334–352.

Uspensky B. A., *Tsar' i patriarch v Rossii (Vizantiiskaia model' i ee russkoe pereosmyslenie)* (Moscow, 1998).

_____, *Tsar' i imperator: Pomazanie na tsarstvo i semantika monarshikh titulov* (Moscow, 2000).

Vernadskii G. V., *Russkoe masonstvo v tsarstvovanie Ekateriny II* (Petrograd, 1917).

Vilinbakhov G. V., "Osnovanie Peterburga i imperskaia emblematika," in *Semiotika goroda i gorodskoi kul'tury: Peterburg. Trudy po znakovym sistemam*, XVIII (Tartu 1984), 46-55.

Vinogradov V. N., "Diplomatiia Ekateriny Velikoi," in *Novaia i noveishaia istoriia*, 4 (2001), 124–148.

Vivanti Corrado, "Henry IV, the Gallic Hercules," in *Journal of the Warburg and Courtauld Institute*, 30 (1967), 176–197.

Woronzoff-Dashkoff, A. *Dashkova: A Life of Influence and Exile*. American Philosophical Society: Philadelphia, 2008.

Wolff Larry, "The Fantasy of Catherine in the Fiction of the Enlightenment: From Baron Munchausen to the Marquis de Sade" in *Eros and Pornography in Russian Culture*. Ed. by M. Levitt and A. Toporkov (Moscow, 1999), 249–261.

Wolff Larry, *Venice and the Slavs. The Discovery of Dalmatia in the Age of Enlightenment* (Stanford, 2003).

Wortman Richard S., *Scenarios of Power: Myth and Ceremony in Russian Monarchy, I: From Peter the Great to the Death of Nicolas I* (Princeton, 1995).

Wraxall, Nathaniel William, *Posthumous memoirs of my own life*, III (London, 1836).

Yates Frances A., *Astraea. The Imperial Theme in the Sixteenth Century* (London, 1993).

Yung M. R., *Hercule dans la littérature française du XVI siècle* (Geneva, 1966).

Zaionnts L. O., "Khvoraniia po mode Nikolaia Strakhova, ili ob odnom neosushchestvlennom zamysle Iu. M. Lotmana," in *Antropologiia kul'tury*, 2 (Moscow, 2004), 171–186.

Zhivov V. M., Uspenskii V. A., "Tsar' i Bog: Semioticheskie aspekty sakralizatsii monarkha v Rossii," in Uspenskii B. A. *Izbrannye trudy*, 1 (Moscow, 1994)., 47–154.

Zhivov V. M., Uspenskii B. A., "Metamorfozy antichnogo iazychestva v istorii russkoi kul'tury XVII–XVIII veka," in Iz istorii russkoi kul'tury, IV (Moscow, 2000), 506–518.

Zorin A. L., *Kormia dvuglavogo oral. Literatura i gosudarstvennaia ideologiia v Rossii v poslednei treti XVIII — pervoi treti XIX veka* (Moscow, 2001).

Zyzykin M., *Tsarskaia vlast' i zakon o prestolonasledii v Rossii* (Sophia, 1924).

Index

Abdul Hamid I 230
Addison, Joseph 195, 196, 202
Akimov I. A. 135
Aleksei Mikhailovich, the tzar
    99, 140, 183
Alembert, Jean Le Rond d' 145
Alexander I (Aleksandr Pavlovich)
    21, 53, 54, 74, 80, 83, 84, 130,
    186, 195
Alexander, John T. 14, 34, 89, 99
Alexander the Great of Macedon 31
Alexandrian S. 270
Altshuller M. G. 219, 268
Ambrosius, the Archbishop 100,
    101
Angiolini, D. M. G. 91
Anna Ioannovna (Anna Ivanovna)
    13–15, 55, 143, 152, 153,
    208–211
Anna Leopol'dovna 13, 15, 55
Anna Petrovna 56
Anne of Austria 53
Anne, the Queen of England 86
Apostolidès J.- M. 12, 192
Argents, Jean-Baptist de Boyer,
    marquis d' 268, 270

Ariosto, Ludovico 52
Astrury, Katerine 195

Babintsev S. M. 274
Baecque, Antoine de 26, 222, 223
Baehr, Stephen Lessing 28, 49, 51,
    54, 77
Barkov, Ivan 227
Barry, Jeanne Bécu, comtesse du 86
Bartlett, R. P. 89, 268
Bazhenov V. I. 183
Bekasova A. V 94
Belinskii V. G. 277
Bentinck, Sophie 18, 19
Berkov P. N. 68, 261, 264
Betskoi I. I. 117, 133
Bezborodko A. A. 198, 242, 248, 249
Bibikov A. I. 77, 108
Biron E. I. 211
Bobrinskii A. G. 72
Bogdanov K. A. 92
Bogdanovich I. F. 36, 115, 119, 160,
    185, 214, 215
Boileau-Despréaux, Nicolas 267
Bolotov A. T. 100, 219, 269
Boucher, François 135

Boufflers, de 280
Bovie, Charles 280
Brikner A. 99, 104, 107
Brounshweigs, the royal family 16
Brown, Horatio Forbes 251
Buffon G.-L. 202
Bulgakov Iakov 230
Burke, Peter 23
Buzheninova A. 209

*C*arcopino, Jerome 50
assirer, Ernst 9, 10
Castéra, Jean-Henri 275
Castle, Terry 16
Catherine I 13–15, 28, 54, 136, 210
Catherine II – passim.
Chappe d'Autéroche J.-B., the Abbot 40
Charles III, the King of Spain 253
Charles IV, the King of Spain 253
Charles V of France 52
Charles XII of Sweden 233
Charles, the Duke of Södermanland 240
Charlotte of Mecklenburg-Strelitz 237–239
Chemesov, Evgraf 24
Cherkasov P. P. 33, 234
Chernov S. N. 27
Chernyshev I. G. 93
Chernyshev Z. G. 77
Chetardie, J.-J. Trotti marquis de la 209
Cleland, John 268
Colbert J.-B. 192, 194
Collot, M. A. 106
Constantine VI 37

Corberon, Marie Daniel Bourrée, marquis de 193
Crébillon, Claude Prosper Jolyot de 224, 268
Crone, Anna Lisa 202, 221, 228, 244
Cross, Antony 30, 70, 268

*D*al' V. I. 240
Dante Alighieri 52
Dan'ko E. Ya. 22
Darnton, Robert 235, 268
Dashkova E. R. 20–22, 66, 139–144, 188, 191, 192, 198, 199, 208, 211, 214, 224, 225, 262
Davies, John 52
Delvau, Alfred 280
Derzhavin G. R. 46, 70, 71, 83–85, 96, 116, 131, 143, 186–191, 193–216, 218–237, 239–255, 264–267, 280n64
Diderot, Denis 27, 127, 202, 223, 268
Dieckmann H. 126
Dimitrii (Samozvanets) 64
Dimitrii (tsarevich) 64
Dimitrii Donskoi 168
Dimsdale, Thomas 89, 93
Dmitriev I. I. 274, 279
Dmitriev-Mamonov A. M. 249, 280
Dolgorukaia, Catherine 87
Dolgorukii I. M. 124
Dolgorukovs 211
Donnels O'Malley, Lurana 78
Druzhinina E. I. 177
Dryden, John 53

Index

$\mathcal{E}$l Greco 151
Elagin I. P. 77, 79
Eliseeva, Olga 231, 249
Elizabeth I of England 52, 55, 56, 70
Elizabeth of Russia (Elizaveta Petrovna) 13, 15–20, 24–28, 33, 35, 36, 42–44, 47, 48, 55–58, 65, 67, 87, 112, 117, 118, 122, 153, 198, 210, 212, 230
Engelgardt L. N. 186
Engelgardt, Varvara 248

$\mathcal{F}$aggionato, Raffaella 78
Falconet E.-M. 106, 122, 126–132, 135, 136
Felten Iu. 123
Fénelon F. 186, 202
Ferdinand I, the King of Naples 234, 235
Florida Blanca, the Count 253
Folz R. 150
Fonvizin D. I. 72, 144
Foucault, Michel 107
Fox, Charles James 237
Frederick II of Prussia 22, 24, 79, 88, 202, 240, 242
Frederick William II of Prussia 79, 240–242, 245

$\mathcal{G}$anulich A. K. 30
Gardzonio S. 148
Garnovskii M. A. 249
Gasparov M. L. 178
Georgi G. I. 277, 288
George III, the King of England 236, 239

Gianetti Michelangelo (1744–1796) 36, 115
Godunov, Boris 64
Goldsmith O. 202
Golenishchev-Kutuzov P. I. 82
Golitsyn F. N. 72
Golitsyn M. 209
Golitsyn S. F. 248
Golitsyn V. V. 151
Golovina V. N. 59
Gordin Ia. A. 278
Goodman Dena 194, 222
Gordin A. M. 261, 262
Gordin M. A. 261, 267, 278
Gordin Ia. A. 267, 278
Greenleaf, Monika 17
Greig S. K. 232
Gribovskii A. M. 123
Grimm, Friedrich Melchior, Baron von 77, 86, 136, 138, 148, 183, 187, 200, 214, 276
Grot Ia. K. 220, 227–229, 237, 240
Gudovich I. V. 220, 225, 249
Gukovskii, G. A. 58, 59, 61, 68, 69, 139, 260, 261, 264
Günther Johann Christian 226
Gustav III, the King of Sweden 78, 79, 113, 232, 234, 240, 241, 283

$\mathcal{H}$amilton, Lady Emma 234, 288
Harris J. 202
Hart Pierre R. 195, 205
Hazlitt, W. Carew 251
Henry IV, the King of France 95
Holstein-Gottorp, Karl August 87
Homer 10

Hopkins, Donald R. 87
Horace 131, 225, 266
Howard, Robert 243

*I*konnikov V. S. 25
Irina, the Byzantine empress 37
Isabella of Austria 87
Isksul' S. N. 113
Ivan V 14
Ivan VI Antonovich 15, 25, 55
Ivanov I. T. 90

*J*ackson, Richard 25, 53
Jommelli, Niccolo 41
Joseph I 87
Joseph II 11, 87, 246, 247, 251
Julius Caesar 38, 120
Jung, Edward 202, 203
Junker, Gottlob Friedrich Wilhelm 56

*K*aganov G. Z. 110, 134
Kaganovich A. 123
Kahn, Andrew 41, 112
Kantorowicz, Ernst H. 13
Kaplan, Herbert 237
Kapnist V. V. 191, 198
Karabanov P. M. 258
Karamzin N. M. 54, 80–85, 134, 135, 170, 264, 274
Kaunitz, Anton Wenzel von 139
Kermode, Frank 10, 31, 38, 51
Khemnitser I. I. 191, 198
Kheraskov M. M. 66, 67, 76, 92, 133–135, 163, 164, 177, 180
Khodasevich V. F. 199, 216
Khrapovitskii A. V. 47, 48, 77, 233, 236, 238–240, 252–254, 278, 283, 284
Khvostov A. S. 136
Kirichenko E. I. 111
Klein, Joachim 205
Kliuchevskii V. O. 12, 139, 148, 185
Klushin Alexander 256, 260–263, 264, 265–267, 269, 274, 284
Knabe G. S. 31, 38
Kniazhnin Ia. B. 259, 261, 262, 264, 272, 281
Kobeko D. F. 72
Kochetkova N. D. 132, 274, 290
Kokorinov A. F. 123
Kostrov E. I. 213, 214
Kozitskii G. V. 167, 196
Kozodavlev O. P. 198, 214
Krylov I. A. 256, 259–265, 267–269, 271–279, 281–285
Kubacheva V. N. 277
Kurakin A. B. 80

L'vov N. A. 187, 191, 198
Laclos, Choderlos de 224
La Fontaine, Jean de 264
Leibniz G. W. 202
Leopold II, the Holy Roman Emperor 283
Levin, Eve 14
Levin Iu. D. 264
Levitskii, D. G. 187, 188
Levitt, Marcus 270
Ligne, Charles Joseph, Prince de 11, 17, 35, 117, 153, 267, 289
Locatelli, Giovanni Battista 273
Locke J. 202

Lomonosov, M. V. 26–29, 35, 36, 40, 44, 53–57, 60, 62, 112, 125, 152, 153, 162, 163, 165, 168, 180, 230, 279
Longinov M. N. 79
Lopukhin I. V. 79
Lotman Iu. M. 14, 38, 49, 110, 111, 259
Louis I of Spain 87
Louis XIV of France 12, 29, 33, 53, 87, 192
Louis XV of France 33, 53, 86, 98, 154
Louis XVI of France 234, 235, 250, 283
Lovejoy, Arthur 202, 203

*M*adariaga, Isabel de 111
Maikov V. I. 39, 45, 63–65, 72, 92, 94–96, 104–107, 115, 116, 135, 180, 184
Manin, Lodovoco 251
Marcus Aurelius 126
Maria Carolina of Austria, the Queen of Naples and Sicily 235
Maria Fedorovna 135
Maria Sushkova 193, 207
Maria Theresa, the Queen of Austria 29, 37, 41, 87, 235, 246
Maria, the Queen of Hungary 37
Marie Antoinette of France 235
Markov Alexander (Ospennyi) 89, 90
Marmontel J. F. 276
Martelli, Alessandro 112

Martynov I. I. 258, 262, 263, 284
Masson, Charles 13, 259, 270, 275, 278, 284
Matseevich, Arsenii 25
Meilhan, Sénac de 270
Mercier, L.-S. 268, 269
Merkuriev I. I. 56
Metastasio, Pietro 56
Mikhail Fedorovich (Romanov) 65
Milton, John 202
Montesquieu Ch.-L. 18, 27, 33, 145, 146, 211
Motonis N. N. 112
Motte, J.-B. Vallen de la 123
Musin-Pushkin V. P. 240
Mustafa III 154

*N*apoleon 251
Naryshkin S. V. 104
Novikov N. I. 80, 81, 126, 259, 281

*O*brezkov A. M. 154
Octavian Augustus 38
Oldfield, Anne 258
Olenin A. N. 228
Orlov A. G. 69, 71, 73, 82, 171, 172, 174, 180
Orlov F. G. 172
Orlov G. G. 34, 69, 72, 93, 99, 103–108, 173
Orlov, brothers 73
Ospovat A. L. 111, 136
Ovid 50, 134

*P*anchenko A. M. 35, 148
Panin N. I. 20, 21, 59, 66, 71–73, 79,

80, 81, 108, 139, 144, 189, 242, 267
Passek P. B. 20
Pavel I (Paul I, Pavel Petrovich) 15, 20, 48, 57, 58, 59, 66, 71–74, 78–83, 88–91, 125, 135, 137, 138, 219, 261, 267, 271, 284
Pavlenko N. I. 25, 281
Peter I (Peter the Great) 14, 15, 21, 22, 25–28, 33, 40, 54–56, 62–64, 73, 80–82, 87, 95, 108–115, 117–120, 122, 124–140, 142–144, 148, 149, 151, 156, 182, 183, 187, 189, 192, 209, 210, 232
Peter II 87, 89
Peter III (Petr Fedorovich) 13, 18, 19, 21–24, 26, 33, 42, 56, 57, 59, 76, 82, 87, 92, 114, 147, 182
Peter Leopold II, Grand Duke of Tuscany 246
Petrov V. P. 26, 27, 29–32, 34–36, 38–44, 63, 69, 70, 73, 74, 115, 120–122, 160–166, 169, 171, 175–178, 181, 191, 212
Philip II, the King of Spain 151
Philip III of Burgundy 179
Pindar 158, 178, 180
Piron, Alexis 270
Pitt the Younger, William 235, 239, 245
Pius VI, the Pope 246
Plutarch 18
Pogodin M. P. 271
Pogosian E. A. 27, 68, 146
Poniatowski, Stanislaw 154, 178, 243, 244

Pope, Alexander 52, 157, 202, 258, 284
Poroshin S. A. 45
Potemkin G. A. 34, 41, 143, 171, 173, 176, 177, 197, 198, 211, 220, 231, 233, 237, 241–243, 246–251, 278, 280, 281
Potemkin P. S. 104, 171, 172
Pototsky Ignatii 244
Prince of Wales, future George IV 237, 238, 245
Prokofiev I. P. 123
Prokopovich, Feofan 14, 130, 134
Proskurin O. A. 163
Prosper, Claude 223
Pugachev, Emelian 182, 188, 196
Pumpianskii L. V. 205, 219, 226
Pushkin A. S. 277
Pushkin, lieutenant 21
Pypin A. N. 40, 77, 286

Quarenghi G. 122

Radishchev A. N. 259, 261, 281
Rakhmaninov I. G. 269
Rasmussen, Karen 118
Raspe R. E. 270
Rastrelli C. B. 112, 122, 129, 137
Raynal, Abbot 261
Razumovskaia M. V. 268
Razumovskii A. K. 117
Razumovskii K. G. 90, 93
Renier, Paolo 251
Repnin N. V. 77
Repnin P. I. 33
Riazanovskii N. V. 118
Riazantsev I. V. 41, 135

Richelieu, A.-J. du Plessis, duc de 192, 194
Rinaldi, Antonio 106, 124, 172, 173
Rivarol, Antoine de 224
Rosa, Salvator 53
Rotari P. 24
Rovinskii D. A. 25, 59
Ruban V. G. 91, 92, 104, 126, 191, 212
Rulhière, Claude Carloman de 24
Rumiantsev P. A. 69, 170, 171, 249
Rumiantsev S. P. 140, 142, 143

Sade D. A. F. marquis de 270
Saltykov P. S. 100
Samoilovich D. 99
Sappho 178
Sechenov Dmitrii, the Metropolitan 24
Ségur, L.-Ph. 18, 47, 123, 238, 250
Serman I. Z. 191, 290
Seznec, Jean 126
Shakespeare W. 219
Shcherbatov M. M. 139, 271, 276
Shcherbatova 93
Shchukin P. I. 79
Shilder N. K. 72
Shmurlo E. 111, 139
Shtelin, Iakov 129
Shternberg I. 275
Shumigorskii E. S. 79
Shuvalov A. P. 198
Shuvalov I. I. 117, 198
Sidney Mary (Herbert), Countess of Pembroke 52
Simolin I. M. 251
Soloviev N. V. 273

Soloviev S. M. 15, 25, 88, 90, 104, 108, 171
Sophia, princess 13, 151
Sorel, Alber 154, 157, 231, 243
Spenser, Edmund 52
Stegnii, P. V. 243
Stepanov N. L. 288
Stepanov V. P. 25, 138, 144
Stroganov A. S. 77
Stroganova E. A. 93
Strong, Roy 12, 38, 52, 173
Suleiman II Magnificent 150, 151
Sumarokov A. P. 24, 36, 44, 57–59, 61–64, 66–69, 71, 73, 74, 112, 114, 125, 165–168, 210, 211, 266

Talyzin, captain 21
Tanner, Marie 10, 31, 33, 38, 52, 179
Tarle E. V. 174, 177
Teplov G. N. 114
Timenchik R. D. 136
Toporov V. N. 111
Torelli, Stephano 22, 23, 59
Tott, baron de 177
Trediakovskii V. K. 186
Trubetskaia 93
Tsimmerman I. G. 243, 286
Tyrell, Wm. Blake 30

Urfé, Honoré d' 53
Ushakov D. N. 240
Uspenskii B. A. 13, 14, 38, 110, 111, 166, 168, 216
Utkin P. P. 106

Vekhter G. Kh. 106

Vernadskii G. V. 75
Viazemskii A. A. 197, 199, 220, 225
Vinogradov, V. N. 231
Virgil 10, 32, 34, 37–39, 43, 44,
　　51–53, 55, 57–60, 62, 63, 68,
　　70–72, 115, 119, 120, 169, 179,
　　180, 185
Vladimir, the Prince 148
Volkonskii P. M. 220
Volkov F. G. 67
Voltaire 31, 33, 34, 78, 97, 98, 100–
　　105, 117–120, 131, 154–161,
　　173, 178, 195, 204, 223, 242,
　　258, 261, 269, 276, 277, 280
Volynskii, Artemii 211
Vorontsov A. R. 248
Vorontsov S. R. 235–239

Warburg, Aby 10
William IV, Prince of Orange 245
Wind, Edgar 10
Wolff, Larry 251, 270
Wortman, Richard 49, 83, 186

Yates, Frances A. 10–12, 31–33, 38,
　　51–53

Zavadovskii P. V. 198, 220, 242,
　　248, 249
Zhivov V. M. 13, 166, 168
Zhukovskii V. A. 83, 130
Zorin A. L. 178, 286
Zubov P. A. 260, 262, 270, 272, 273,
　　277–279, 283
Zyzykin M. 54

www.ingramcontent.com/pod-product-compliance
Lightning Source LLC
Chambersburg PA
CBHW051110230426
43667CB00014B/2519